THE
Herb
BIBLE

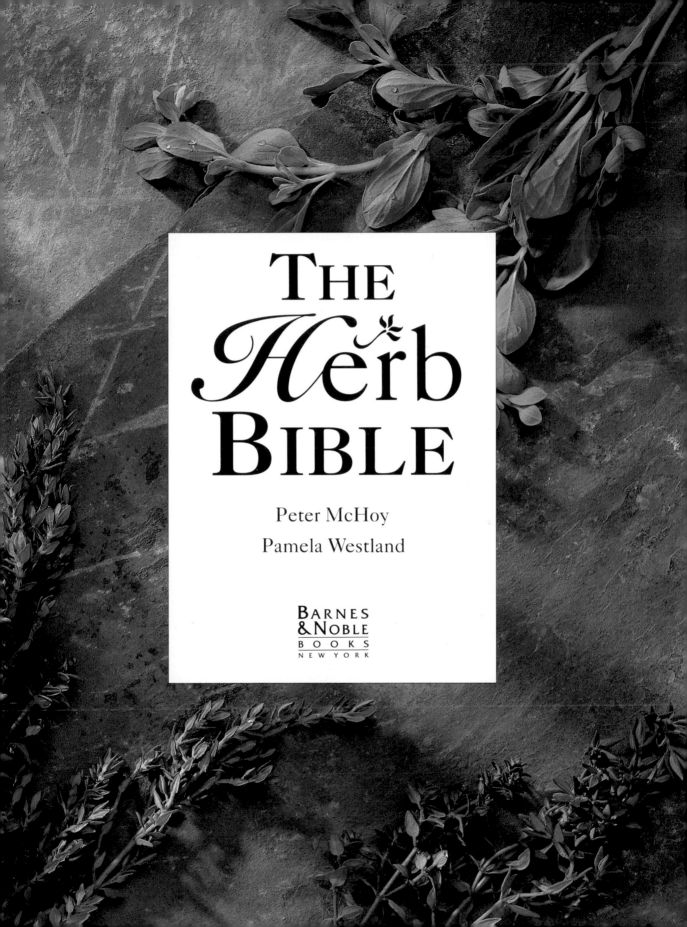

THE
Herb
BIBLE

Peter McHoy

Pamela Westland

BARNES
&NOBLE
BOOKS
NEW YORK

A QUARTO BOOK

This edition published by
Barnes & Noble Inc.,
by arrangement with
Quarto Inc.

1994 Barnes & Noble Books

ISBN 1-56619-569-1

This book was designed and produced by
Quarto Inc.
The Old Brewery
6 Blundell Street
London N7 9BH
England

Senior editors Honor Head and Ellen Sarewitz
Senior art editor Penny Cobb
Designer Anne Fisher
Editor Barbara Haynes
Editorial consultant Richard Marshall
Photographers Nelson Hargreaves and Chas Wilder
Illustrators Elisabeth Dowle, Sally Launder and Sharon Smith
Picture research Susannah Jayes
Picture research manager Giulia Hetherington
Editorial director Sophie Collins
Art director Moira Clinch

Typeset by Genesis Typesetting, Rochester, Kent, England
Printed in China by Leefung-Asco Printers Holdings Ltd, Hong Kong
Manufactured by Regent Publishing Services Ltd, Hong Kong

IMPORTANT NOTICE

The *Herb Bible* is intended to be a general introduction to the use of herbs. The
information contained in this book is neither comprehensive nor prescriptive, and
the advice does not address individual circumstances and conditions. Any person
may develop an allergic reaction at any time to a plant-derived substance, whether
taken internally, as a food or for self-medication, or used topically. Some plants are
toxic if taken in large quantities or over a long period of time. Others may have an
unpleasant effect in specific circumstances. The authors and publisher cannot be
held responsible for adverse reactions to plant substances used inappropriately.
This book is not a guide to self-diagnosis and treatment, and professional advice
should be sought before using any herb remedy except for minor and self-limiting
symptoms. Always consult a physician or qualified herbal practitioner if you are
already receiving treatment for a medical condition. Herbal remedies are not
innocuous and the effects of concomitant medication are potentially dangerous.
Professional advice should be sought for any persistent condition.

CONTENTS

INTRODUCTION

Most of us have a clear idea of what is meant by an herb, yet the word is exceedingly difficult to define in precise terms. At its loosest, an herb can be any plant with a useful property, such as a source of dye, medicine, or insect repellent. Such a definition obviously includes edible plants, but that leads to the inclusion in some herb books of fruits such as rhubarb, pomegranates, and oranges; similarly chicory and Welsh onion are sometimes considered as herbs and at other times as vegetables.

Some experts debate the difference between an herb and a spice, the argument being that an herb is an annual, perennial or biennial that can be grown from seed and that has practical or

Philipsburg Manor, in New York State, was built in the late seventeenth century. The adjoining herb garden is still arranged as it would have been at that date, with all the herbs which would have been in day-to-day use at the time.

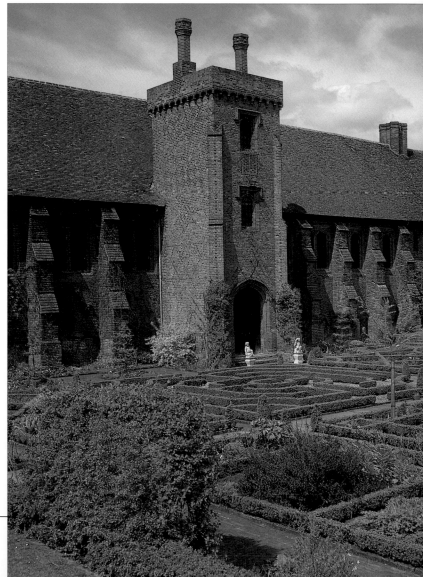

The Elizabethan palace at Hatfield in Hertfordshire, England, showing the formal knot-garden made in the seventeeth century, much of which is given over to herbs.

Dandelion (left), one of the herbs recommended by John Gerard.

Selfheal (right) was gathered from the wild for use long before it was added to the cultivated herb garden.

culinary uses – woody plants and those not grown from seed are spices. This seems a fruitless debate, as plants such as bay (*Laurus nobilis*) and sage would be classed as spices, while almost every cook regards them as herbs.

In this book, a pragmatic approach has been taken. We have included plants that have a culinary, medicinal, or practical use that you would expect to find in a traditional herb garden – along with some that you may prefer to gather from the wild rather than introduce into your garden, like nettles and horsetail. A few are no longer used for their original purpose, or are impractical to harvest on a small scale (you will not extract a useful amount of oil from a couple of evening primrose plants, for example, nor harvest sufficient woad to yield enough dye to make the effort worthwhile). However, both plants are traditional inhabitants of the herb garden. Growing herbs that are of historical importance makes the herb garden more interesting, and often more ornamental, too.

THE HERB HERITAGE

Wild plants were used for food and medicines long before records were kept, and their culinary and medicinal uses must have been discovered largely by accident – no doubt with disastrous consequences for those who experimented with the poisonous ones! At first only native plants would have been used, and not non-native species cultivated in gardens. The widespread use of introduced plants began when trade routes became established, enabling the dissemination of knowledge and plants to pass between different cultures and lands.

We know that the Hebrews used herbs to flavor their food in biblical times, and most well-known culinary herbs, such as rosemary, thymes, and marjorams grew in the Middle East.

Early documented evidence of medicinal use is sparse, but records from Babylon dated

Ancient Egyptian musicians (above) wear cones of scented grease, heavily perfumed with herbs.

An illustration from a fourteenth century Italian herbal (below).

about 2000 B.C. give instructions for the preparation and administration of medicinal herbs. The ancient Egyptians were importing oils and spices from India and other places, for medicine, cosmetics, perfumes, dyes, and disinfectants, as well as for the highly skilled art of embalming. The Greeks also possessed considerable knowledge of the uses of herbs. In about 400 B.C. students of Hippocrates, the "father of medicine", were learning about the use of herbs for easing pain and curing diseases. By the first century A.D., the Greek physician Dioscorides listed 500 plants with medicinal properties in his *De Materia Medica*.

The Romans also used medicinal herbs extensively. As they conquered most of Europe, they took this vast knowledge of herbs with them, together with many of the actual plants and seeds. It has been estimated that over 200 herbs were introduced to Britain by the invading Romans.

After the demise of the Roman Empire, the source of herbal knowledge in Europe lay largely with the Christian monks, who often had a "physick" garden attached to their monasteries. Throughout the Middle Ages, herbal knowledge and folklore also proliferated in towns and villages, largely passed on by word of mouth.

Herbals distilled and disseminated the accumulated knowledge of centuries. John Gerard's *Herball* was published in England in 1579, and although based on a translation of an earlier Latin text, contained much original information. In 1640, this was followed by John Parkinson's massive *Theatrum Botanicum*, which covered about 3,800 plants.

Both authors combined fact and received wisdom and were prone, at times, to flights of vivid imagination. Nicolas Culpeper was even more wide-ranging in his herbal, *The English*

Frontispiece to John Gerard's Herbal, dated 1597 (above).

Plan (left), of the Chelsea Physic Garden in London, dated 1751.

Physician (also called *The Complete Herbal*), published about 1651. In it, he propounded the theories of astrological botany and the Doctrine of Signatures – the idea that the shape and appearance of a plant indicates its medicinal uses. His books were the accepted orthodoxy of the day, and were very successful.

So important are these volumes in the history and development of herb growing that hardly a book on herbs is published that does not make reference to them.

The "Age of Herbals" was succeeded by a more scientific approach to the study of herbs. By 1673, the Worshipful Society of Apothecaries had established a physic garden at Chelsea in London, with the objective of advancing the understanding of the botany of medical plants. This typified the more rational and scientific approach stemming from the development of the scientific method, which began to influence herbal medicine.

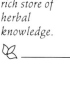

THE NEW WORLD

Colonists of the New World took with them their books by Gerard, Parkinson, and Culpeper, along with some of the herbs they used. Culinary and medicinal plants would have been particularly important to settlers who knew little or nothing of the qualities of the native flora. However, the settlers soon discovered that the indigenous peoples also had a vast herbal knowledge of their own. A cross-fertilization of knowledge between the two peoples

Bee balm (above), which was used by the Oswego tribe to make a form of tea.

An early print of Native Americans transporting the fruits of a gathering trip (right). Incoming Europeans found the Native Americans had a rich store of herbal knowledge.

The Indian pepper harvest, from a fifteenth-century illumination.

resulted in the development of a new body of herbal lore. This was recorded primarily by the naturalized Americans.

A Mexican Indian doctor named Juan Badianus gave us the first recorded written evidence of native American herb lore. In 1552, he wrote a manuscript, in Latin, recording medical practices of the time.

DECLINE AND REVIVAL

Since the late 18th century, herbal medicine has come to be supplanted as conventional practice by allopathic medicine, although the culinary uses of herbs have always been retained. However, since the 1960s, people have become more aware of the practical value of fresh herbs, and nowadays few people would consider a garden complete without at least a small patch devoted to them. Even urban gardeners often like to grow a small selection in windowboxes and containers.

Most herbs are now grown for culinary or decorative use, or for fragrant or cosmetic products, but herbal medicine still has a vital role to play alongside conventional medicine. Controlled trials by physicians have shown that some herbs used in Chinese medicine, for instance, achieved better results in the treatment, for example of eczema, than the strongest preparations available from the pharmaceutical industry.

Herbal medicine is not really a do-it-yourself job, however. Although the tisanes and mild preparations suggested in this book are unlikely to do you any harm, this is *not* a medical manual, and self-diagnosis of any medical condition is not a good idea. Do not embark upon self-treatment of any serious illness without professional advice – from a medical practitioner or a qualified herbalist.

Though caution has to be advised when using herbs medicinally, culinary experiment-ation can be indulged in more enthusiastically.

As we travel more freely and further afield, most of us are eager to discover the delights of new herbs and spices, and to try new tastes.

Although the main uses of herbs are culinary and medicinal, they have many other potential uses, such as in perfumery, cosmetics, and around the house. Many creative ideas for using herbs will be found within this book, and if you are prepared to experiment, you will discover many interesting and useful arts and crafts that may become part of your way of life.

Chinese medicine makes extensive use of herbal remedies. Here, herbs are displayed in the window of a Chinese chemist.

DIRECTORY

OF *H*ERBS

HOW TO USE THE DIRECTORY

This directory includes all the useful herbs that you are likely to want to grow in a practical working garden, with hints and tips on how to get the best from them. You will find uses of all the herbs in the Directory summarized in the chart on pages 212–217. The plants are listed alphabetically by botanical – Latin – name. If this is not known, you can find it in the index under its common name.

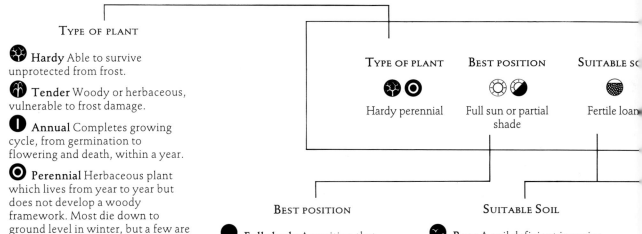

Type of plant

Hardy Able to survive unprotected from frost.

Tender Woody or herbaceous, vulnerable to frost damage.

Annual Completes growing cycle, from germination to flowering and death, within a year.

Perennial Herbaceous plant which lives from year to year but does not develop a woody framework. Most die down to ground level in winter, but a few are evergreen.

Biennial Herbaceous plant that completes its growing cycle, from germination to flowering and death, in two years.

Subshrub Low-growing plant that is woody at the base but lacks the stature of a normal shrub, or has a woody base which develops only soft, herbaceous shoots.

Shrub Perennial plant that develops a permanent framework of woody branches.

Deciduous Perennial plant that produces a new growth of leaves at the beginning of each season and drops them at the end.

Evergreen Perennial plant that has foliage lasting more than one growing season.

Grass Members of the Gramineae family with blades that grow out of a sheath and generally have a hollow stem. Sedges and rushes have solid stems.

Best position

Full shade A position that receives little or no direct sunlight. Bear in mind that a dark gloomy position may be unsuitable, and some plants will not thrive in very dry soil often associated with shade.

Sheltered Growing position protected from the full effects of ambient conditions such as frost and wind. Shelter may be provided by walls, hedges or other plants, or natural terrain.

Partial shade Either dappled shade provided by a tree with a light canopy (such as birches), or in the shade of walls, buildings or other plants for *part* of the day.

Full sun Thrives in bright light and tolerates strong sun, and the dry soil that often goes along with this.

Suitable Soil

Poor A soil deficient in major nutrients. A few plants, such as nasturtiums, flower better in such soils.

Fertile A soil to which fertilizer has been added if it was deficient in nutrients.

Wet Poorly-drained soil which retains water. It is often lacking in nutrients and is colder than surrounding soil.

Moist A soil that does not dry out quickly – usually one that contains plenty of decomposing organic material. Some soils are moist because of their position and a high water table.

Well drained A soil that does not become waterlogged. "Moist but well drained" means that although the soil never becomes very dry, the moisture can drain away freely and plant roots do not stand in waterlogged ground.

If you are unable to find a particular herb in the Directory, it may be because the plant is potentially very hazardous for amateurs to use medicinally. For example, foxgloves (which yield the powerful heart drugs digitalin and digitoxin) and opium poppies are decorative herbs that you might want to grow ornamentally, but not to use herbally. Other herbs, such as horsetail and nettles, are not suitable for cultivating in the confines of an herb garden.

The Directory has been designed as a quick source of information on the main characteristics of a herb, how to grow it and where to plant it. The main uses are also outlined. Even if you already grow the plant in your garden, the cross-reference will open up many possibilities you may not have thought about.

To include as much information as possible the key facts for each herb are summarized at the end of the main entries as shown in the panel below. The following explanation of terms will help you get the best from the Directory.

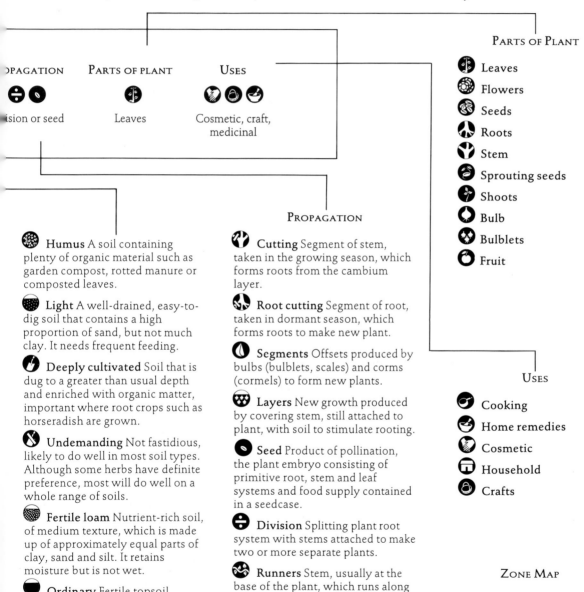

PROPAGATION

PARTS OF PLANT

Leaves

USES

Cosmetic, craft, medicinal

PARTS OF PLANT

Leaves

Flowers

Seeds

Roots

Stem

Sprouting seeds

Shoots

Bulb

Bulblets

Fruit

SOIL

Humus A soil containing plenty of organic material such as garden compost, rotted manure or composted leaves.

Light A well-drained, easy-to-dig soil that contains a high proportion of sand, but not much clay. It needs frequent feeding.

Deeply cultivated Soil that is dug to a greater than usual depth and enriched with organic matter, important where root crops such as horseradish are grown.

Undemanding Not fastidious, likely to do well in most soil types. Although some herbs have definite preference, most will do well on a whole range of soils.

Fertile loam Nutrient-rich soil, of medium texture, which is made up of approximately equal parts of clay, sand and silt. It retains moisture but is not wet.

Ordinary Fertile topsoil, containing some nutrients and soil organisms.

PROPAGATION

Cutting Segment of stem, taken in the growing season, which forms roots from the cambium layer.

Root cutting Segment of root, taken in dormant season, which forms roots to make new plant.

Segments Offsets produced by bulbs (bulblets, scales) and corms (cormels) to form new plants.

Layers New growth produced by covering stem, still attached to plant, with soil to stimulate rooting.

Seed Product of pollination, the plant embryo consisting of primitive root, stem and leaf systems and food supply contained in a seedcase.

Division Splitting plant root system with stems attached to make two or more separate plants.

Runners Stem, usually at the base of the plant, which runs along the ground and forms roots where the leaf joins the stem.

USES

Cooking

Home remedies

Cosmetic

Household

Crafts

ZONE MAP

See p. 218 for the Zone Map and an explanation of the growing zones.

Achillea millefolium
YARROW

THE NAME YARROW is applied to several achilleas, but this is the one most often used as an herb. A common roadside plant in many parts of America and Europe, it is tough with creeping roots that enable it to spread rapidly. It will thrive in almost any soil and position other than shade and may be a weed in lawns. In a mown lawn, it is no more than 2

Wild yarrow is usually white, but it's best to grow a colored variety such as 'Red Beauty'.

inches tall, but elsewhere grows to about 24 inches.

The foliage is feathery with a pleasant smell when crushed. The species has small white flowers carried in flat heads from early summer to late fall. Less invasive are colored varieties such as 'Paprika' (24 inches), 'Red Beauty' (20 inches), the pink 'Rosea' (24 inches), or, alternatively, 'White Beauty' (24 inches). These achilleas look good, but must be kept in check.

Although the species can be raised from seed, named varieties are propagated by cuttings or division. If you choose to grow the species in an herb garden, you may be able to transplant "weed" plants growing elsewhere in the yard.   ZONE 2

WARNING Avoid large doses during pregnancy.

TYPE OF PLANT	BEST POSITION	SUITABLE SOIL	PROPAGATION	PARTS OF PLANT	USES
Hardy perennial	Full sun or partial shade	Undemanding. Tolerates poor and dry soil	Cuttings, division, seed	Leaves and flowers	Cosmetic, craft, culinary, household, medicinal

Agrimonia eupatoria

AGRIMONY

THIS MODEST PLANT with slender spikes of flowers blooms all summer. All parts of the plant – flowers, downy leaves, even the root – are slightly aromatic with a smell reminiscent of apricots, fainter than the similar but less common *A. odorata* (syn. *A. repens*).

Agrimony is very undemanding. It will even tolerate partial shade and dry soil. It grows on hedge banks and wild edges of fields in the southern United States and in many parts of Europe, a clue to its undemanding nature.

A creeping rootstock means that it can spread, but

Agrimony is a rather weedy-looking plant, at its best in a wild part of the yard.

it often develops just a single upright stem with a few weak branches. Its appearance does not warrant a prime site, so plant it where its unpredictable habit will not spoil a neat, formal herb garden.

It is perennial, but tends to be short-lived, so it is worth growing spare plants. Plants can be bought from nurseries and garden centers, but the herb is easy to grow from seed.   ZONE 6

TYPE OF PLANT	BEST POSITION	SUITABLE SOIL	PROPAGATION	PARTS OF PLANT	USES
Perennial	Full sun or partial shade	Undemanding, but well drained	Cuttings or seed	Leaves	Household, cosmetic, medicinal

Alchemilla vulgaris
LADY'S MANTLE

THIS SPECIES RESEMBLES the widely grown *A. mollis*, so popular with gardeners and flower arrangers. The small yellowish green flowers are carried in fuzzy heads above folded and pleated leaves that collect dew or raindrops after a shower. The first flush is in early summer, but flowering can continue into early fall. Lady's mantle is one of the most appealing herbs to grow and can make a fluffy edging in a formal herb garden or border. Alternatively, try planting it with catnip or lavender for a happy color combination. This trouble-free plant grows to a height of about 12 inches.

Lady's mantle, *A. vulgaris*, is the species traditionally grown for herbal use. However, some herb growers treat *A. mollis* in the same way. If you already have the latter in the flowerbed, and simply want to include it in the herb garden for its decorative effect, you are almost sure to find self-sown seedlings in the herbaceous border or between paving stones to transplant. ZONE 3 WARNING Do not consume during pregnancy.

TYPE OF PLANT	BEST POSITION	SUITABLE SOIL	PROPAGATION	PARTS OF PLANT	USES
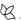					
Hardy perennial	Full sun or partial shade	Fertile loam	Division or seed	Leaves	Cosmetic, craft, medicinal

Allium cepa, Proliferum group
EGYPTIAN ONION

THIS PLANT, ALSO KNOWN as the top onion, has bulbs on the stem tops as well as at the base. The 3-foot-high flowering stems produce inconspicuous white flowers which are followed by clusters of small bulbs which sprout leaves. Both types of bulbs are used like onions to season soups, sandwiches, and salads. If you need only a small quantity for seasoning, use the stem bulblets so the ground bulbs form a large clump – especially if the plant is growing in a border. The bulbs are small in comparison with an onion, so regard them as a variation rather than a substitute for onions.

This culinary herb is simple to propagate – most easily from the bulblets that form on the tall, hollow stems. When harvesting, save a few bulbs to replant.

ZONE HA

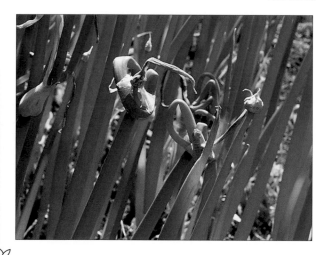

Egyptian onions are neat, well-behaved plants, sure to fascinate when the stem bulbs appear.

TYPE OF PLANT	BEST POSITION	SUITABLE SOIL	PROPAGATION	PARTS OF PLANT	USES
❋ ❶	⊛	⬤	◗ ✿	◗ ◗ ✿	⬲
Hardy annual	Full sun	Fertile loam	Bulbs, bulblets	Leaves, bulbs, bulblets	Culinary

Allium fistulosum

WELSH ONION

T HE WELSH ONION or Japanese bunching onion is a compact, well-behaved, clump-forming plant that does not become invasive. White "drumstick" flowerheads form on hollow stems about 18–30 inches tall, then new leaves sprout around the base of the plant. Although the flowers are less attractive than chives, they are bold enough for a place in the border, and their ability to form clumps makes them suitable as a tall edging in a vegetable plot.

The bulbs, although small, can be used like onions and the thinly sliced young leaves will provide an

Welsh onions form neat clumps that make quite an attractive edging in the kitchen or herb garden.

onion-flavored garnish similar to chives.

Once a clump of Welsh onions is established, self-sown seedlings will provide an ample supply of new plants, but never enough to be a nuisance. The clumps are also easy to divide, and this is a simple method of propagation in spring.   ZONE HA

TYPE OF PLANT	BEST POSITION	SUITABLE SOIL	PROPAGATION	PARTS OF PLANT	USES
Hardy annual	Full sun or partial shade	Fertile loam, preferably moist	Division or seed	Leaves, bulbs	Culinary

Allium sativum

GARLIC

THE TASTE AND SMELL of garlic is familiar to practically everyone, and in many countries it is one of the most widely used culinary herbs. Garlic has flat gray-green leaves about 1 inch wide and 12 inches long. The willowy flower stalks produce clusters of mauvish white flowers which can reach 2 feet or more.

If you like garlic, this is an herb you will certainly want to grow. The "cloves" are tightly clustered bulblets, each sheathed in a papery skin, and "tissue-wrapped" to hold them together.

Plant individual bulblets in early spring, 1 inch deep and 6–8 inches apart. If spring planting gives disappointing results, producing "solid" bulbs that have not split into cloves, try planting in late fall. Alternatively, plant in spring but put the bulbs in the refrigerator a week before to give them a cold spell before planting. Where summers are cold and damp, the crop can be disappointing, but early planting in the fall usually improves results. Garlic responds well to feeding, so apply a general garden fertilizer if growth seems poor.   ZONE 3

TYPE OF PLANT	BEST POSITION	SUITABLE SOIL	PROPAGATION	PARTS OF PLANT	USES
Hardy perennial	Full sun	Fertile loam	Segments of bulb "cloves"	Bulb	Cosmetic, culinary, medicinal

Allium schoenoprasum
CHIVE

Chives make a very pretty edging, bright enough for a flower garden.

THE COMMON, OR ONION, CHIVE is such a versatile plant that you can use it all around the garden. It makes compact clumps of grass-like foliage about 12 inches tall, covered with pink or purple flowers in early summer. A clump of chives is just as attractive as thrift (*Armeria maritima*), which it resembles from a distance, and makes an excellent edging for a flower-bed or border. Use it as well in herb pots and windowboxes. You can even grow it indoors by a light window.

If you want chives primarily for culinary use, remove the flowers to prevent the plants from becoming exhausted. Harvest the young leaves by pinching them off at the base to keep the stubs from dying back and leaving unsightly brown edges. By using protection in spring and fall, the harvesting period can be extended to last about nine months.

As even young leaves can be harvested for an onion-flavored garnish, try raising some plants from seed by a light window, perhaps in a glass kitchen jar for a more interesting effect. Otherwise, grow them in seed trays and transplant them into flowerpots.　　　　ZONE 2–3

TYPE OF PLANT	BEST POSITION	SUITABLE SOIL	PROPAGATION	PARTS OF PLANT	USES
Hardy perennial	Full sun or partial shade	Fertile, moist but well-drained	Division or seed	Leaves	Cosmetic, culinary

Allium tuberosum

GARLIC CHIVE

THE GARLIC CHIVE OR Chinese chive is a vigorous plant forming upright clumps about 24 inches tall. The snowy white flowerheads which appear in summer are surprisingly sweetly scented despite the strong garlic smell of the leaves and bulbs. With its height and attractive flowers it has a place in borders as well as herb gardens, and it forms clumps which are easy to divide.

The flavor is not as strong and pungent as true garlic, so this is a useful herb for those who prefer a milder flavor.   ZONE 4

If you find garlic difficult to grow, or the flavor too strong, try garlic chives instead.

TYPE OF PLANT	BEST POSITION	SUITABLE SOIL	PROPAGATION	PARTS OF PLANT	USES
Hardy perennial	Full sun or partial shade	Fertile, moist but well-drained	Division or seed	Leaves	Medicinal culinary

Aloysia triphylla
LEMON VERBENA

Lemon verbena is one of those plants that has suffered from renaming, and it may also be sold as *Lippia citriodora*. But whatever its name, this is an excellent herb to grow. The pale purple flowers, clustered along the stems in late summer, are not very showy, but the plant's main attraction is the foliage, which gives off a strong citrus scent when crushed. Lemon verbena is at its most aromatic in the early evening.

Grow lemon verbena in a warm, protected position as it is not frost-hardy and needs protection during winter except in the mildest areas. It is a wise precaution to take cuttings unless you choose to grow the herb in a container and overwinter it in a conservatory or greenhouse. Where the weather is mild enough for it to survive outdoors, lemon verbena will grow into a bushy shrub 5 feet high and as much across. However it will be smaller when grown in a container.

Prune in mid-spring to remove dead wood and cut the main stems to about 12 inches from the ground to keep the shrub compact.

Although lemon verbena can be raised from seed, it is easier to take softwood cuttings in late summer to overwinter under glass.   ZONE 8

TYPE OF PLANT	BEST POSITION	SUITABLE SOIL	PROPAGATION	PARTS OF PLANT	USES
Tender deciduous shrub	Full sun or partial shade	Fertile loam	Cuttings or seed	Leaves	Cosmetic, culinary, medicinal, household

Althaea officinalis

MARSH MALLOW

THE CONFECTION OF MARSH MALLOW was formerly made from the mucilage present in the stems, leaves, and especially the roots, but substitutes are now used commercially. The herb has other uses, however, and it is such a pretty perennial that little justification is needed to include it in the garden. The pale pink, or occasionally white, saucer-shaped flowers in late summer have a country-garden appeal, and where conditions suit it will make a bushy plant about 4 feet tall.

Marsh mallow can grow rather tall and straggly for a formal herb garden, and is more at home in a moist area of an informal flowerbed where it looks best planted with border plants or in front of shrubs.

You are unlikely to grow enough marsh mallow to make the confection, but it's a pretty plant to enjoy as an ornamental herb.

As its common name implies, this is a plant that grows wild in marshes, mainly near the sea. It is often disappointing in the hot, dry soils that most herbs prefer and needs watering freely in dry weather unless the ground is naturally moist.

It is easy to increase by pulling pieces from the crown of large plants in the fall. It can also be raised from seeds sown in spring. ZONE 5

TYPE OF PLANT	BEST POSITION	SUITABLE SOIL	PROPAGATION	PARTS OF PLANT	USES
Hardy perennial	Sun or partial shade	Moist	Division or seed	Leaves, roots, stems	Cosmetic, culinary, medicinal

Anethum graveolens

DILL

Dill is a very aromatic annual herb and one that is quick and easy to grow. With its feathery dark blue-green leaves and starry clusters of yellowish green flowers in midsummer, it looks rather like a small version of fennel (with which it will hybridize if planted too close).

Its fine-cut foliage looks attractive in a border, but avoid an exposed position as strong winds can flatten the plants. Because the seeds are allowed to ripen on the plant, they multiply freely, and self-sown seedlings may be a problem. So a corner on its own in the herb garden may be a more practical planting position than a border.

Dill is attractive enough to grow in a border, but self-sown seedlings can be a problem.

Seed is usually sown in spring, but in mild areas, fall sowing produces earlier plants. For a succession of young leaves, make a regular sowing every two or three weeks throughout early and midsummer. The seedlings do not transplant well and respond by flowering prematurely, so sow where they are to grow.

ZONE HA

TYPE OF PLANT	BEST POSITION	SUITABLE SOIL	PROPAGATION	PARTS OF PLANT	USES
Hardy annual	Full sun, sheltered	Light, well-drained	Seed	Leaves, seeds	Craft, culinary, medicinal

Angelica archangelica
ANGELICA

Use angelica as a bold focal point in the herb garden or as a group at the back of a border. In its second year, this biennial will make a huge plant with 2-foot-high bright green leaves topped in mid or late summer by its spectacular clusters of yellowish green flowerheads on stems about 6 feet tall. All parts of this distinctive herb are fragrant to the touch.

Its large size will mean that unless you have lots of space, only two or three plants can be accommodated in an herb garden. The noble stature of angelica makes it an eye-catching feature.

Although technically a biennial, if you prevent it from flowering by cutting off stems that show signs of blooming it may keep growing for a third year.

Sow a few seeds each year to make sure new plants are available to replace those that die. The seed soon loses its viability, however, and to be sure of good germination try to save your own seed and sow within a couple of weeks if possible. If you have trouble germinating the seed, buy small plants in the spring. Once angelica is established, self-sown seedlings should make sure of a continuing supply of plants without much effort on your part.   ZONE 4
WARNING Avoid large doses during pregnancy. Diabetics should avoid this herb.

TYPE OF PLANT	BEST POSITION	SUITABLE SOIL	PROPAGATION	PARTS OF PLANT	USES
Biennial	Partial shade	Moist, fertile	Seed	Leaves, roots, seeds, stems	Culinary, medicinal

Anthemis nobilis/Chamaemelum nobile
CHAMOMILE

T HE CORRECT BOTANICAL NAME for chamomile is *Chamaemelum nobile*, but it is usually sold by herb nurseries as an anthemis. Various related plants are sometimes called chamomile, so check descriptions and names before you buy. The plant illustrated is the type most often grown and is sometimes described as lawn or Roman chamomile.

The dainty white daisy flowers with yellow centers are carried among feathery leaves. The plant has a spreading habit and seldom exceeds 12 inches in height. It can be used for paths in an herb garden as it is a popular grass substitute. The variety usually selected for this use is the non-flowering 'Treneague.' This variety is suitable for a lawn but not as an herb, for it is the flowers that have the useful properties.

Chamomile looks best planted in a bold drift as ground cover, as individual plants can look weedy. It will, in any case, self-sow freely. ZONE 4 WARNING Avoid excessive doses of chamomile.

Chamomile is sometimes used as a grass substitute. In the herb garden it will make an attractive green carpet.

TYPE OF PLANT	BEST POSITION	SUITABLE SOIL	PROPAGATION	PARTS OF PLANT	USES
Hardy perennial	Full sun or partial shade	Undemanding, does well on poor soil	Division or seed	Flowers	Craft, cosmetic, household, medicinal

Anthriscus cerefolium
CHERVIL

Chervil is a pleasant, leafy herb that readily self-seeds.

CHERVIL RESEMBLES ITALIAN PARSLEY, with bright green, divided leaves and growing to about 24 inches. The flavor is very different, however, with a hint of licorice. It is one of the ingredients of *fines herbes*, so it is widely used in French cooking. Grow plenty because it can be used generously.

Chervil is an ideal herb to grow troughs, large pots, containers or even windowboxes, but keep it well watered or plants will run to seed prematurely. This is because this delicate-looking plant prefers a position in moist shade. It quickly deteriorates and runs to seed in extremes of heat or cold.

Sow a short row every two or three weeks in spring and summer for a succession of young leaves. In mild areas or when plants are under protection, try sowing some seed in the fall. Always sow where the plants are to grow as the seedlings are too fragile to transplant, and thin them to about 4 inches apart when they are large enough to handle.

To avoid the need for resowing every year, allow a few plants in each row to produce their dainty white flowers and set seed. Self-sown seedlings should maintain a supply of plants in the bed.   ZONE HA

TYPE OF PLANT	BEST POSITION	SUITABLE SOIL	PROPAGATION	PARTS OF PLANT	USES
Hardy annual	Partial shade	Fertile, moist	Seed	Leaves	Cosmetic, culinary, medicinal

Artemisia abrotanum
SOUTHERNWOOD

Try planting southernwood where you will brush against the aromatic foliage.

cold, it will become shabby in winter, especially if exposed to chilling winds. (The bedraggled appearance in winter may have given rise to another of its colloquial names, that of "old man.") Leave this old growth on as protection, but cut it back to 18 inches in late spring to stimulate fresh shoots and to keep the plant compact.

Propagate by softwood cuttings from division in the spring or fall. Cuttings root easily.   ZONE 5

T HIS IS AN HERB with many common names besides the one given here. They all indicate its value as a traditional herb. In some the link is obvious, such as the French *garde-robe*, a reference to its use as a moth deterrent. Others, like "maiden's ruin," "lover's plant," and "lad's love," are less obvious (it was used as a love charm).

The soft green aromatic foliage is silky to touch, so grow it where you can brush it with your hand as you walk past to release its aroma of camphor. It is a compact shrub that grows to about 5 feet with a spread of 2 feet. With its feathery foliage, sometimes topped with small yellow flowers in late summer, it looks perfectly at home in a herbaceous border. Try it in a container too.

Although hardy in most areas except the very

TYPE OF PLANT	BEST POSITION	SUITABLE SOIL	PROPAGATION	PARTS OF PLANT	USES
Shrub	Full sun, sheltered	Ordinary but well drained	Cuttings, layers	Leaves	Cosmetic, culinary, medicinal, household

Artemisia absinthium
WORMWOOD

Lɪᴋᴇ ᴍᴏsᴛ ᴀʀᴛᴇᴍɪsɪᴀs, wormwood is an attractive and extremely aromatic foliage plant, useful in shrub and mixed borders as well as the herb garden. A subshrub, it makes a rounded bush about 3–4 feet tall covered with dainty, finely cut foliage. The leaf color is silvery when young but ages to pale green. However, 'Lambrook Silver' retains its attractive silvery color well. Yellowish green flowers are produced in midsummer, but they are insignificant compared with the foliage.

Plants become leggy unless trimmed back in spring. Be drastic and prune them back to about 6 inches above the ground – new growth will soon have them looking good again.

Wormwood needs annual pruning for the best foliage effect.

Wormwood can be raised from seed, but it is easier to propagate from cuttings or division. Dividing the plant also encourages vigorous new growth.   ᴢᴏɴᴇ 2–3

ᴡᴀʀɴɪɴɢ Wormwood should not be used without medical supervision, and should never be taken in pregnancy, or by people suffering from liver disease.

Tʏᴘᴇ ᴏғ ᴘʟᴀɴᴛ	Bᴇsᴛ ᴘᴏsɪᴛɪᴏɴ	Sᴜɪᴛᴀʙʟᴇ sᴏɪʟ	Pʀᴏᴘᴀɢᴀᴛɪᴏɴ	Pᴀʀᴛs ᴏғ ᴘʟᴀɴᴛ	Usᴇs
Subshrub	Full sun	Ordinary, well drained	Cuttings, division, seed	Leaves	Medicinal

Artemisia dracunculus
FRENCH TARRAGON

Tarragon is a valuable culinary herb but lacks ornamental value.

TARRAGON IS ONE OF the most sought-after culinary herbs, but beware what you buy. French tarragon has excellent flavor, but Russian tarragon (*A. dracunculoides*) is very inferior. Superficially they look similar, but the leaves of French tarragon are long, narrow, and willowy, while those of the Russian form are larger, coarser, and more indented at the margins. The taste test will confirm genuine French tarragon. Before buying a plant chew a leaf: French tarragon has a distinctive, slightly licorice flavor, but Russian tarragon is bitter and less pleasant.

French tarragon makes a thick, bushy plant 2–3 feet tall, with a spread of about 18 inches. It rarely flowers successfully, which is why it needs to be grown from cuttings or by division. (Russian tarragon is often grown from seed.) To encourage leaf growth, pinch out any flowering shoots that appear.

Cold, damp winters pose a problem as tarragon does best in a warm, sunny position where the climate is mild throughout the year. To help it through the winter, cut back the top growth in the early fall, and cover the plant with straw, conifer shoots, or a plastic sheet. Otherwise, pot up some small pieces of the plant, or take cuttings and overwinter them in a light, frost-free greenhouse or conservatory.

Try moving a plant to a cold frame for the winter: you may be able to enjoy fresh tarragon for a few more months.   ZONE 5

TYPE OF PLANT	BEST POSITION	SUITABLE SOIL	PROPAGATION	PARTS OF PLANT	USES
Hardy perennial	Full sun or partial shade	Ordinary, well drained	Cuttings, division	Leaves	Culinary

Artemisia vulgaris
MUGWORT

Despite its lack of visual appeal, this is a useful herb for flavoring that is easy to grow. It is a herbaceous perennial with 3–5 foot purplish stems. The coarsely divided leaves are often slightly rolled at the edges and felted white beneath. The yellowish brown flowers, which scarcely protrude from their scaly protection, appear between midsummer and early fall.

The plant is easy to raise in a seedbed outdoors in spring or summer. Seed is available from wildflower specialists. However, if you have trouble buying seeds, you may be able to gather them from the wild; mugwort is a common weed over most of the northern hemisphere including North America and Central Asia. Improved varieties are available as plants from specialist herb nurseries, including a variegated form. ZONE 3

WARNING Do not consume during pregnancy.

Mugwort can look rather weedy, but provides a useful filler in a herbaceous or mixed border.

TYPE OF PLANT	BEST POSITION	SUITABLE SOIL	PROPAGATION	PARTS OF PLANT	USES
	⚙	✖		⚭	
Hardy perennial	Full sun	Undemanding	Division, seed	Leaves	Medicinal

Borago officinalis
BORAGE

root means it does not transplant easily nor does it do well in containers. Bees and wasps are attracted by borage, so do not plant it too close to a path.

For summer use, sow in mid or late spring where the plants are to grow, and again in early and mid-summer for succession. In mild areas or if seedlings are under protection, sow in the fall to flower in late spring and early summer. Borage is an annual, so plants will die at the end of the season, but self-sown seedlings germinate freely and you should always have replacement plants coming up.

For winter use only, a few seeds can be sown in a large pot and thinned to one if more germinate. Keep the pot near a very light window, or better still in a conservatory or greenhouse. ZONE HA

Borage is loved by bees and gardeners alike. It's very decorative and thrives in a sunny position.

Decorative borage has bright blue star-like flowers, each with a cone of prominent black anthers, often described as a "beauty spot." Occasionally, a plant may have pink, or more rarely white, flowers. The stems, leaves, and flower buds are all covered with silvery hairs which catch the light and give the whole plant a rough feel.

Grow borage in a border among ornamental herbaceous plants if there is no space in a more formal herb garden. However, its long, fleshy tap

TYPE OF PLANT	BEST POSITION	SUITABLE SOIL	PROPAGATION	PARTS OF PLANT	USES
Hardy annual	Full sun or partial shade	Undemanding	Seed only	Flowers, leaves	Cosmetic, culinary, medicinal

Calendula officinalis
POT MARIGOLD

THE POT MARIGOLD IS essential for any herb garden. Apart from bringing color to salads and other dishes, its bright orange or yellow flowers introduce a cheerful note to an herb garden that may otherwise be dominated by grays and greens.

You can buy single calendulas of the traditional country-garden type, but most seed companies sell

Pot marigolds are so decorative that many people grow them purely as ornamentals.

the larger and more decorative double varieties. Both can be used herbally, so choose whichever fits in with your style of garden. If you allow them to self-sow, they will, in any case, deteriorate over the years and become dominated by small single flowers. Dwarf varieties grow to about 12 inches, while the traditional varieties, more suited to an herb garden, reach about 18 inches.

In spring, sow seed where the plants are to grow. Thin out the seedlings when large enough to handle, leaving about 9 inches between plants. For a succession, sow every two or three weeks throughout. In mild areas a fall sowing will produce flowers by mid or late spring.　　　　ZONE HA

TYPE OF PLANT	BEST POSITION	SUITABLE SOIL	PROPAGATION	PARTS OF PLANT	USES
Hardy annual	Full sun	Undemanding	Seed	Flowers, leaves	Cosmetic, craft, culinary, household, medicinal

Carum carvi

CARAWAY

This is an invaluable herb to include in the garden despite its somewhat weedy appearance. The thread-like bright green leaves that resemble carrot tops have a mild flavor somewhere between dill and parsley. Stems 18–30 inches high are topped by clusters of small white flowers, which eventually produce the ribbed seeds used to flavor candy, cookies, cakes, and breads. Even the finger-thick, parsnip-like roots can be eaten.

Caraway looks best in a large clump or bold drift, so plants can grow into each other and provide mutual support, rather than in rows. If you intend to use their roots, however, it is probably more convenient to grow them in rows.

A biennial, caraway can be sown in both spring and fall for a succession of young foliage. In either case, the plants will flower the following summer. Caraway does not transplant well, so always sow the seeds where the plants are to grow. Thin the seedlings to about 6 inches apart when they are about 3 inches high.

Harvest the seed before it drops, but allow a few plants to shed their seeds to provide a supply of self-sown seedlings if space permits. ZONE 3

Caraway is an easy-to-grow biennial, best sown in bold drifts if you want to harvest its seeds.

Type of plant	Best position	Suitable soil	Propagation	Parts of plant	Uses
Hardy biennial	Full sun, sheltered	Undemanding, well drained	Seed	Leaves, roots, seeds	Craft, culinary, medicinal

Chenopodium bonus-henricus

GOOD KING HENRY

Good King Henry does not look particularly attractive, but it has many culinary uses, and you can crop it over a long period.

IN COMMON WITH MOST herbs this has several other colloquial names, including goosefoot. Described and sold as either an herb or a vegetable, good King Henry can certainly be cooked like spinach or eaten raw in salads, or the young emerging shoots can be blanched and used like asparagus. It is a good standby to have in the yard as it needs the minimum of attention. Lamb's quarters (*C. album*), native to North America, can be used in a similar way.

The plants form clumps of dark green spear-shaped leaves about 18–24 inches tall. Small spikes of insignificant flowers develop in spring, but pinch these out to encourage more leaf growth.

To stimulate young, succulent growth, mulch the area with garden compost or rotted manure after the top growth has died down. Apply a balanced garden fertilizer in spring. You should be able to crop good King Henry for several years, but after three or four it is worth starting again with new plants.

Sow in early or mid-spring and thin the plants to about 12 inches apart when large enough to handle. Small plants may be obtainable through specialist herb nurseries. ZONE 5

TYPE OF PLANT	BEST POSITION	SUITABLE SOIL	PROPAGATION	PARTS OF PLANT	USES
Hardy perennial	Full sun	Fertile	Seed	Leaves, shoots	Culinary

Chrysanthemum balsamita/Balsamita major
COSTMARY

Costmary is also sold under the name of *Balsamita major*. Also known as alecost, it is a leafy herb that forms an upright clump 24–36 inches tall and looks best mixed with more attractive border plants. Alternatively, grow it where the foliage can be brushed in passing to release its scent. The name "Bible Leaf" is sometimes applied to the plant in America and alludes to the fact that early settlers sometimes used the dried leaves as aromatic page markers.

Both leaves and pale yellow flowers are mint-scented. The young leaves are used mainly for culinary purposes and as a mint substitute, but the herb can be used to make herb pillows.

It is best not to let flowers develop; otherwise, the plant will soon become leggy. Even with flowers removed, the center of the clump may die out after a few years, so propagate new plants regularly.

There are several ways to propagate costmary. If you can obtain seeds, sow them in spring. However, if you already have an established plant, the best way is to take root cuttings as described on page 135, or simply cut and replant a creeping rooted portion in spring. ZONE 4

Type of plant	Best position	Suitable soil	Propagation	Parts of plant	Uses
Hardy perennial	Full sun or partial shade	Fertile	Division, root cuttings, seed	Leaves	Cosmetic, culinary, household, medicinal

Chrysanthemum parthenium/Tanacetum parthenium
FEVERFEW

This has always been an important herb and, today, is again regarded as having considerable medicinal potential. It is also a pretty plant, with soft, light green serrated leaves that form mounds 9–24 inches high, generously sprinkled with white or yellow, single or double flowers for most of summer and into the fall. In addition, it is undemanding to grow and does well in any well-drained soil. It will even self-sow into crevices in walls and between paving stones. Feverfew really is a plant of many virtues.

You will find feverfew sold under other names; in seed catalogs it may be listed as *Matricaria eximia*. The varieties with double and yellow flowers or golden foliage can be used in the same way. Many of the compact double varieties look attractive in containers. 'Aureum' has golden foliage that re-

mains bright even in partial shade and into winter.

Feverfew is a short-lived perennial, so maintain a supply of new plants. Seed sown in spring or cuttings taken in summer are easy and reliable methods of propagation; division and leaf cuttings are possible but difficult.　ZONE 4

Feverfew is an attractive plant with white daisy flowers, but the golden form is especially appealing.

Type of plant	Best position	Suitable soil	Propagation	Parts of plant	Uses
Perennial (often grown as a half-hardy annual)	Full sun, partial shade	Undemanding	Cuttings, division, seed	Leaves	Cosmetic, household, medicinal

Cichorium intybus
CHICORY/BELGIAN ENDIVE

CHICORY IS AN EXTREMELY useful plant to grow. The leaves are eaten as a vegetable, the roots can be ground to make a flavoring for coffee, and the very pretty blue flowers, once used to produce soothing eye drops, can simply be enjoyed.

Sow the seeds in rows in late spring or early summer and thin the plants to about 12 inches apart. Some varieties produce heads rather like a romaine lettuce that can be cut and eaten in late fall or early winter; others need to be lifted and forced as a winter vegetable.

To produce tight heads of blanched leaves (chicons), lift the parsnip-like roots in late fall or early winter. Plant them in deep pots or boxes after trimming off the leaves and bottom of the root. Then keep them in a dark place at a temperature of at least 55°F. After three or four weeks, a head of new leaves should have grown that can be harvested when about 6 inches. Consult seed catalogs to identify the particular varieties which are recommended for the different uses.

If you want chicory to flower, do not cut or lift the plants at the end of the first year but leave them to bloom in their second season.   ZONE 3

WARNING Excessive and continued use of chicory may impair the function of the retina.

TYPE OF PLANT	BEST POSITION	SUITABLE SOIL	PROPAGATION	PARTS OF PLANT	USES
Hardy perennial (usually treated as a hardy annual)	Full sun	Fertile	Seed	Leaves, roots	Culinary

Cochlearia armoracia/Armoracia rusticana

HORSERADISH

Horseradish is not normally an attractive plant, but the variegated form can become a focal point.

Horseradish is a coarse-looking plant with dock-like leaves about 24 inches long. There is a variegated variety with leaves splashed with white that makes a more decorative plant.

The useful part of the plant is the pungent thick fleshy root rather than the leaves. So despite the fact that it can be invasive, prepare the ground well before planting. Cultivate the soil to about 18 inches, working in plenty of garden compost or rotted manure. Plant about 12 inches apart, and keep well watered to prevent the roots from becoming coarse. Plant dormant roots of horseradish, known as thongs, with the top of the root about 2 inches below the soil surface. Spikes of tiny white flowers may appear in late spring or early summer, but remove these to concentrate the plant's energy on leaf and root production.

The easiest way to propagate horseradish is to break off and replant small pieces of root in spring. These should soon grow new shoots.

Being soft and fleshy, the leaves are prone to attack by a plethora of leaf-eating insects, and snails can be a particular problem. ZONE 4

Type of plant	Best position	Suitable soil	Propagation	Parts of plant	Uses
Hardy perennial	Full sun or partial shade	Ordinary but deeply cultivated	Root cuttings, seed	Roots	Cosmetic, culinary, medicinal

Coriandrum sativum

CORIANDER

leaves are also called Chinese parsley, a reference to their inclusion in many Chinese dishes. The seeds that follow the mauve-tinted white flowers are also strongly but more pleasantly aromatic. The seeds are an important spice and have been used for centuries.

Sow this easy-to-grow annual in mid-spring, where it is to grow. Choose a position sheltered from strong winds because the stems are weak and the plant tends to loll about, a problem that twiggy stakes should overcome. Water regularly in dry weather, especially if you want a long-lasting supply of fresh leaves. ZONE HA

Coriander is an easy annual, best sown in a bold drift. Individual plants can look weedy.

CORIANDER HAS LACY, feathery foliage and a frothy profusion of tiny white flowers in early and midsummer. It grows to about 24 inches and tends to look best as single plants surrounded by colorful herbs like pot marigolds or in bold drifts in a wilder part of the yard. It can also be grown in large pots, provided you sow *in situ*. It also looks good in an herb border supported by other plants, so allowing its feathery foliage to fill in any gaps.

The leaves have a pungent smell that has been described as a cross between lemon peel and sage; it is one that many people find unpleasant. The fresh

TYPE OF PLANT	BEST POSITION	SUITABLE SOIL	PROPAGATION	PARTS OF PLANT	USES
Hardy annual	Full sun	Undemanding, well drained	Seed	Leaves, seeds	Culinary, household, medicinal

Cuminum cyminum
CUMIN

Sow seed in spring where the plants are to grow, and thin them out to a few inches apart if too many germinate. The crop of seeds should be ready to harvest about three or four months later; the hotter and drier the summer, the better the crop should be.

ZONE HA

Cumin is an unimposing plant, so sow it in bold drifts. Provide a sunny spot for successful results.

THIS USEFUL SPICE WAS out of favor as a plant for the herb garden until interest increased in Indian and Middle Eastern cooking, not to mention spicy Mexican cuisine. Now there is every reason to grow it.

Cumin is a small and unimposing plant grown solely for its seeds. It does not reach much more than 12 inches, and has grass-like leaves on branching stems that are topped with small heads of tiny lilac or white flowers.

A sunny spot is essential to ensure that a good crop of seed matures and ripens, so grow cumin massed in a bed where it can be allowed to set seed.

TYPE OF PLANT	BEST POSITION	SUITABLE SOIL	PROPAGATION	PARTS OF PLANT	USES
Hardy annual	Full sun	Undemanding	Seed	Seeds	Culinary, medicinal

Cymbopogon citratus
LEMONGRASS

ALTHOUGH COMMERCIALLY CULTIVATED in Florida, this lemon-scented tender perennial is not widely grown outside tropical climates. The grass rarely flowers, and it is grown for its long, slender, bright green, strap-shaped leaves, which are used to impart a lemon flavor to candy and are also used to make a refreshing tea.

A few specialist nurseries do sell plants. In areas where the winters are mild and frost-free, it will survive outdoors over winter. Where conditions suit, the plant will make an upright clump up to 6 feet tall. Elsewhere grow it in a container placed in partial shade, but where the aromatic leaves can be

Lemongrass is only suitable for growing outdoors in warm areas, but can be grown in a container and overwintered in a conservatory or in a greenhouse.

touched to release their fragrance as you pass. The leaves will only reach 36 inches, and the plant can overwinter indoors, preferably in a frost-free greenhouse or conservatory.

In mid or late spring, cut the leaves back to just above the soil to stimulate new growth. An established clump should be divided in spring once it becomes too large for the container.   ZONE 9

TYPE OF PLANT	BEST POSITION	SUITABLE SOIL	PROPAGATION	PARTS OF PLANT	USES
Tender perennial grass	Partial shade	Fertile	Division	Leaves	Culinary, household

Filipendula ulmaria
MEADOWSWEET

Meadowsweet is a medicinal herb, attractive enough to be grown as an ornamental plant. Also called "Queen-of-the-meadow," it develops basal rosettes of leaves from creeping roots in spring, followed in early and midsummer by leafy stems topped with many-branched heads of small white flowers. Massed flowerheads create a foam-like effect to a height of 3–5 feet. Both leaves and flowers are aromatic; the leaves smell rather like

The golden variety 'Aurea' is a much more attractive garden plant than the green meadowsweet.

wintergreen, yet the flowers have a sweet almond-and-honey fragrance in the evening air.

In the wild, meadowsweet grows mainly near water, a clue to the need this plant has for ample moisture in the soil. It performs poorly in the hot, dry conditions that suit most herbs.

The variegated and golden cultivars are ornamental. 'Aureo-variegata' has dark green leaves marked with deep yellow. Another cultivar, 'Plena', has attractive double flowers.

The easiest way to propagate is to divide clumps in the fall. Alternatively the species can be raised from seed sown in the fall.   ZONE 2–3

TYPE OF PLANT	BEST POSITION	SUITABLE SOIL	PROPAGATION	PARTS OF PLANT	USES
Hardy perennial	Full sun or partial shade	Moist	Division	Flowers	Craft, medicinal

Foeniculum vulgare
SWEET FENNEL

THERE ARE TWO WIDELY available forms of common, sweet or Roman fennel, one with green and the other with bronze foliage, *F. vulgare* 'Purpureum'. Both types are much used as an herb and as an ornamental garden plant – the green as a background to show off the bronze. Both are attractive from the moment the feathery new shoots appear in spring until the 6-foot stems with distinctive seedheads need cutting down in the fall.

The thread-like leaves smell strongly of licorice and develop into great plumes. The stems, however, are strong and rigid, and by late summer bear flat heads of minute yellow flowers.

Fennel should be grown at the back of an herb border, or ornamentally in an herbaceous border. It will also make a striking focal point in a more open position, such as in a graveled plot, where the many insects that the flowers attract can be studied.

For best results, sow in spring where the plants are to grow. Once you have a plant you will never be

Fennel is one of the most decorative herbs, pleasing enough to grow in a flower border.

short of self-sown seedlings unless the flowerheads are cut off before the seeds ripen and fall – a wise precaution to prevent seedlings from becoming a nuisance. Plants can be increased by division, but the deep tap root is difficult to lift.   ZONE 6

TYPE OF PLANT	BEST POSITION	SUITABLE SOIL	PROPAGATION	PARTS OF PLANT	USES
Tender perennial	Full sun	Undemanding, but well drained	Seed	Leaves, seeds	Cosmetic, craft, culinary, medicinal

Foeniculum vulgare var. *azoricum*

FLORENCE FENNEL

THE SEEDS AND LEAVES of the Florence fennel or finocchio can be used like sweet fennel, though they have a slightly milder flavor. However, Florence fennel is grown as a vegetable, primarily for its bulb-like stems, which have a taste somewhere between licorice and celery.

It is a compact plant, growing to about 24–36 inches, but attractive enough to be grown in groups in the flower border.

Florence fennel needs a long growing season with plenty of moisture. Sow about ½ inch deep in late spring, and thin seedlings to 8 inches apart. Earth up to blanch the "bulbs" once they have reached the size of golf balls. Flowerheads should be removed unless wanted for the seeds. The bulbs should be ready to harvest by late summer.   ZONE A

Florence fennel is commonly grown as a vegetable, but makes a pretty foliage plant too.

TYPE OF PLANT	BEST POSITION	SUITABLE SOIL	PROPAGATION	PARTS OF PLANT	USES
Annual	Full sun	Fertile	Seed	Leaves, seeds, stem	Culinary

Galium odoratum
SWEET WOODRUFF

THIS GROUND-HUGGING CARPETER was once scattered on floors to improve the smell of musty rooms, but nowadays it is grown as an outdoor carpet for a shady area.

Clusters of tiny white, delicately scented flowers appear in spring, set off by whorls of pointed leaves on square stems. The low-growing plants will reach about 6–12 inches. As this is a woodland plant, it will not do well in the hot, sunny conditions that most herbs prefer. Use it instead as a dainty edging to the shady side of an herb garden and work in plenty of moisture-holding garden compost, rotted manure, or rotted leaves before you plant.

When the leaves wilt in the fall they fill the air with the sweet smell of hay as they dry. This

distinctive smell is scarcely present during the spring and summer, and it only develops when the herb is dried.

Divide plants in spring. Otherwise, raise them from seed in spring also, but be prepared for slow germination. Sweet woodruff may still be sold under its old name of *Asperula odorata*.   ZONE 4

Grow sweet woodruff in a bold drift or as a carpet. It's useful for a shady area.

TYPE OF PLANT	BEST POSITION	SUITABLE SOIL	PROPAGATION	PARTS OF PLANT	USES
Hardy perennial	Shade or partial shade	Moist, rich in humus	Division, seed	Leaves	Culinary, household

Glycyrrhiza glabra
LICORICE

LICORICE HAS BEEN CULTIVATED in Europe and the New World for centuries. Old people still remember the true licorice sticks: roots stripped of their bitter bark that are held like a lollipop and chewed as candy. They are still sold in some health-food stores.

Despite the well-known uses of licorice, surprisingly few people recognize the plant. It has graceful ash-like foliage, and in summer the spikes of pale violet-blue pea-like flowers are a bonus.

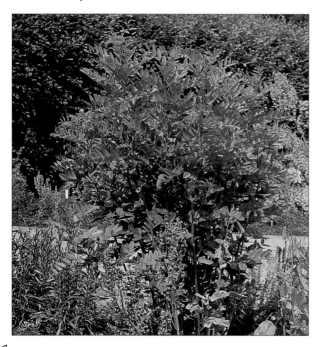

You need plenty of space for licorice. Despite being an herbaceous perennial, it can reach 6 feet once it has become established for a few years and the roots spread. However, a more usual height is 3–4 feet. Cut down the foliage in the fall as it begins to die back, and at the same time remove creeping stems close to the roots if you need to control the spread. The roots are ready to be harvested the third year after planting.

To propagate, plant pieces of root, each with a bud, about 6 inches apart in the fall or at any time during the dormant season.   ZONE 9
WARNING Licorice may increase fluid retention and blood pressure. It should not be used by people with hypertension, or in conjunction with digitalis drugs.

TYPE OF PLANT	BEST POSITION	SUITABLE SOIL	PROPAGATION	PARTS OF PLANT	USES
Tender perennial	Full sun	Light	Division, root cuttings	Roots	Culinary, medicinal

Hyssopus officinalis
HYSSOP

Hʏssop ɪs ᴡᴇʟʟ ᴡᴏʀᴛʜ growing for its decorative contribution to the herb garden and pleasant aroma. It resembles lavender in appearance, and the blue, sometimes white or pink, flower spikes open from midsummer into the fall. Both flowers and foliage have a strong, slightly musky smell.

The plant makes a neat dwarf shrub about 24 inches tall, with a spread about half that. This compact shape makes it suitable for growing in a container or as a low informal hedge within the herb garden, but bear in mind that it will attract bees and wasps. Plant rooted cuttings for a hedge in spring, 12 inches apart, and once established clip regularly to maintain a neat profile.

Cut back plants in beds or borders to just above soil level in early spring to stimulate bushy new

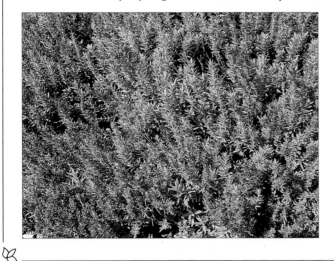

growth; shoots may, in any case, be damaged by a severe winter. The plant will deteriorate with time and is best replaced after four or five years. Self-sown seedlings will probably have established themselves in the bed to replace old plants. Otherwise, new plants can be raised from cuttings taken in the fall.   ᴢᴏɴᴇ 2–3

Try hyssop as an edging or low "hedge." It also makes an attractive plant in a container.

ᴛʏᴘᴇ ᴏf ᴘʟᴀɴᴛ	ʙᴇsᴛ ᴘᴏsɪᴛɪᴏɴ	sᴜɪᴛᴀʙʟᴇ sᴏɪʟ	ᴘʀᴏᴘᴀɢᴀᴛɪᴏɴ	ᴘᴀʀᴛs ᴏf ᴘʟᴀɴᴛ	ᴜsᴇs
Hardy perennial	Full sun	Fertile, well drained	Cuttings, division, seed	Flowers, leaves	Culinary, household, medicinal

Iris ✕ *germanica* var.*florentina*
ORRIS ROOT

ORRIS ROOT LOOKS LIKE a pale bearded iris, with the familiar fan of stiff sword-shaped leaves rising from thick rhizomes that lie at soil level. The white flowers with a hint of blue appear in early summer and last for a couple of weeks. The plant usually makes a clump about 24 inches tall, but in warm areas can be larger.

The flowers have a faint but pleasant fragrance, but the true orris aroma – like vanilla or violets – is only released after the rhizomes have been dried. (Before drying they have an earthy smell.)

Do not expect to harvest rhizomes until the third year after planting, and if possible establish an area where a colony can be left to grow undisturbed for a few years. If you do not have enough space in the herb garden, plant it in the herbaceous border or in front of shrubs.

The easiest method of propagation is by lifting and dividing the rhizomes in midsummer after flowering, making sure there is a fan of leaves on each piece that you replant. Keep the rhizome horizontal to the surface and do not plant too far below the surface.

Orris root may be sold as *Iris florentina* or as *I.* 'Florentina'.   ZONE 4

TYPE OF PLANT	BEST POSITION	SUITABLE SOIL	PROPAGATION	PARTS OF PLANT	USES
Hardy perennial	Full sun	Undemanding, well drained	Division	Roots	Cosmetic, household

Isatis tinctoria
WOAD

Woad is also known as dyer's weed in some countries. It was the traditional blue dye used in medieval Europe for coloring cloth and decorating the body. The dye is slow to prepare and the smell disgusting as the crushed leaves ferment, so only the most enthusiastic traditionalist would want to use woad for this purpose nowadays. However, it is an interesting plant to have in any herb collection because of its fascinating history.

The plant is a biennial that grows to about 3–5 feet. It looks rather leggy and uninteresting during

its first year of growth, but when it flowers in early summer the following year, a group will make a bold splash of yellow that is difficult to ignore. The flowers resemble those of the yellow mustard and rape plants now widely grown for the oil their seeds yield. If woad is grown for its dye, however, the leaves are regularly cropped before the plant flowers.

You can buy plants from specialist herb nurseries, but it is easy to grow from seed sown in spring or late summer. ZONE 3–4

Woad is quite pretty in flower, but you may need to stake it as the growth can be rather leggy.

TYPE OF PLANT	BEST POSITION	SUITABLE SOIL	PROPAGATION	PARTS OF PLANT	USES
Hardy biennial	Full sun	Fertile	Seed	Leaves	Household

Laurus nobilis

SWEET BAY

No HERB GARDEN IS complete without a bay, and trained and clipped into a formal shape such as a pyramid or "lollipop," it makes an excellent centerpiece for a formal design. Clipped bays also make stylish patio plants, and a pair in large pots on each side of the front or back door are always impressive. The small creamy flowers that appear in late spring are insignificant.

Where conditions suit, bay can make a very large bush or small tree, but it is possible to keep it to about 6 feet by regular clipping and pruning. Use pruning shears to clip sweet bay, not shears. This avoids slashing the large, dark green, glossy leaves which would then turn brown at the cut edges.

Sweet bay is an excellent, easily shaped, shrub for a container.

Bay will not survive frost or cold winters, and even in milder climates some of the leaves may be damaged in cold weather. Cold temperatures and strong winds make the worst combination, so erect a wind shelter for the necessary protection. Where winters are very cold, bay should be grown in a container and taken into a greenhouse or light porch for the winter.

When growing plants in containers or large pots, use a loam-based potting soil and remember to feed occasionally during summer. Repot in spring.

Cuttings are the preferred method of propagating sweet bay. It can also be raised from seed, but germination is often slow and erratic. ZONE 7

TYPE OF PLANT	BEST POSITION	SUITABLE SOIL	PROPAGATION	PARTS OF PLANT	USES
Tender shrub	Full sun or partial shade	Well drained	Cuttings, seed	Leaves	Craft, culinary, household, medicinal

Lavandula
LAVENDER

Lavandula
angustifolia
'Hidcote'

THE SCENT OF LAVENDER is familiar to all. Whether grown in a border or bed, in a large pot, or as a hedge, it is one of the most attractive and fragrant of all herbs. Lavender is also a traditional country-garden plant. It has gray-green aromatic foliage and fragrant spikes of blue or mauve flowers from midsummer to early fall.

There are many species and varieties from which to choose, so it is worth considering growing a collection. Some of the best to start with are: *L. angustifolia* (syn. *L. spica*) 'Hidcote' blue' (violet-blue); *L. angustifolia* 'Munstead,' English lavender (lavender-blue, green leaves); *L. stoechas* French lavender (dark purple flowers in congested terminal heads rather than long spikes); and *L. dentata* var. *candicans* French gray lavender. There are also white- and pink-flowered cultivars, though these lack the impact of the more traditional colors. All grow to about 24–36 inches.

Clip over the plants lightly with shears in the fall or the following spring to keep them neat and compact. Even clipped plants deteriorate in time, so raise some replacements every few years.

Lavenders can be grown from seed, but the preferred method of propagation is taking cuttings which will root readily in spring or late summer. Cuttings also mean that named varieties will be the same as their parent.   ZONE 5
WARNING Avoid high doses during pregnancy.

TYPE OF PLANT	BEST POSITION	SUITABLE SOIL	PROPAGATION	PARTS OF PLANT	USES
Hardy shrub	Full sun	Undemanding, well drained	Cuttings, seed	Flowers, leaves	Craft, cosmetic, culinary, medicinal, household

Use lavenders liberally . . . not only in the herb bed but in borders and among shrubs. They are excellent companions for roses.

Lavandula
angustifolia
'Munstead'

Lavandula x
intermedia
'Twickle Purple'

Lavandula
stoechas

Levisticum officinale
LOVAGE

Lovage is a tall, leafy perennial herb that grows to about 5–6 feet. Umbrella-like clusters of small yellow flowers are produced in mid or late summer, but the leaves are the main feature of the plant, resembling those of celery but much larger. The flavor and smell is also celery-like.

As lovage is so tall, it is best grown at the back of a border, where its size will not be a problem. It is difficult to place in a formal herb garden with small beds. However, it is useful for corners that are too shady for sun-loving herbs to thrive, as it grows happily in full sun or partial shade. Do not allow young plants to dry out, and always keep lovage well watered in dry weather. A balanced fertilizer applied in early summer will keep plants vigorous and lush.

The seed should be sown in late summer or early fall. Sprinkle a few seeds where you want the plant to grow, and thin the seedlings to one in each position if more germinate. Otherwise, start them off in pots or trays indoors and plant out the seedlings. Established plants do not divide successfully, but you can take root cuttings.   ZONE 6

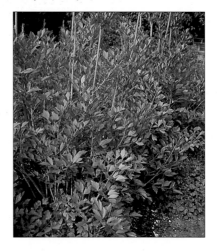

Lovage demands plenty of space, but you can use it as a leafy border filler as well as in the herb garden.

TYPE OF PLANT	BEST POSITION	SUITABLE SOIL	PROPAGATION	PARTS OF PLANT	USES
Hardy perennial	Full sun or partial shade	Fertile, moist	Root cuttings, seed	Leaves, stems, roots, seeds	Cosmetic, culinary, medicinal

Marrubium vulgare

HOREHOUND

herbs. To maintain a compact bushy appearance, old plants should be clipped with shears each spring. Horehound is a versatile plant for although it prefers full sun, it also performs satisfactorily in partial shade.

Horehound is almost always grown from seed sown in mid-spring, indoors or in a seedbed outdoors. Transplant the seedlings to where they are to grow, spacing them about 10 inches apart, or take cuttings during the summer. ZONE 3

Horehound is unspectacular but useful and easy to grow.

HOREHOUND IS SELDOM GROWN nowadays, but it is worth finding space for a clump as this perennial tolerates poor, impoverished soil and can look after itself. It makes a bushy plant about 2 feet high, with small wrinkled leaves and crinkled edges that turn down. The small white flowers clustered along the stems in summer are much loved by bees.

Grow a couple of plants in an herb border or formal herb garden or use it as an ornamental edging. It can also be used in a container with other

TYPE OF PLANT	BEST POSITION	SUITABLE SOIL	PROPAGATION	PARTS OF PLANT	USES
Hardy perennial	Full sun or partial shade	Undemanding	Cuttings, seed	Leaves	Medicinal

Melissa officinalis
LEMON BALM

Melissa
officinalis

L EMON BALM IS A country-garden plant grown for its lemon-scented leaves as much as its herbal use. No herb garden should be without this plant, which is as decorative as it is useful. It should be placed next to a path or in a low raised bed, where the strong lemon scent of the foliage will be released as the leaves are brushed in passing.

The small white flowers clustered up the stem during the summer are insignificant visually, but very attractive to bees, as the botanical name *melissa* suggests. The plant makes a rounded mound 2–3 feet high, with leaves that resemble those of mint. In warm climates it can grow up to 4 feet. Although it will grow in dry soils, the scent is stronger and more agreeable if the ground is moist and fertile.

This is an herbaceous perennial that can easily be

Plant lemon balm where you can brush against its aromatic foliage.

TYPE OF PLANT	BEST POSITION	SUITABLE SOIL	PROPAGATION	PARTS OF PLANT	USES
Hardy perennial	Full sun or partial shade	Fertile, moist	Cuttings, division, seed	Leaves	Cosmetic, culinary, medicinal, household

'Variegata' (syn. 'Aurea')

propagated by division, cuttings or seed. Seed tends to be slow to germinate, but some self-sown seedlings can usually be found around an existing plant. The easiest way to multiply lemon balm is by dividing the clump in spring. If you need more than a few plants, take cuttings in late spring.

It is worth replacing plants every two or three years. This is because old plants are often over-large and have lost the neat form of youth.   ZONE 4

Variegated Cultivars

The golden and variegated varieties look good toward the front of an herbaceous border or in front of shrubs, if the position is not too dark. The cultivar **'All Gold'** will bring a splash of yellow to a shady or partially shaded border. In full sun the leaves tend to scorch and turn brown.

'Variegata' (also called 'Aurea') will tolerate full sun. Its leaves are boldly splashed and speckled with yellow, and the foliage looks especially striking in early summer.

The cultivar 'Variegata' is perhaps the brightest lemon balm, and the best choice for a border position.

The cultivar 'All Gold' is a bright choice for a shaded position.

'All Gold'

Mentha
MINT

Mentha spicata
(spearmint)

No HERB GARDEN IS complete without a couple of different mints. All those described on the following pages are upright-growing to about 1–2 feet and a spread that constantly increases as the plant expands its territory by underground stems unless restrained by some means (see pages 61, 62 and 63). (*Mentha pulegium*, pennyroyal, is a creeping plant described on page 64.)

There are a dozen or more mints widely available from garden centers and herb specialists, and a collection of six or so will add interest to the garden as well as your meals.

The mint most commonly grown is spearmint (*M. spicata*), the flavor and scent of which is readily associated with chewing gum. This and all the mints described have the same cultural requirements. They also have similar spikes of small, bluish mauve or purple flowers in late summer. As these are not very attractive, you may prefer to cut them off with shears to make more of a feature of the foliage.

Despite the ability of mints to cling to life tenaciously and challenge their neighbors for space, they respond well to care and attention. They do least well in hot, dry positions, when diseases such as mildew and rust can be a problem. To encourage lush growth with succulent leaves, grow them in moist soil and partial shade. Once the shoots begin to age and the leaves look old, try cutting some of the shoots back to just above ground level to stimulate a fresh flush of growth.

Work plenty of garden compost or rotted manure

Type of plant	Best position	Suitable soil	Propagation	Parts of plant	Uses
Hardy perennial	Full sun or partial shade	Moist, fertile	Division, runners	Leaves	Cosmetic, craft, culinary, household, medicinal

Mentha spicata, *spearmint, is perhaps the best for culinary use.*

into the ground before planting. Set plants about 9–12 inches apart. To propagate mint, either divide an established clump in fall or spring or separate pieces of runners (underground stems) and bury 2 inches deep, ideally in spring.

To help combat disease, cut off the shoots at ground level in the fall, using shears. Burn or otherwise dispose of the material so that disease spores cannot reinfect the garden.

If mint is cropped heavily, top-dress plants with a layer of well-rotted manure during the winter, and if possible start a new bed every third year.

Extend the harvesting period by potting a few plants in late summer. Cut the top growth down to about 6 inches and take the pot into a greenhouse or place by a light window indoors. Lift some runners in the fall and plant them about 2 inches deep in pots or trays. Keep in a warm greenhouse or a cold frame; you will have young fresh mint to enjoy a month or so before that growing outdoors is ready. ZONE 3

SELECTED SPECIES AND HYBRIDS

The illustrations and main identification features given should help you to recognize most of the common mints, but they can be confusing and even the experts make mistakes in identification.

Apple mint (*M.* ×*suaveolens*) Also known as **round-leaved mint**, this has very hairy stems and

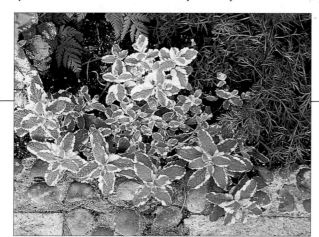

Variegated apple mint looks good tumbling over a path.

Mentha suaveolens *(variegated apple mint)*

rounded, rather wooly wrinkled leaves. It is sometimes called *M. ×rotundifolia*, and you might find it sold under either name   ZONE 4.

The variegated apple mint *M. ×suaveolens* var. *variegata* is sometimes called **pineapple mint**. Its leaves are blotched and splashed with creamy white and some may be almost all white. The allusion to a pineapple scent is rather fanciful, but perhaps created to distinguish it from the plain-leaved apple mint.

Apple mint, especially the variegated form, is a compact plant that grows to about 12 inches, making it a good choice for the front of a border or in a container.

Corsican mint (*M. Requinii*). This bright green, low-growing mint makes good ground cover, but it is not as hardy as other *Mentha* species. Its strong peppermint flavor and fragrance were used to make crème de menthe.   ZONE 6

Curly mint This mint is difficult to ascribe to a particular species. The name is given to several different mints, many of them hybrids, with waved, twisted, or curled leaves. Curly leaves add nothing

If you crush the leaves of the bergamot mint, you will know why it has been given this name.

Mentha ×piperita citrata
(bergamot mint)

Like the other mints, variegated apple mint will soon spread, but a bed of it can be really eyecatching.

Mentha ×villosa
alopecuroides
(Bowles' mint)

Mentha ×gentilis 'Variegata'
(variegated ginger mint)

Use the variegated ginger mint to provide a bold splash of foliage color in the herb garden.

to culinary merit, but contribute variety and interest to a mint collection.

Bergamot (*M.×piperita* var. *citrata*) A hairless mint with thin smooth leaves and purple runners, it has purplish flowers. In full sun it develops a strong citrus scent and the whole plant is tinged purple. In shade the color is more coppery. Use it as an aromatic herb in potpourri or to make a honey-sweetened drink. The flavor is not so good for cooking.   ZONE 3

Red mint (*M. ×gentilis*) This strongly scented mint smells like spearmint. The short-stalked leaves are pointed at both ends, but the variegated form is the one usually grown and very distinctive with contrasting stripes of yellow along the midrib and main veins.

Horse mint (*M. longifolia*) The grayish and very hairy leaves are much longer than broad and have a rather musty smell. It is not a good choice for culinary use.

Peppermint (*M. ×piperita*) This has thin, hairy, stalked leaves. Two forms are widely available: black peppermint has deep purple stems and leaf blades up to about 2½ inches long; white peppermint is a lighter green and has leaf blades up to about 3 inches long. Its distinctive smell means it cannot be mistaken for any other mint. Peppermint is used to make a refreshing mint tea.   ZONE 3

Pineapple mint see apple mint.

Round-leaved mint see apple mint.

Spearmint (*M. ×spicata*) This mint is the most generally cultivated of the culinary mints. The leaves are almost or completely stalkless, lance-shaped, bright green and hairless.   ZONE 3

Curly mint

Mentha ×piperita
(peppermint)

Mentha pulegium

PENNYROYAL

Pennyroyal makes a good ground-cover plant, with small oval leaves spaced evenly along slender 16–18 inches tall stems that grow from creeping roots. Some forms of the plant are more compact, however, and grow only 6 inches tall. The foliage has a peppermint smell, but the leaves have a strong, rather bitter taste. The clusters of small lilac-pink flowers in midsummer are an attractive bonus.

Apart from its use as a ground cover (it can even be used as a grass substitute for lawns), it will grow in crevices and tumble over paving, but regular watering in very dry weather is essential. It is also worth planting in a windowbox or other container.

This is an undemanding plant that is not fussy about soil and will grow in sun or shade. It is generally much lusher and healthier in moist shady conditions, however, and even where conditions suit it, it may require renewing after about four years. In very cold climates, pennyroyal benefits from protection in winter.

It is easy to grow from seed sown in spring, but propagation is easiest by division.   ZONE 7

WARNING   Pennyroyal should not be consumed at any time during pregnancy. It can also be toxic if used to excess by anyone.

TYPE OF PLANT	BEST POSITION	SUITABLE SOIL	PROPAGATION	PARTS OF PLANT	USES
Perennial	Full sun or partial shade	Undemanding but well drained	Division, seed	Leaves	Cosmetic, household, medicinal

Monarda citriodora

LEMON MINT

Although less commonly grown than *Monarda didyma*, lemon mint makes an attractive border plant 3–5 feet tall topped with crowns of pale pink flowers. It makes a bushy clump that expands with age. The oval, pointed leaves smell strongly of lemon when bruised and can be used in a similar way to those of the scarlet bee balm.

Monarda citriodora is highly ornamental, and is also very attractive to butterflies and bees.

The plant makes a bold splash of color when it flowers in midsummer, and you can be sure it will attract plenty of bees and butterflies. It is grown as an annual in northern climates, but farther south it is a good plant for the herbaceous border. Try to find space for it in the herb garden, where it will add both height and color.

Lemon mint should be obtainable from herb growers or nurseries specializing in more unusual plants. To propagate a large number of plants, take cuttings in spring. Otherwise, divide a large clump into several pieces; it benefits from division every third year, anyway.   ZONE 5

TYPE OF PLANT	BEST POSITION	SUITABLE SOIL	PROPAGATION	PARTS OF PLANT	USES
◉	❂ ◐	🌊 🌊	🌱 ⊖	🌿	⊘
Perennial	Full sun or partial shade	Fertile, moist	Cuttings, division	Leaves	Culinary

Monarda didyma
BEE BALM

This useful herb, also known as bergamot or Oswego tea, is a popular border plant grown for its decorative flowers as much as for its aromatic foliage. The tubular flowers, held like a crown at the top of the 3–4-foot stems in mid and late summer are normally bright scarlet. There are also varieties with pink, salmon, crimson, mauve, purple or white flowers, so you can create a really colorful show. As the common name implies, bee balm attracts bees which are appreciative of nectar-rich flowers and hummingbirds are also attracted to the plant.

Although flowers are the main attraction for many people, it is the dark green, aromatic leaves that are its justification in the herb garden. They are a prime ingredient of Earl Grey tea and have other culinary uses. There is even a pleasant fragrance when the top growth has died down. The roots are also sweetly aromatic.

Work plenty of garden compost or rotted manure into the ground before planting, and apply a mulch of organic material each spring.

For a plentiful supply of plants, raise them from seed or by taking cuttings. Otherwise, just divide an established clump in autumn. The plants benefit from division every second year or they become bare in the center. Named cultivars must always be propagated from cuttings or by division.   ZONE 4

Type of plant	Best position	Suitable soil	Propagation	Parts of plant	Uses
Hardy perennial	Full sun or partial shade	Fertile, moist	Cuttings, division, seed	Leaves	Cosmetic, craft, culinary, household, medicinal

Myrrhis odorata
SWEET CICELY/GARDEN MYRRH

The flowers are dull, but sweet Cicely is a pleasant foliage plant.

THIS TALL PERENNIAL HERB grows to about 3 feet. It has attractive ferny foliage and small creamy white flowers arranged in umbrella-like heads in late spring and early summer. In spring, it is one of the first plants to produce new growth. Despite this, it usually retains its foliage until midwinter.

The claw-like clusters of long, brownish black seeds are quite attractive, but if you grow sweet Cicely primarily for its leaves, cut off the flower-heads to prevent seeding. Both the leaves and seeds give off a strong aroma that leaves a hint of licorice and aniseed.

This herb prefers a partially shaded spot with cool soil for the carrot-like tap roots (these can be eaten as a vegetable) to penetrate. It does not like the hot dry positions that suit most herbs. If you cannot find an appropriate space in the herb garden, grow it at the back of an herbaceous or mixed border. Its fresh green foliage is a good foil for more colorful plants and they in turn offer support, as sweet Cicely has a tendency to sprawl.

Seed can sometimes be slow to germinate, but there are nearly always some self-sown seedlings that can be transplanted while still young. Small pieces of root will usually grow if planted in spring, provided they have a bud, or eye, but the parent plant will object to being lifted. ZONE 4

TYPE OF PLANT	BEST POSITION	SUITABLE SOIL	PROPAGATION	PARTS OF PLANT	USES
Hardy perennial	Partial shade	Fertile	Division, seed	Leaves, roots, seeds	Craft, culinary, household

Myrtus communis
MYRTLE

Myrtle is a charming evergreen shrub with small, aromatic, dark green leathery leaves, and fragrant white flowers about 1 inch across from early to late summer. These are sometimes followed by purple-black oval berries. For decorative impact, 'Variegata' with its creamy white and green leaves is a better plant.

Where conditions suit, the green-leaved species will make a shrub 10 feet or more high, but 'Variegata' is less vigorous. Both types can be kept to about 3 feet if grown in a large pot. Keep well watered in dry weather; this is especially important for container-grown plants.

If space is at a premium a number of low-growing cultivars, including 'Compacta', 'Microphylla', 'Minima', and 'Nana' are available, along with the dwarf subspecies *M. communis tarentina*, (sometimes sold as 'Jenny Reitenback'). There is also a variegated dwarf cultivar available.

Myrtle will tolerate a light frost which will only cause superficial damage, but does best when kept above 41°F. This can be achieved by growing plants in large containers that can be moved indoors into a greenhouse or conservatory for winter. Outdoors, it needs to be planted beside a warm wall in a sheltered position. Prune out any frost-damaged shoots in spring.

Propagate by cuttings in late summer.   ZONE 8–9

Myrtle is a charming evergreen, but it is one that does best in a warm area.

TYPE OF PLANT	BEST POSITION	SUITABLE SOIL	PROPAGATION	PARTS OF PLANT	USES
Tender evergreen shrub	Full sun, sheltered	Light, well drained	Cuttings	Leaves, fruit	Culinary

Nasturtium officinale
WATERCRESS

THIS LEAFY PLANT GROWS from 2–24 inches depending on conditions. It remains low and compact in cool running water, but grows tall and runs to seed in hot weather or in dry conditions. It spreads by the thread-like roots which may arise from each leaf joint. The tiny white flowers are uninteresting, and their development is a sign that the plant is past its best.

The natural habitat for watercress is in a flowing stream, but it may be grown without natural running water. To do this, a special bed must be made and kept wet by constant watering. Dig a trench about 12 inches deep in a partially shaded position, and place 6 inches of well-rotted manure or garden compost in the bottom. Cover it with a layer of about 3 inches of soil, to which has been added as much moisture-retaining material as possible.

If starting from seed, sow directly into the finished trench in mid-spring, water thoroughly, and make sure that the trench never dries out. For this reason, it is sensible to dig the trench close to a water supply or outside faucet.

Alternatively, grow your watercress in a shallow trough half-filled with soil. Plant the seedlings into the soil, which must be kept moist. Gradually increase the level of the water in the trough as the cress grows. About once a week, drain the old water and refill with fresh. ZONE 4

TYPE OF PLANT	BEST POSITION	SUITABLE SOIL	PROPAGATION	PARTS OF PLANT	USES
Hardy perennial	Full sun or partial shade	Moist, preferably wet but not stagnant	Cuttings, division, seed	Leaves	Culinary, medicinal

Nepeta cataria
CATNIP/CATMINT

SEVERAL SPECIES of nepeta have been given the name of catnip, but *N. cataria* is the one that cats really love to sniff and rub against. The herb is sometimes used to fill "toys" for cats. The gray-green leaves feel soft and crushing them releases the characteristic minty aroma. The shaded mauve to white flowers, on shoots up to 24–36 inches high, are borne in clusters where the leaves join the stem.

Although not as showy as *N.* ×*faassenii* and *N. mussinii* (syn. *N. racemosa*) which are more popular for the garden, try planting *N. cataria* as an ornamental in the herbaceous border if you are short of room in the herb garden. Bear in mind that it is likely to be squashed flat by cats lying on it, so it is worth protecting with a low fence of wire netting.

Like other catnips, it makes an attractive edging for a shrub or mixed border, or to divide the herb garden into sections. But avoid using it where it will cascade over the edge of a path as it attracts bees and wasps.

Catnip is easy to propagate from seed, but unless you need a large number, divide established clumps in early or mid-spring; this will give you larger plants more quickly. Cuttings of basal shoots can also be taken in mid-spring. ZONE 3

Nepeta cataria is not as bright as the more popular catnips, but your cats will love it!

TYPE OF PLANT	BEST POSITION	SUITABLE SOIL	PROPAGATION	PARTS OF PLANT	USES
Hardy perennial	Full sun	Undemanding	Cuttings, division, seed	Leaves	Cosmetic, medicinal

Ocimum basilicum

SWEET BASIL

The pungent foliage of basil is usually green, but try a colored one such as 'Dark Opal' for a change.

Sᴡᴇᴇᴛ ʙᴀsɪʟ ɪs ɢʀᴏᴡɴ for its foliage which has a pungent smell. It can be grown indoors in pots or outside in the garden during summer. The kind most often seen has soft, dark green leaves, though the shape and size can vary, and some are ruffled. In poor light the plants soon become leggy, so keep pinching out the growing tips to encourage branching and a bushy shape. (This is worth doing even with outdoor plants.) The white flowers are not a feature of basil, so do not hesitate to pinch out flowering spikes.

For contrast grow green-leaved basil in combination with one of the purple-leaved cultivars such as 'Dark Opal,' *O. basilicum* 'Purpurascens,' or the lemon-scented 'Citriodorum.' These purple-leaved basils can look dull on their own, but are a good foil to their green counterpart. They also make attractive companions as patio plants in a container.

Unless you buy plants, propagate each year from seed sown indoors in spring. You then have the choice of growing them in pots by a light window, or planting them in the herb garden when there is no risk of frost and they have been acclimatized (this is very important as a sudden chill or very cold winds may kill basil even without a frost). If growing them outside, space plants about 12 inches apart.

Bush basil (*O. basilicum* 'Minimum,' sometimes listed as *O. minimum*) has much smaller leaves and grows to about 12 inches rather than the 24 inches or more of sweet basil.   ZONE A

TYPE OF PLANT	BEST POSITION	SUITABLE SOIL	PROPAGATION	PARTS OF PLANT	USES
Tender annual	Full sun	Ordinary, well drained	Seed	Leaves	Craft, culinary, household, medicinal

Oenothera biennis
EVENING PRIMROSE

THE EVENING PRIMROSE, also called night willow herb or German rampion in North America, has the sort of wildflower charm that looks good in a country garden. In the herb garden, it makes a bold splash of yellow to contrast with the predominant greens. It is a biennial which in its first year forms a flat rosette of pale green leaves, then in the second produces upright stems about 3–4 feet tall. These stems carry large fragrant yellow flowers from early summer into the fall. Where conditions suit, flowers may even be produced late in the first year. The flowers are short-lived and are at their best in the evening, when the scent increases in intensity.

Evening primroses are now grown commercially on a large scale for the essential oil, which is regarded as having important medicinal properties. On a garden scale, the yield will not make harvesting a practical proposition. It is, however, such an attractive plant that it needs no excuse for a place in any herb garden.

Sow the seeds where the plants are to grow in late spring or early summer and thin out the seedlings when large enough to handle. Seeds are available from specialist nurseries or those dealing in wild-flower seeds; otherwise, buy seedlings from an herb nursery. Once plants are established, self-sown seedlings should provide a supply of plants for subsequent years. ZONE 4

TYPE OF PLANT	BEST POSITION	SUITABLE SOIL	PROPAGATION	PARTS OF PLANT	USES
Hardy biennial	Full sun	Undemanding	Seed	Leaves, stems, seeds	Medicinal

Origanum majorana
SWEET MARJORAM

THIS DESIRABLE CULINARY HERB needs to be treated as a half-hardy annual in most areas, although it is in fact a tender perennial that will overwinter outside where frosts are not a problem. The plant grows to about 10 inches, with tough trailing stems, covered in summer with clusters of small but dainty flowers, usually mauve-pink but sometimes white or purple. The plant's flowers are produced from pea-like buds that resemble knots, which is why it became commonly known as knotted marjoram. The small oval leaves are pungently aromatic.

Sweet marjoram makes an attractive container plant, and by taking it indoors and placing it where it

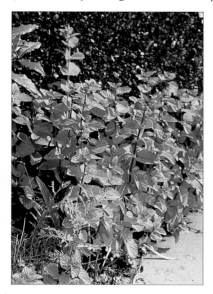

Sweet marjoram makes an attractive edging, but remember that it's not frost-hardy.

gets natural light, you should be able to keep it through the winter.

Sow seeds indoors or, if possible, in a greenhouse and transplant into trays or pots. Plant out in early summer after hardening off. Sow seed outdoors in late spring where the plants are to flower, but cover them to aid germination.

Overwintered plants can be propagated by cuttings or division, but it is usually easier to raise new plants from seed each year.　　　ZONE A

TYPE OF PLANT	BEST POSITION	SUITABLE SOIL	PROPAGATION	PARTS OF PLANT	USES
Annual	Full sun	Fertile	Cuttings, division, seed	Leaves	Cosmetic, craft, culinary, household, medicinal

Origanum vulgare
OREGANO/WILD MARJORAM

Oregano is an invaluable culinary herb. Also called wild marjoram or hardy pot marjoram, it is easy to grow and a highly decorative garden plant. Unlike sweet marjoram, it is hardy and will overwinter without problems. It dies down for the winter, but when growth starts in spring, it will soon make a bushy plant which will grow to 24 inches tall. An established plant will have a spread of about 18 inches, making an attractive mound of aromatic foliage studded with masses of small pink flowers from mid to late summer.

The flowers are very attractive to many kinds of insects, including butterflies, bees, and wasps. Therefore, although it is useful as an edging plant in summer, do not plant it where it will overhang a path if insects bother you.

The golden-leaved cultivar makes an ideal edging

plant as it is smaller and more compact than the green-leaved species. The flowers can be trimmed with shears to keep it as a neat foliage plant. Oregano tends to become woody and less attractive after about four years, so consider dividing and replanting, or raising new plants from cuttings, after the third year. ZONE 3

Origanum vulgare *is pretty in flower, and 'Aureum' makes an attractive foliage plant.*

TYPE OF PLANT	BEST POSITION	SUITABLE SOIL	PROPAGATION	PARTS OF PLANT	USES
Hardy perennial	Full sun	Ordinary, well drained	Cuttings, division, seed	Leaves	Culinary

Panax quinquefolius

GINSENG

Health food and herb enthusiasts rank ginseng as a medicinal herb of major importance. Chinese ginseng is a different species, but the two look similar and are used in the same way. The five-fingered leaves are held hand-like on 12–18 inch stems that arise from the base of the plant. Smallish green flowers appear on mature plants in early summer – usually three or four years after sowing. Like the plant itself, the fleshy roots develop only slowly.

The plant is of no great ornamental value, but it can be used as a foliage ground cover in the right conditions. It is worth trying to grow as a curiosity, even if it struggles to thrive. In the wild, it grows in moist woodland, so prepare a special small bed in partial shade, enriching it with plenty of humus-forming material such as garden compost, rotted manure, or decomposed leaves.

It can be grown from seed, but this may not be easy to obtain. Some herb nurseries also sell ginseng plants, but you are unlikely to find this herb in garden centers.

ZONE 3

TYPE OF PLANT	BEST POSITION	SUITABLE SOIL	PROPAGATION	PARTS OF PLANT	USES
Hardy perennial	Partial shade	Moist, fertile	Division, seed	Roots	Medicinal

Pelargonium
SCENTED GERANIUMS

THE SCENTED GERANIUMS ARE species and hybrid species belonging to the same genus as the popular border plants known as geranium. In some species, the scent released by the crushed leaves is unmistakable, but in others the aroma is more elusive and difficult to define. What one person describes as orange, another may consider smells of lemons, or even roses!

Most scented geraniums grow 12–24 inches tall,

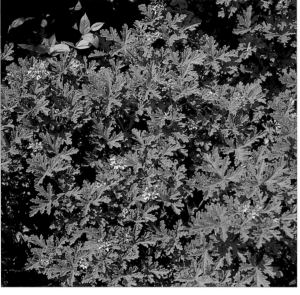

Pelargonium graveolens has been described as smelling of lemons, oranges, and roses!

Pelargonium
graveolens

but the shape and size of leaf vary considerably, and some are attractively variegated. The flowers are relatively unspectacular when compared to the showy display given by summer bedding geraniums.

All scented geraniums make good potted plants for home or greenhouse, but outdoors they lack the impact of their more floriferous cousins. Once there is no risk of frost, however, they can be planted in

TYPE OF PLANT	BEST POSITION	SUITABLE SOIL	PROPAGATION	PARTS OF PLANT	USES
Tender perennial	Full sun or good light	Well-drained, light (fill pots with loam-based compost)	Cuttings	Flowers, leaves	Cosmetic, culinary, household

Pelargonium
'Lady Plymouth'

Pelargonium
crispum

the herb garden for the summer. Alternatively, a collection can be grown in a raised bed, perhaps on the patio where visitors will enjoy doing a "sniff test"!

Lift plants in the fall and cut them back by about two-thirds before overwintering in a frost-free place. Keep on the dry side during the winter. You may find it more convenient to keep them in large pots throughout the year and plunge them, complete with pot, into the soil for the summer.

If the plants become straggly, pinch back the growing tips to keep them compact and induce branching. Feed during the summer, whether in pots or outdoors. Cuttings taken in the fall and spring root easily. ZONE 10

SELECTED SPECIES

Most herb growers sell scented geraniums, but to extend your collection you may have to obtain plants from a specialist nursery. There are many other species and varieties besides the ones listed here, some with different scents.

P. ×*asperum* Pine scent (which some people find unpleasant); lilac flowers; rough gray-green leaves.

P. capitatum Rose scent; rose-purple flowers; hairy leaves; sometimes sold as 'Attar of Roses;' variegated cultivar available.

P. ×*citrosum* Orange scent; mauve flowers.

P. crispum Lemon scent; mauve flowers; small crinkled leaves; variegated varieties available; sometimes sold as the finger-bowl pelargonium (geranium) because it was used to scent finger bowls.

P. ×*fragrans* Nutmeg/spice scent; white flowers; small gray-green leaves; a variegated cultivar with mauve flowers, 'Variegatum', is also available.

P. graveolens Scent difficult to define, variously described as lemon, orange or rose; pink and purple flowers; gray-green leaves; **'Lady Plymouth'** is a variegated cultivar. **'Little Gem'** has a lemon scent.

P. grossularioides Coconut scent; purple flowers; small leaves; creeping habit.

P. ×*nervosum* Lime scent; lavender flowers; small crinkled leaves.

P. odoratissimum Apple scent; small white flowers; sprawling habit.

P. tomentosum Peppermint scent; small white flowers; pale green leaves.

Pelargonium
quercifolium,
*the oak-leaved or
Almond Geranium*

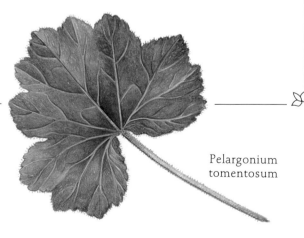

Pelargonium
tomentosum

Petroselinum crispum
PARSLEY

Curled parsley

year. But by the time it flowers, the plant is past its best and should be discarded.

Parsley seed has a reputation for being slow or difficult to germinate, but it will usually succeed if the ground is warm and moist. If you have problems, try soaking the seeds in lukewarm water for a couple of hours before sowing in drills or furrows that have been well watered beforehand. Make sure the soil never dries out before the seeds germinate.

By sowing at various times, you should be able to pick fresh parsley at any time of the year. The earliest sowing can be under glass in late winter or early spring, followed by regular sowings outdoors

Curled varieties of parsley are the most attractive. Grow them in blocks, rows, or as an edging.

Pᴀʀsʟᴇʏ ɴᴇᴇᴅs ʟɪᴛᴛʟᴇ ɪɴᴛʀᴏᴅᴜᴄᴛɪᴏɴ. It is probably one of the most universal of culinary herbs, and a familiar sight in vegetable and herb gardens with its tightly curled leaves.

Although a hardy biennial and easily overwintered, it is most often grown as an annual. The almost moss-like foliage will form a plant 9–12 inches tall which will eventually produce tiny clusters of greenish yellow flowers in the second

Tʏᴘᴇ ᴏғ ᴘʟᴀɴᴛ	Bᴇsᴛ ᴘᴏsɪᴛɪᴏɴ	Sᴜɪᴛᴀʙʟᴇ sᴏɪʟ	Pʀᴏᴘᴀɢᴀᴛɪᴏɴ	Pᴀʀᴛs ᴏғ ᴘʟᴀɴᴛ	Usᴇs
Hardy biennial	Full sun or partial shade	Fertile, humus-rich	Seed	Leaves, roots	Cosmetic, culinary, household, medicinal

*Plain-leaved
parsley*

in spring and summer. In the fall sow seed in a cold frame for a winter crop. You can also try growing parsley in pots in a greenhouse or by a very light window indoors. ZONE 4

SELECTED VARIETIES

Italian parsley (*P. crispum* var. *neopolitanum*) This is also known as flat-leaved parsley. It does not make such an attractive edging plant as the more familiar curled parsley (sometimes called French parsley), but it has a stronger flavor. The leaves are flat and resemble those of coriander. Cultivation is the same as for curled parsley.

Hamburg parsley (*P. crispum* var. *tuberosum*) Also known as turnip-rooted parsley, the leaves of this distinctive type look like Italian or plain-leaved parsley, and they can be used in the same way. But this is a dual-purpose plant, and the parsnip-like roots can be eaten as a vegetable.

Sow Hamburg parsley in early or mid-spring, where the plants are to grow, and lift the roots in the fall or winter.

WARNING Parsley should not be consumed during pregnancy. It can also cause inflammation of the nerves if used to excess.

*Hamburg
parsley*

*Hamburg
parsley has
leaves that can
be used like
ordinary parsley,
and roots that
can be eaten as
a vegetable.*

Pimpinella anisum

ANISE

ANISE IS GROWN PRIMARILY for its seeds, which have the distinctive aniseed flavor. However, a piquancy can be given to soups and salads by adding a few of the leaves. The mature leaves of this annual are feathery and resemble a coarse carrot, but those produced while the plant is still young are more rounded and less divided. Umbrella-like flower-heads of tiny white blooms resembling those of dill are produced in mid or late summer.

The plant grows to about 18–24 inches and is best used as a filler in an herb bed or border. The young plants are rather fragile, so put them in a sheltered position protected from strong winds. Be sure to

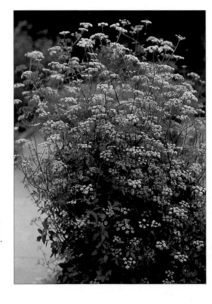

This rather flimsy annual does best in a sheltered position. Use it as a filler in a herb bed or border.

sow where you want the plants to grow, as seedlings do not transplant well.

The main sowing time is spring, and the herb is best grown as an annual. Once the plant is established, you are assured of more in future years, although the self-sown seedlings are unlikely to become a major problem. Because it is grown for its seeds, these must be allowed to form after flowering and mature to harvest. Just put away a small quantity to sow the next spring in case insufficient self-sown seedlings appear. ZONE A

TYPE OF PLANT	BEST POSITION	SUITABLE SOIL	PROPAGATION	PARTS OF PLANT	USES
Annual	Full sun	Light, well drained	Seed	Leaves, seeds	Culinary, household, medicinal

Poterium sanguisorba
SALAD BURNET

ONCE POPULAR IN ENGLISH cottage gardens and taken to North America by early settlers, salad burnet has become a rather neglected culinary herb. Its leaves have a flavor reminiscent of cucumber, and they are well worth including in summer salads.

The long cascading stems splay out from the center of the plant, making a mound about 12 inches tall. The small, toothed, blue-green leaves grow in opposite pairs along the stems, and in early summer these are topped by small reddish flowerheads. Although not evergreen, the plant is in leaf for most of the year as the new leaves appear very early and are retained well into winter.

Salad burnet is undemanding and will take care of itself once established. In the wild it grows especially well on chalk, but it will grow satis-

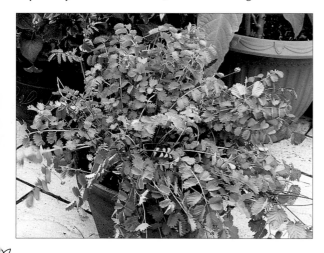

factorily in most beds, given a sunny position.

The plant can be divided, but once established, self-sown seedlings will almost certainly be available. In fact, it is advisable to cut off flowerheads to prevent seedlings from becoming a problem. ZONE 3

*Try growing salad burnet in a container
if you can't find space in the herb garden.*

TYPE OF PLANT	BEST POSITION	SUITABLE SOIL	PROPAGATION	PARTS OF PLANT	USES
Hardy perennial	Full sun	Undemanding	Division, seed	Leaves	Culinary, medicinal

Prunella vulgaris
SELFHEAL

Selfheal varies in height according to conditions; although normally a ground-hugger just a few inches high, it will grow to more than 18 inches in poor light and moist soil. Mauve, purple, pink, or white flowers appear in dense heads in mid and late summer.

It can be used as a ground cover or as an edging plant for beds and borders. However, use it with care as it can become a persistent weed. For instance, it is not advisable to plant selfheal at the front of a border adjoining a lawn as it will easily spread into the grassed area and become a problem. Grow it instead in an area of the herb garden contained by paving to restrict its spread. Alternatively, plant it in a large container, perhaps placed at the base of a tree or group of shrubs.

Selfheal can be bought as a plant, but it is easy to raise from seed. However, you may have to order from a nursery specializing in herbs or wildflowers. Sow at any time between spring and fall. Division is the easiest method of propagating established plants. The prostrate stems root freely, so there are plenty of young plants that can be separated from their parents.   ZONE 3

TYPE OF PLANT	BEST POSITION	SUITABLE SOIL	PROPAGATION	PARTS OF PLANT	USES
Hardy perennial	Full sun or partial shade	Undemanding, well drained	Leaves	Leaves	Medicinal

Pulmonaria officinalis
LUNGWORT

Lungwort is a popular garden plant, grown mainly for its appealing spring flowers that are pink or red when they open, then turn violet and blue, creating a multi-colored effect. There are also white cultivars. The first flowers, on 9–12 inch stems, appear in early spring, and the plant continues to bloom until late spring. The blotched, silvery-white variegated leaves, remain attractive for many months.

The spots on the foliage were thought to resemble diseased lungs in early times, and made the plant popular in folk medicine as a treatment for lung

Pulmonaria officinalis
'Sissinghurst white'

diseases such as tuberculosis. It contains mucilage, tannin, saponins, and silicic acid, and some of these can have a beneficial effect on the respiratory system. An infusion of the dried leaves is sometimes used for coughs and sore throats. Some herbalists prescribe lungwort to control diarrhea.

Lungwort makes effective ground cover for a shaded area, but it also looks good in bold clumps at the front of herbaceous or mixed borders, as well as in the herb garden. The plant is undemanding provided there is sufficient moisture. Water freely in dry weather if the soil appears dry.

Division, preferably at the end of the season, is the easiest method of propagation. ZONES 2–3

TYPE OF PLANT	BEST POSITION	SUITABLE SOIL	PROPAGATION	PARTS OF PLANT	USES
Hardy perennial	Shade or partial shade	Moist	Seed, division	Leaves	Medicinal

Rosa gallica 'Officinalis'
APOTHECARY'S ROSE

FRAGRANCE ALONE WOULD BE justification enough for including some roses in the herb garden. But they also qualify on other counts. Rose water is used medicinally and in cooking, rose petals can be crystallized or used fresh in salads and desserts, and the hips are made into teas and syrups. So have no qualms in planting plenty of roses to bring beauty and color to your herb collection. However, try to restrict yourself to those that have been used traditionally as herbs or are a source of fragrant oils, such as the apothecary's rose. Others which should be considered are *R.* ×*damascena* 'Trigintipetala' (a form of the damask rose much used for the production of attar of roses in Bulgaria), *R.* ×*alba,* and *R.* ×*centifolia* (the cabbage or Provence rose). Modern hybrid roses should be avoided as they seldom look right in an herb garden.

If you have space for just one shrub rose, the apothecary's rose combines the qualities of beautiful blooms with intense fragrance, petals of substance that dry well, and a good herbal pedigree. It makes a shrub 3–4 feet tall with a similar spread, and the semi-double flowers have crimson petals with a central cluster of golden anthers, and red hips in the fall. ZONE 5

TYPE OF PLANT	BEST POSITION	SUITABLE SOIL	PROPAGATION	PARTS OF PLANT	USES
Hardy shrub	Full sun	Fertile	Cuttings	Flowers	Cosmetic, craft, culinary, household, medicinal

Rosmarinus officinalis
ROSEMARY

Rosemary is one of the essential culinary herbs and should be included in every herb garden. It is worth planting purely as an ornamental herbaceous plant. The small gray-green leaves are evergreen in southern climates, and simply brushing against them releases their distinctive resinous fragrance. The small flowers – which vary from dark blue to very pale blue or even white according to cultivar – nestle close to the stem among the foliage. The flowers sometimes begin to open in late winter in mild districts, though late spring is the main flowering period.

Rosemary varies considerably in size depending on the cultivar. Some remain bushy and compact at about 36 inches or less; others like 'Tuscan Blue' are

Rosemary is a first-rate ornamental perennial, at home in the flower garden. This cultivar is 'Sissinghurst Blue'.

taller and more erect. A plant of a tall cultivar can easily reach 6 feet.

Rosemary can be a centerpiece to a formal herb garden, form an informal dividing hedge, or be planted in a decorative shrub border. It makes an elegant patio plant for a large pot and, in a cold area, growing it in a container makes winter protection easier. Rosemary tolerates clipping, so you can keep it small and compact if necessary.

Although hardy in milder climates, in colder areas or in cold, exposed districts, protection is necessary. Cuttings can be taken in summer.   ZONE 6

TYPE OF PLANT	BEST POSITION	SUITABLE SOIL	PROPAGATION	PARTS OF PLANT	USES
Tender perennial	Full sun or partial shade	Light, well drained	Cuttings	Leaves	Cosmetic, craft, culinary, household, medicinal

Rumex acetosa
SORREL

Sorrel looks like a weed, so don't give it a conspicuous position.

Sorrel is grown for the tangy flavor of its leaves. It is sometimes known as the broad-leaved sorrel as the leaves are up to 2 feet. The mature plant reaches about 3 feet, but the leaves are best eaten before the spikes of small rust-colored flowers appear. The flavor is best if the soil is moist and cool. So in hot and dry areas, apply a thick mulch around the plants after watering thoroughly. Pick the plants over frequently and remove flower buds to ensure a continuing supply of young succulent foliage.

Sorrel is a deep-rooted perennial plant that can be difficult to eradicate. If allowed to flower and set seed, the resulting self-sown seedlings will become a nuisance. Therefore to avoid these problems and because fresh young leaves have a more refined flavor, sorrel is best treated as an annual.

Sow in spring, where the plants are to grow, and thin the seedlings to about 12 inches apart. Try to remember to remove the flowering stems before they can set seed.

Seeds can usually be bought from nurseries specializing in herbs and wildflowers, and many herb nurseries sell established plants.   ZONE 3

TYPE OF PLANT	BEST POSITION	SUITABLE SOIL	PROPAGATION	PARTS OF PLANT	USES
Hardy perennial	Sun or partial shade	Fertile, moist	Division, seed	Leaves	Craft, culinary, household, medicinal

Rumex scutatus
FRENCH SORREL

THIS PLANT PROVIDES PLENTY of spinach-like leaves that are milder in taste than some of the other sorrels. The pale green, distinctively shaped wavy leaves are about 4 inches long and arise from ground level to form a clump. Insignificant small greenish flowers appear on stalks about 12–18 inches tall in late spring or early summer.

Water the plants well in dry weather to encourage a plentiful supply of tender leaves. The flowering stems should be removed as soon as they appear to

French sorrel lacks eye-appeal and is best grown in rows like spinach.

help promote more leafy growth and also to prevent self-sown seedlings from becoming a problem.

If you prevent flowering in this way, the plants will continue to flourish for several years. However, they are best divided and replanted after three years. French sorrel can also be raised easily from seed. Sow it in spring where it is to grow, or in seed trays to plant out later.

Slugs, snails, and caterpillars also find the leaves make a succulent feast, so be prepared to control these pests.   ZONE 4

TYPE OF PLANT	BEST POSITION	SUITABLE SOIL	PROPAGATION	PARTS OF PLANT	USES
Hardy perennial	Full sun or partial shade	Fertile, moist	Division, seed	Leaves	Culinary

Ruta graveolens

RUE

THIS SMALL HERBACEOUS PERENNIAL grows about 18–36 inches tall and is covered with attractive, rounded, and divided foliage which is green or blue-green. The leaves have an acrid smell, and in very cold areas the plant may lose some of them in winter. In summer it bears bright yellow flowers which some people prefer to remove.

A variegated rue with leaves flecked creamy white is available, but the most attractive varieties have bright glaucous-blue foliage. 'Blue Mound' is popular in America, and 'Jackman's Blue' is the one usually grown in Europe.

Rue can be grown as single plants in an herb or herbaceous border, but a row planted as a low dividing "hedge" within the herb garden can look particularly decorative. Don't be afraid to clip the plants with shears in spring to encourage new bright foliage and compact growth.

Sow seeds in spring or cuttings of non-flowering shoots can be taken in summer.   ZONE 4

WARNING   Take care when handling rue. The foliage can cause a very severe reaction in some people, especially if handled in sunshine. Particularly severe reactions can need hospital treatment. Use it with caution medicinally, too – it can be toxic in high doses. It should never be used during pregnancy. Use it sparingly as a culinary herb, as the flavor is very strong.

TYPE OF PLANT	BEST POSITION	SUITABLE SOIL	PROPAGATION	PARTS OF PLANT	USES
Perennial	Full sun	Undemanding	Cuttings, division, seed	Leaves, roots	Household, medicinal

Salvia elegans
PINEAPPLE SAGE

THE SOFT, DOWNY LEAVES which smell strongly of pineapple are the main attraction of the plant. Where conditions suit, however, an attractive display of tubular red flowers on slender spikes is a bonus in late summer. These are attractive to many insects and to hummingbirds in search of nectar.

This tender perennial never makes a large plant and normally only reaches 24–36 inches. To encourage a bushy shape, pinch out the growing tips of the plants when they are small. It will grow happily in a large pot. This makes the winter protection this shrub requires easy, as you can simply move the container into a greenhouse or conservatory. However, where the winters are mild,

pineapple sage might survive outdoors if it is protected by a sunny wall. It is always worth taking a few cuttings each year to overwinter in a frost-free place as an insurance against winter losses.   ZONE 9

Growing pineapple sage in a container makes it easier to move to a frost-free place for the winter.

TYPE OF PLANT	BEST POSITION	SUITABLE SOIL	PROPAGATION	PARTS OF PLANT	USES
Tender perennial	Full sun	Well drained	Cuttings	Leaves	Culinary

Salvia officinalis
GARDEN SAGE

Salvia
officinalis

The useful sage can be surprisingly beautiful in flower.

GARDEN SAGE IS A classic culinary herb. It is also one of the most ornamental, particularly if one of the cultivars with variegated or colored foliage is chosen. It is a dwarf, semi-evergreen subshrub that usually grows no more than about 24 inches. In summer it forms a neat mound of aromatic foliage that looks equally good alongside herbaceous plants and shrubs as it does in the herb garden.

Decorative spikes of white, pink, or pale blue flowers usually appear in late spring and early summer, but you may prefer to remove them as this plant is primarily grown for its foliage. In any case sage is reluctant to flower unless the climate and conditions are favorable.

Although hardy, sage often suffers damage in a harsh winter. In less than favorable areas it will look ragged at the onset of spring with many damaged

TYPE OF PLANT	BEST POSITION	SUITABLE SOIL	PROPAGATION	PARTS OF PLANT	USES
Hardy subshrub	Full sun	Undemanding, well drained	Cuttings, seed	Leaves	Culinary, cosmetic, household, medicinal

Salvia officinalis
'Tricolor'

Salvia officinalis
'Purpurascens'

leaves, and in the extreme north it may be killed by winter cold. However, by early summer most plants will again be well clothed with fresh young leaves and in mild areas sage will come through the winter looking good.

After three or four years plants often begin to lose their compact shape and are then best replaced. The species itself can be raised from seed, but for variegated and colored-leaved cultivars you need to take cuttings. In any case it is always worth taking a few cuttings to overwinter in a cold frame as insurance against winter losses. ZONE 3

SELECTED CULTIVARS

The species itself has leaves that open pale green but harden to almost gray. This garden sage, as it is known, is a perfectly acceptable foliage plant and looks pleasing in an herb garden. However, it has some outstanding cultivars which should be seriously considered for any garden. Try to include one or two varieties of *S. officinalis* to add color and interest to the herb garden, or grow them in beds and borders with other ornamentals. They look good in raised beds and in patio containers, where they will add summer-long color and the leaves can be crushed to release the distinctive aroma.

The most popular cultivars are listed below, but there are many others from which to choose, such as the white-flowered **'Albiflora'**, red-flowered **'Rubiflora'**, and golden-leaved **'Aurea'**. Nurseries offer both broad-leaved and narrow-leaved forms of the garden sage, but the one sold as narrow-leaved may be a distinct species called *S. lavandulifolia*.

'Icterina' Sometimes called 'Variegata,' it is known as golden sage and has particularly bright coloration. The new foliage in spring is marbled primrose, gold, and green, and it retains a good gold and green contrast throughout summer and into fall.

'Purpurascens' This is purple sage with velvety gray-green leaves suffused with purple. Violet-blue flowers may be produced in summer. It makes a splendid companion for yellow-leaved plants, with which it contrasts well.

'Tricolor' A compact cultivar with bright leaves that manage to combine green, cream, white, purple and pink. Although very attractive, it tends to be less hardy than some of the others.

WARNING Sage should not be consumed during pregnancy.

The variegated sages are better garden plants, and can be used like plain sage. This one is 'Icterina.'

Salvia officinalis
'Icterina'

Salvia sclarea

CLARY

look good growing in front of shrubs, or you can include a few plants in the herbaceous border. It is probably at its best as a country-garden plant in an informal setting.

Clary is usually grown as a biennial, sown in late spring to flower the following year and will self-sow. It can also be propagated by division in early fall or spring. But as it is the leaves and not the flowers that are used, you can treat it as an annual. This is useful in a cold area as otherwise the plant needs a warm, sheltered position to survive the rigors of a harsh winter.

Seed is usually available from specialists, but be careful when buying from general nurseries not to buy the ornamental *Salvia horminum*, also described as clary.   ZONE 3–4

Clary has large leaves that can make the plant look ungainly at first, but it's stunning in flower.

THE NAME CLARY IS sometimes applied to other salvias, but *S. sclarea* is the one usually grown in herb gardens. It is a striking plant with large, wrinkled leaves covered with white, wooly hairs. Pale pink or violet-flushed flowers with papery bracts appear in late summer and bring the plant to a height of about 3 feet.

True clary is an imposing plant with its large leaves and striking flowerheads, but it is not an easy plant to place. Try it in a mixed herb border as it can

TYPE OF PLANT	BEST POSITION	SUITABLE SOIL	PROPAGATION	PARTS OF PLANT	USES
Biennial	Full sun	Undemanding	Seed	Leaves	Culinary, medicinal

Santolina chamaecyparissus
LAVENDER COTTON

Lavender cotton, or cotton lavender, is more widely grown as an ornamental plant than as an herb, but its use as an insect repellent justifies its inclusion in the herb garden. It was once used to treat parasitic worms in children, but its medicinal applications have fallen into disuse.

The plant makes a small mound of finely cut, silvery-white aromatic foliage that acts as a good foil to other plants. Like box, it is suitable as a dwarf hedge for use in knot gardens and as a divider in formal herb gardens. It can also edge a formal herb bed or a centerpiece containing a bay tree or rosemary.

Lavender cotton will grow to about 18 inches as a foliage plant if pruned regularly, and about 2 feet if allowed to flower. The masses of button-like yellow flowers in summer can be attractive on single plants, but where lavender cotton is grown as a hedge or edging, cut them off with shears to retain a neat and compact outline.

This pleasing foliage plant should not be confined to an herb garden.

The cultivar *S. chamaecyparissus* 'Nana' (syn. *S. chamaecyparissus cosrica*) is a particularly compact form (10 inches), which is dwarf enough for a rock garden, and which makes a neat edging.

Lavender cotton can be raised from seed or from cuttings taken in summer. ZONE 6–7

TYPE OF PLANT	BEST POSITION	SUITABLE SOIL	PROPAGATION	PARTS OF PLANT	USES
Perennial	Full sun	Fertile, moist but well drained	Cuttings, seed	Leaves	Cosmetic, culinary, household

Saponaria officinalis
SOAPWORT

Before commercial soap production started in the 1800s, soapwort was an important herb. The leaves produce a cleansing lather when crushed and rubbed in water, although it is the tough root that provides most of the saponins – the active ingredients. It was also once used medicinally, but now it is only used cosmetically and as a water softener.

This perennial plant produces spreading shoots in spring which emerge from the fleshy roots as thick as a finger. Delicate-looking, slightly fragrant, pinkish white flowers open over a long period during the summer. The individual flowers are about 1 inch across, borne in loose heads on stems 12–36 inches high. Double cultivars with both white and pink flowers are also available.

Where the plant grows naturally, it shows a preference for stream sides and damp woods, and in a moist position in partial shade, it will grow taller and much better than in the dry, sunny conditions that many herbs prefer.

Soapwort mixes in well with country-garden plants grown informally to give a rustic atmosphere. It needs plenty of space in order to grow well and to allow it to spread and flop about, and where conditions suit it, it will spread enthusiastically by runners. It can also be raised from seed sown in spring.

ZONE 2–3

TYPE OF PLANT	BEST POSITION	SUITABLE SOIL	PROPAGATION	PARTS OF PLANT	USES
Hardy perennial	Sun or partial shade	Moist, rich in humus	Division, seed	Leaves, roots	Cosmetic, household, medicinal

Satureja hortensis
SUMMER SAVORY

Summer savory is a small-leaved, rather modest annual, but pungently flavored. Most cooks find the flavor of summer savory superior to that of the similar looking, but perennial winter savory.

Summer savory is a bushy, spreading plant that grows to about 12 inches tall. It tends to be top-heavy as the season advances and if not supported is likely to flop over. The dainty pale lilac flowers bloom intermittently between midsummer and early fall, but are too insignificant to make much of a show.

Sow the seed in spring where the plants are to grow and later thin the seedlings to about 6 inches apart. Seed can also be started off under glass and the seedlings planted out, but the plant generally resents transplanting.

Reserve an area in the herb garden for summer savory as you can depend on a supply of self-sown seedlings in subsequent years, and the seedlings are less likely to become a nuisance among other plants. Summer savory also does well in containers such as pots and windowboxes. ZONE HA

Summer savory is best grown in its own bed, where self-sown seedlings will not be a problem.

TYPE OF PLANT	BEST POSITION	SUITABLE SOIL	PROPAGATION	PARTS OF PLANT	USES
Hardy annual	Full sun	Light	Seed	Leaves	Culinary, medicinal

Satureja montana
WINTER SAVORY

Winter savory is an evergreen perennial, though it may shed its leaves in very cold areas or a particularly harsh winter. A slow-growing plant, it makes a neat mound about 12 inches high and 8 inches across. In late summer, tiny pale lilac, white or pinkish white flowers cover the plant. It is worth clipping the tops of plants in spring to encourage a supply of fresh young leaves for picking. In addition, trimming will keep the plant looking neat and stimulate dense growth. This tolerance of clipping means that winter savory can be grown as a low hedge within the herb garden with plants spaced about 8 inches apart.

Winter savory prefers a soil that is not too fertile, and provided it is given a sunny position, it is a trouble-free herb to grow. In cold areas it will benefit from winter protection by placing in a cold frame.

Try growing winter savory in a pot or other container. If the pot is small enough to be taken indoors and kept in a very light position, you will be able to keep the plant cropping through the winter months. Pinch back the tips of the shoots regularly to prevent the plant from becoming leggy.

Winter savory can be raised from seed, and when allowed to flower it will self-seed. It can also be propagated from cuttings.   ZONE 5

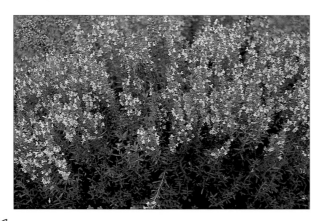

Although it may shed its leaves in winter in northern climates, winter savory is a useful perennial.

TYPE OF PLANT	BEST POSITION	SUITABLE SOIL	PROPAGATION	PARTS OF PLANT	USES
Hardy semi-evergreen subshrub	Full sun	Undemanding, well drained	Cuttings, seed	Leaves	Culinary, household, medicinal

Stachys byzantina (syn. *S. lanata, S. olympia*)
WOOLY BETONY

THIS EXCELLENT ORNAMENTAL, ALSO called lamb's ears, looks good in the herb garden proper, combined with herbaceous plants or as a ground cover in front of shrubs. Some herb enthusiasts may challenge its place in an herb garden as it has no medicinal or culinary uses, but it is stocked by some herb nurseries as a cottage-garden plant and is listed in some herb books. It is used to enhance herbal wreaths, so let it enhance the beauty of your herb garden, too.

The plant forms a dense, slowly spreading mat of

Don't confine this excellent ground cover plant to the herb garden. It's a first-rate general garden plant.

soft, wooly, silvery-gray leaves said to resemble a lamb's ears. Its ground-hugging habit and light color make it a particularly attractive plant during the summer. The foliage grows to about 9–12 inches, but the spikes of pink to purple flowers in midsummer bring the height to about 18 inches.

Many people find the flowers attractive, others prefer the low carpeting foliage alone. In the latter case 'Silver Carpet' would be a good choice as it seldom flowers. For a carpet of pale yellow early in the year, try 'Primrose Heron.' The color of the new leaves tones down during the summer, and by winter the leaves are a silvery gray.

An evergreen in the mildest climates, the winter-damaged leaves of wooly betony usually look messy by the end of winter and should be cleared to make way for the new growth.   ZONE 4

TYPE OF PLANT	BEST POSITION	SUITABLE SOIL	PROPAGATION	PARTS OF PLANT	USES
◉	✷			❀	◓
Perennial	Full sun	Fertile, well drained	Division, seed	Leaves	Craft

Symphytum officinale
COMFREY

Comfrey is decorative enough to include in the herbaceous border. Its trusses of mauve-pink, bell-shaped flowers begin to open in early summer and continue for many weeks. The flowers bring a touch of color to what is otherwise a rather unassuming clump of leaves about 24 inches tall.

It grows naturally in damp ground near river banks, so a moist, fertile soil will produce the tallest plants and yield the best crop of lush leaves.

Division is the easiest and quickest method of propagating this perennial. Plants grown from seed are often slow to mature.

Be prepared to protect the leaves from the ravages of slugs and snails if these are a problem in your garden or herb bed. ZONE 3

WARNING Comfrey should not be taken internally.

This medicinal herb does not look amiss in an herbaceous border, but it demands plenty of space.

COMFREY HAS SUCH A tremendous reputation for its medicinal qualities that no herb garden would be complete without a clump. Although it is no longer recommended that it be taken internally, you can use its foliage as a valuable addition to the compost pile. Many organic gardeners grow comfrey for this specific purpose.

TYPE OF PLANT	BEST POSITION	SUITABLE SOIL	PROPAGATION	PARTS OF PLANT	USES
Hardy perennial	Full sun or partial shade	Fertile, moist	Division, seed	Leaves, roots	Cosmetic, household, medicinal

Tanacetum vulgare
TANSY

*Don't confine tansy to the herb garden.
It is also a worthwhile herbaceous
border plant.*

Tansy's bright yellow heads of button-like flowers show up well against its feathery, dark green leaves which have a very pungent taste. The foliage is most attractive and worthy to cut for use in fresh or dried arrangements. The flowers can be dried for winter arrangements.

This hardy perennial herb is undemanding and easy to grow. It does well even in poor soil. In an exposed position, it may become ragged and look untidy after strong winds. Inserting supports in late spring will help to overcome this minor drawback.

Tansy soon forms a dense clump about 3–4 feet tall and spreads rapidly by underground rhizomes. It is advisable to divide and replant established plants every second or third year. Plants can also be propagated from seed.   ZONE 3

WARNING   Tansy should not be eaten at any time during pregnancy.

TYPE OF PLANT	BEST POSITION	SUITABLE SOIL	PROPAGATION	PARTS OF PLANT	USES
Hardy perennial	Full sun	Undemanding	Division, seed	Leaves	Craft, culinary, household, medicinal

Taraxacum officinale
DANDELION

Many gardeners spend hours each year trying to eliminate dandelions from their garden, and it sometimes comes as a surprise to find it grown as a crop. In fact it has a long history of medicinal use – especially as a diuretic, hence the colloquial names piss-the-bed or French *pis-en-lis*.

Nowadays, it is more likely to be grown for its culinary properties. The young leaves, rich in vitamins and minerals, can be used in salads or cooked like spinach. The roots are used to make a coffee-substitute, and home winemakers use the flowers or the leaves. The quality of the leaves is improved by blanching like frisée. Some roots can be lifted in the fall and forced in the dark, like chicory, to supply crisp young leaves in the winter.

Dandelion seed can be bought from some nurseries, and the selections they offer are likely to be superior to wild dandelions. But you may prefer to dig up and replant some roots from another part of the yard or gather them elsewhere. Bear in mind that the deep tap roots are difficult to lift without leaving some behind, which is why dandelions are so difficult to eradicate. Deadhead before it self-seeds.

ZONE 3

TYPE OF PLANT	BEST POSITION	SUITABLE SOIL	PROPAGATION	PARTS OF PLANT	USES
Hardy perennial	Full sun	Undemanding	Root cuttings, seed	Flowers, leaves, roots	Cosmetic, culinary, household, medicinal

Teucrium chamaedrys

GERMANDER

Germander used to be grown for medicinal use, and a tea brewed from its leaves was a popular remedy for gout. Nowadays, it is more often grown as an edging plant for an herb bed or border. It can also be used to form patterns in knot gardens and parterres. It is a good plant to grow in a dry stone wall or at the edge of a raised bed.

A dwarf, bushy, aromatic plant with creeping roots, germander forms low, bushy growth about 12 inches high. The small but dainty pink flowers are never spectacular, but they occur over a long period from midsummer through to the early fall. In cold areas, or during severe winters, it may drop its leaves, but in southern climates it remains evergreen. In very cold regions, it is worth mulching around the roots in the fall to give some protection during winter.

The creeping roots make germander suitable for division, but take cuttings if you need a lot of plants, for instance to create an edging.   ZONE 5

Germander is a useful edging for an herb bed or border. It can also be grown in dry stone walls.

TYPE OF PLANT	BEST POSITION	SUITABLE SOIL	PROPAGATION	PARTS OF PLANT	USES
Perennial	Full sun	Fertile	Cuttings, division	Leaves	Medicinal

Thymus
THYME

Thymus
vulgaris

N<small>O HERB GARDEN WORTH</small> the name should be without some thyme. There are many species and cultivars, all highly aromatic and attractive. If space permits, start a collection – there are dozens to choose from, all widely available. Most of them flower in mid and late summer.

The one most commonly used in the kitchen is *T. vulgaris* (English or common thyme), but many others can be used for culinary, medicinal, and aromatic purposes. Some, such as golden and variegated lemon thyme, can be used for cooking, but the flavor is not as good as common thyme. Creeping, mat-like species, such as *T. pulegioides*, have tiny interwoven branches that have leaves too small to make the effort of harvesting worthwhile.

It makes sense to grow a few culinary varieties in greater numbers for harvesting, and a selection of

Thymus vulgaris,
*the thyme most
used for culinary
purposes, is very
appealing in
flower.*

T<small>YPE OF PLANT</small>	B<small>EST POSITION</small>	S<small>UITABLE SOIL</small>	P<small>ROPAGATION</small>	P<small>ARTS OF PLANT</small>	U<small>SES</small>
Hardy evergreen subshrub	Full sun	Undemanding	Cuttings, layers, seed	Leaves	Cosmetic, culinary, household, medicinal

There are many varieties of thyme, with variations in flower and foliage color. A collection of them makes a very pleasing feature.

other thymes for their decorative effect. All the thymes described on the following pages are undemanding low-growing perennials that have the same cultural requirements.

They require little attention once established but tend to become straggly and messy after a few years. Therefore, it is best to propagate a few new plants every year to use as replacements. Layering is possible, but for more than one or two plants cuttings are a better proposition.

Although hardy in most areas, in the northern United States or exceptionally severe winters losses are not uncommon – another reason for overwintering young plants in a cold frame. ZONE 5

THYME IN THE GARDEN

Thymes are versatile plants to use around the garden. If you want to grow them purely as a crop to harvest, a massed group in a bed or herb garden is both practical and pleasing. You can, however, make more of a feature by growing thyme between paving stones, as edging plants, for ground cover, or in containers.

Scented thyme lawns These are a practical proposition provided you consider using thyme as a grass substitute for a small area seldom walked on, or for secondary paths within the herb garden.

The best thymes for a lawn or path are the creeping thyme (*T. praecox arcticus*, syn. *T. drucei*) and

Thymus praecox
arcticus

Thymus
pseudolanuginosus

the wooly thyme (*T. pseudolanuginosus*, syn. *T. languinosus*). Both are low creepers that grow about 2 inches high; wooly thyme makes an especially low ground-hugging carpet. As selective weedkillers cannot be used on a thyme lawn, it is essential to make sure the ground is as weed-free as possible before planting. You will have to weed by hand.

Between paving stones The two thymes mentioned above are also a good choice to plant in the crevices between paving stones. But at the very edge of a path, which will have the least amount of wear, you can also grow varieties of *T. vulgaris*.

Around a garden seat Thyme is a delightful plant to grow between paving stones under a bench or in a raised bed where the leaves are conveniently close to be crushed to release their aroma. But remember, thyme attracts bees and wasps, so this idea may not appeal to everyone.

IN CONTAINERS

Thymes are ideal for growing in a windowbox or other kind of container, either alone or together with other plants. To maintain a supply of leaves for the kitchen, plant a windowbox with *T. vulgaris* if you have no space in the yard, or no herb garden. Otherwise, grow the more decorative thymes in containers. Good ones to use are the golden *T. ×citriodorus* '**Bertram Anderson**' (syn. '**Anderson's Gold**'), variegated *T. ×citriodorus* '**Variegatus**' (syn. *T. ×* '**Silver Posie**') and good flowering cultivars like *T. doerfleri* '**Bressingham Pink**'.

AND INDOORS . . .

Thyme can be grown indoors by a very light kitchen window, but this is best regarded as a novelty venture or as a way of supplementing the outdoor supply. Kits can sometimes be bought with everything necessary: container and seed. Unless light conditions are excellent, however, you would do better to buy a small plant from a garden center and pot it in an attractive container. Then when it deteriorates and ceases to be attractive or useful, plant it outside to recover.

SELECTED SPECIES AND CULTIVARS

The following thymes are species and cultivars worth including in a collection. Many other thymes will be obtainable from specialist nurseries.

The commonly used synonyms have been included in the following list. Plants may be sold

Thymes are small enough for you to be able to grow a collection in a container.

Thymus ×
citriodorus
'*Bertram Anderson*'

This group of thymes in a terra-cotta trough shows varieties grown for foliage and flowers. 'Bressingham Pink' sits next to a golden thyme.

under any of the names given. Varieties of *T. drucei, T. serpyllum, T. vulgaris,* and *T.* ✕*citriodorus* are often attributed to different species, which can cause much confusion, but the varietal name should give a good indication as the identity of the plant.

T. ✕*citriodorus* (lemon thyme) Broader leaves than *T. vulgaris* and strongly lemon-scented when crushed; 9 inches.

T. ✕*citriodorus* 'Aureus' (golden thyme) Leaves edged yellow; less hardy and robust than most thymes; 8 inches.

T. ✕*citriodorus* 'Bertram Anderson' (syn. 'Anderson's Gold') A dwarf carpeter with bright golden foliage that holds its color well even through the winter; 2 inches.

T. ✕*citriodorus* 'Golden King' Bushy, upright

habit, with gold-edged leaves; 9–12 inches.

T. ✕*citriodorus* 'Silver Queen' Leaves edged cream; not as hardy and robust as most thymes; 8 inches.

T. ✕*citriodorus* 'Variegatus' (syn. 'Silver Posie') Silver-edged leaves and pinkish flowers – an attractive plant for a container; 6 inches.

T. doerfleri 'Bressingham Pink' Bright pink flowers; carpeting habit; 2 inches.

T. herba-barona (caraway thyme) Forms a mat of

Thymus citriodorus 'Silver Queen' with a group of other thymes in a terra-cotta trough.

Thymus ✕ citriodorus *'Silver Queen'*

Thymus
herba-barona

dark green leaves with a strong smell of caraway seed; pinkish mauve flowers; 4 inches.

T. praecox arcticus (syn. *T. drucei*) Low-growing, with small gray-green leaves, red or pink flowers; 'Albus' has white flowers; 1 inches.

T. pseudolanuginosus (syn. *T. lanuginosus*) (wooly thyme) Grows into a mat of minute wooly leaves; it seldom flowers; 2 inches.

T. serpyllum (creeping wild thyme) Forms a flat green mat, with tiny pale lavender flowers; 2 inches.

T. serpyllum 'Coccineus' A crimson-flowered cultivar of the above.

T. serpyllum 'Pink Chintz' Loose cushions of soft, wooly leaves with pale pink flowers; 4 inches.

T. vulgaris (common, English, or garden thyme) More upright than the other thymes; usually mauve or purple flowers, but sometimes white; 6–10 inches.

T. vulgaris 'Doone Valley' Low mat-forming plant with dark green leaves heavily marked with gold; mauve flowers; 3 inches.

WARNING Do not take large doses of thyme during pregnancy.

*Caraway thyme (*T. herba-barona) *is a ground-hugger that forms a mat of caraway-scented foliage.*

Thymus
serpyllum
'Albus,' a white
form of creeping
thyme.

Thymus
serpyllum

Trigonella foenum-graecum
FENUGREEK

THIS TENDER ANNUAL will grow into an erect plant 18–24 inches tall if allowed to reach maturity. But it is usually harvested before it even becomes a seedling. This is because fenugreek is grown mainly as a "sprouting seed." However, the seeds are also an important ingredient in curry powder, and they yield a yellow dye. The mature plant, as depicted in the illustration, has culinary and medicinal uses.

Use the sprouting seeds at the stage shown in the photograph to add a spicy tang to a salad or as a sandwich filling. The fully developed leaves are bitter and strong-tasting, but can be used in some Asian dishes.

To grow fenugreek outdoors, start the seed off under glass and plant out when there is no risk of frost, or sow directly outdoors in late spring.

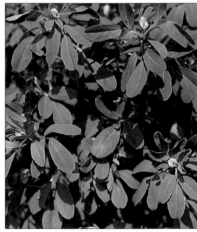

Fenugreek is usually grown as sprouted seeds, but you can grow it to maturity.

To produce the curry-flavored sprouts, germinate the seed on layers of moist paper towels in a light position indoors. Keep the towel moist, and harvest the seedlings when ready – which can be as little as six days. Wash, then drain. Special jars for sprouting the seeds are obtainable, or improvise with a glass jar, a piece of cloth, and a rubber band – the trick is to keep the seeds moist, but to drain off excess water so that they do not rot.   ZONE TA

TYPE OF PLANT	BEST POSITION	SUITABLE SOIL	PROPAGATION	PARTS OF PLANT	USES
Tender annual	Full sun (outdoors)	Fertile, well drained	Seed	Leaves, seeds, sprouting seeds	Culinary, household, medicinal

Tropaeolum majus

NASTURTIUM

Tᴴɪꜱ ᴘᴏᴘᴜʟᴀʀ ᴀɴɴᴜᴀʟ ɪꜱ easy to grow and a favorite with children. It is always worthy of a place in the herb garden. Both flowers and leaves are edible, and the seeds can be pickled as capers.

Nasturtium flowers are so bright and colorful that even one or two plants will enliven a part of the herb garden dominated by foliage plants. Although the climbing varieties can be used, they tend to smother other plants. The compact varieties that grow to about 24 inches are more practical and are good container plants.

This is one plant that you don't need to feed or provide with very fertile soil – rich soil is positively detrimental. Too fertile a soil or too much watering will produce a mass of leaves but few flowers, most of which are likely to be hidden underneath the foliage. Poor conditions are needed to produce plants with compact growth and masses of flowers carried above the foliage.

Sow nasturtiums where they are to flower, or start them off in pots to plant out in late spring or early summer. Although usually described as hardy annuals, the seedlings are likely to be killed by the first sharp frost, so avoid early sowing outdoors.

It is difficult to grow nasturtiums without attracting aphids and caterpillars. To avoid having to use an insecticide on an edible crop, pick off affected leaves at the first sign of attack. ZONE HA

Tʏᴘᴇ ᴏꜰ ᴘʟᴀɴᴛ	Bᴇꜱᴛ ᴘᴏꜱɪᴛɪᴏɴ	Sᴜɪᴛᴀʙʟᴇ ꜱᴏɪʟ	Pʀᴏᴘᴀɢᴀᴛɪᴏɴ	Pᴀʀᴛꜱ ᴏꜰ ᴘʟᴀɴᴛ	Uꜱᴇꜱ
Hardy annual	Full sun	Undemanding, poor	Seed	Flowers, leaves, seed	Cosmetic, culinary, household, medicinal

Valeriana officinalis
VALERIAN

The true valerian is a tall plant best at the back of an herb border.

Valerian was formerly valued for its root, which was used for a number of medicinal purposes, but nowadays it is grown mainly as an ornamental plant. Although not the most attractive herb, it is useful at the back of a border. The finely divided blue-green leaves are attractive, and the white or pink flowers held on stiff, 4–5-foot stems in spring have a pleasant vanilla-like fragrance.

When the plant is grown for its root, the flowers are usually removed so that all the plant's energy goes into the development of what is, in fact, the rhizome. If you are growing it simply as an interesting herb to have in your collection, let it flower – the tall spikes look especially attractive viewed against the dark background of a hedge. However, staking is prudent in an exposed position.

The plant can be raised from seed, and where conditions are suitable, self-sown seedlings will usually be found if you need more plants. Clumps can also be divided.

The plant is attractive to cats . . . and to rats (it is reputedly the charm the Pied Piper of Hamelin used to lead the rats away). ZONE 3

TYPE OF PLANT	BEST POSITION	SUITABLE SOIL	PROPAGATION	PARTS OF PLANT	USES
Hardy perennial	Full sun or partial shade	Moist but well drained	Division, seed	Roots	Medicinal

Verbena officinalis
VERVAIN

Vervain is an herbaceous perennial with toothed leaves on branching stems that arise from spreading roots. It usually makes a clump about 3 feet tall and 18 inches across. It is primarily a leafy plant, and the insignificant mauve flowers borne at the tips of the shoots from midsummer to the middle of fall contribute little.

Use it as a "filler" in a border of mixed herbs rather than in a prominent place. Although it has no culinary use, its inclusion in a practical herb garden can be justified. A tisane is made from the dried leaves which is said to be a mild sedative.

Vervain is easily grown from seed sown in spring, or from cuttings taken in summer. But division in

spring is the quickest and easiest method of propagation for just a few plants.

Although a perennial, vervain can be raised annually from seed and discarded at the end of the season. Seed will probably have to be bought from a specialist nursery stocking herbs or wildflowers.

ZONE 5

WARNING Do not consume during pregnancy.

Vervain is not a spectacular plant, but it does produce a show of small flowers from midsummer.

TYPE OF PLANT	BEST POSITION	SUITABLE SOIL	PROPAGATION	PARTS OF PLANT	USES
Hardy perennial	Full sun	Fertile, well drained	Cuttings, division, seed	Leaves	Medicinal

Viola odorata
SWEET VIOLET

THE DELICATE FRAGRANCE OF sweet violets has won them a place in the hearts of most gardeners. The plant seldom grows more than 6 inches tall, and the flowers themselves – like pansies with a spur at the back – are diminutive, only about ½ inch across. Early to mid-spring is the main flowering time, but a few flowers may appear in a mild winter.

The most common color is violet-blue, but there are other shades of blue, and white violets are not uncommon. Parma violets are probably hybrids, with *V. odorata* as a parent. These were once very popular, with collectors attracted to the larger,

Sweet violets are one of the delights of spring. Cut some to enjoy their fragrance indoors.

sometimes double, and more fragrant flowers.

Although violets are now grown primarily for their scent and delicate beauty, they have culinary uses, too, and they were once widely used medicinally. They grow naturally in damp shady hedges and grassy banks in or near woodland. Although they will grow in a sunny position, they thrive in partial shade in moist and fertile soil. Plant them in drifts, like ground cover, as individual plants are easily overlooked. The front of an herb border would suit or near a hedge or wall, provided the soil is not too dry.

Sweet violets self-sow freely once established. Clumps can also be divided. ZONE 6

TYPE OF PLANT	BEST POSITION	SUITABLE SOIL	PROPAGATION	PARTS OF PLANT	USES
Hardy perennial	Partial shade	Fertile, moist	Division, seed	Flowers, leaves, root	Cosmetic, culinary, medicinal

GROWING

HERBS

MAKING PLANS

Before you launch into anything more ambitious than buying a pot or two of culinary herbs to flourish on a kitchen windowsill, take stock of your backyard, patio, terrace, balcony or even windowbox if that is the extent of your territory; your home interests and hobbies, and the time you have available or are prepared to give to tend and nurture the plants.

IF YOU ENJOY COOKING and have only a small balcony but are prepared to give even a few minutes a day to the plants' care, then the world of herbs is your oyster. If your interest lies more strongly in home remedies, your property is north-facing and largely unsheltered, and time is even more of the essence, then these factors will influence your choice of plants at the planning stage. The details given in the *Directory of Herbs* will be invaluable in helping you to assess the possibilities of achieving just the right balance between time and effort and results. Traditionally herbs were grown in geometrically formal knot gardens found in European monasteries and large estates established in medieval times or higgledy-piggledy in country gardens. Somewhere between these two extremes there is a style of planting herbs that is appropriate to each of us, whether it is a designated herb patch or a few herbs intermingled with other flowers and vegetables.

Before planting, it is important to take a critical look at your growing space and helpful to draw up a scale plan. In this way you can be sure of making the closest possible match between the native environments of your chosen herbs and the situation you are about to offer them. You do not need to be a landscape architect to measure your plot and transfer the details onto graph paper. Draw in boundary walls and fences, paths and ponds, hedges, trees and screens, and any other existing features, such as raised beds and rock gardens, terracing and steps, and structures such as garages, compost bins, and so on. Indicate the north-south aspect of the garden and you will at once be able to identify and mark areas that receive maximum, medium, and minimum amounts of light: those that receive the full glare of the noon-day sun, those that are partially shaded, and those that never enjoy the benefits of direct sunlight.

Since many herbs originate from the warm and sunny

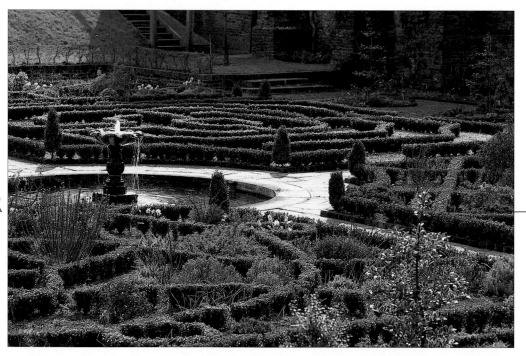

Neatly clipped hedges outline a series of geometrical herb beds in the knot garden at Hatfield House, Hertfordshire in England.

Scented geranium and sage grow side by side with brightly colored flowers and vegetables in a backyard garden.

climes of the Mediterranean region, a well-drained soil plus a sunny aspect match up to the general requirements of those such as basil, coriander, marjoram and rosemary. But as the *Directory of Herbs* shows, all is not lost if your garden has a largely shady character. Among the herbs that would settle happily for such conditions are mint, woodruff and sweet violet. And you may be able to elevate sun lovers to a more favorable spot, where the sun will reach them, on a flat roof for example, by growing them in containers.

Water is another essential requirement for plant development, and in this case, too, a plant's specific needs are largely determined by its native habitat. Those that originate from damp and temperate regions – chiefly broad-leaved plants – have a higher requirement and a higher tolerance of moisture than their Mediterranean counterparts. If you have a patch in your yard which is well drained but does not dry out completely, even in summer, you can plant it with a selection of moisture-tolerating herbs, such as valerian.

Conversely, if your yard has a sandy soil which does

Even in a small garden you can make room for a wide variety of herbs. Simply create as many different growing conditions as you wish.

1. *North-facing – lavender*
2. *Fertile loam, sunny – catnip, clary*
3. *Partial shade – bee balm, yarrow*
4. *Moist and sunny – comfrey, soapwort*
5. *South-facing – oregano, tansy*
6. *Full sun, dry – borage, sage*
7. *Full sun, well drained – apothecary's rose, evening primrose*
8. *Container – sweet bay*

not retain moisture and you wish to cultivate plants such as bergamot, marsh mallow or meadowsweet which require a damp spot, then you can easily adapt your growing conditions to suit. Dig a broad trench or a patch of the required shape at least 12–18 inches deep. Line it with a sheet of heavy-duty plastic pierced at intervals with holes and fill it with garden soil enriched with plenty of well-rotted manure or garden compost to retain moisture. The polythene will prevent the moisture from draining away quickly, yet ensure that the area does not become waterlogged. (Few herbs thrive if their roots are permanently in water.) In a dry spell, remember to keep the area damp by frequent watering.

Preparing the ground

Most herbs are unfastidious and some of the most useful herbs, such as sages and thymes, naturally grow in poor or shallow soils that are often dry and impoverished.

It is seldom that you will have to abandon trying to grow a particular herb because of your soil, but you will achieve results if you can try to give them the kind of soil conditions suggested for each herb.

When preparing the ground for a herb garden, concentrate on removing perennial weeds, and dig the soil to a depth of about 10 inches. For deep-rooting plants like horseradish and lovage, loosen the soil to twice this depth – using a fork to break up the lower level and adding plenty of compost or rotted manure.

Sandy soils are light to dig but because they are free-draining tend to dry out very quickly. If you want to grow herbs that prefer a moist, fertile soil, dig in humus-forming material – rotted farmyard manure, garden compost or composted seaweed – then mulch the plants annually. As sandy soils are often impoverished, add a balanced general garden fertilizer before planting, following the manufacturer's recommended rates. If you want to grow herbs described as needing a fertile or rich soil, hoe or rake in a fertilizer annually.

Clay soils are heavy to dig, often becoming waterlogged in wet weather, and clumps stick together in a mass if you pick up a handful and squeeze it in your hand. A clay soil is usually slow to warm up in spring, can become almost hard in hot, dry weather, and is generally unpleasant to dig. The treatment suggested for sandy soil will also improve clay soils.

Loam soils are easy to dig and fairly rich in nutrients. Except for adding fertilizer annually for those herbs described as needing a fertile or rich soil, you should not have to add anything to the soil routinely.

Soil testing

A simple test which gives some indication of general soil types, known as the kitchen jar test, can be carried out as follows:

1 Put a few tablespoons of soil in a large jar, fill it with water and put on the lid.

2 Shake the jar vigorously and leave the soil and other material to settle for a day or two.

The table right is intended to provide an at-a-glance guide to soil types and the herbs best suited to them. However, don't be afraid to take a chance, as most herbs are not fastidious and will grow well in most soils.

CLAY SOIL
A narrow band of sand and stones covered by a thicker band of closer-textured clay.

MEDIUM SOIL
Shown by roughly equal layers of sand and clay beneath the surface of the water.

LIGHT SOIL
A thick layer of sand and possibly stones, and a light covering of clay.

Soil types and herbs – the perfect marriage

It is important to know what type of soil you have and whether it differs from one part of the yard to another. Soil type affects not only the water-holding properties but also the nutrients naturally available to the plants. Most herbs will survive and even thrive in a wide range of soil types, but for healthy plants, with abundant foliage and prolific flowering, it is best to grow them in soil which closely resembles that of their native habitat.

SANDY SOIL

Water drains rapidly from light sandy soil taking nutrients with it, but all the undemanding Mediterranean herbs will thrive in such soils.

Borage	*Borago officinalis*
Chamomile	*Anthemis nobilis*
Coriander	*Coriandrum sativum*
Evening primrose	*Oenothera biennis*
Fennel	*Foeniculum vulgare*
Lavender	*Lavandula*
Tarragon	*Artemisia dracunculus*
Thyme	*Thymus*
Wild marjoram	*Origanum vulgare*
Winter savory	*Satureja montana*

Lavender 'Hidcote'

CLAY SOIL

Because this type of soil bakes solid in summer and is uncompromisingly sticky in winter, it is not a favorite with gardeners. Clay does, however, favor a number of herbs, predominantly those with deep roots. These will, incidentally, help to break up the large soil mass. Working generous amounts of garden compost into the top layer will make clay soils more suitable for the herbs listed under loam and moist loam.

Bee balm	*Monarda didyma*
Comfrey	*Symphytum officinale*
Mint	*Mentha*
Wormwood	*Artemisia absinthum*

Bee balm

MOIST LOAM

Poorly drained medium loam can be improved by frequent forking over. It favors deep-rooted herbs and those which naturally occur on heavy soil.

Angelica	*Angelica archangelica*
Bee balm	*Monarda didyma*
French sorrel	*Rumex scutatus*
Lady's mantle	*Alchemilla*
Lemon balm	*Melissa officinalis*
Meadowsweet	*Filipendula ulmaria*
Mint	*Mentha*
Parsley	*Petroselinum crispum*
Sweet Cicely	*Myrrhis odorata*
Valerian	*Valeriana officinalis*

WET SOIL

Most herbs dislike having permanently wet roots, but the following are worth a try in poorly drained soil.

Angelica	*Angelica archangelica*
Bee balm	*Monarda didyma*
Marsh mallow	*Althaea officinalis*
Meadowsweet	*Filipendula ulmaria*
Valerian	*Valeriana officinalis*
Watercress	*Nasturtium officinale*

Watercress

LOAM

Usually rich in nutrients and well drained, this type of soil is ideal for most herbs.

Basil	*Ocimum basilicum*
Bay	*Laurus nobilis*
Caraway	*Carum carvi*
Catnip	*Nepeta cataria*
Chervil	*Anthriscus cerefolium*
Chives	*Allium schoenoprasum*
Coriander	*Coriandrum sativum*
Dill	*Anethum graveolens*
Fennel	*Foeniculum vulgare*
Lady's mantle	*Alchemilla*
Lovage	*Levisticum officinale*
Rosemary	*Rosmarinus officinalis*
Rue	*Ruta graveolens*
Sage	*Salvia officinalis*
Thyme	*Thymus*

DESIGNING YOUR HERB GARDEN

Sun and soil are important considerations, since they affect the plants' chances of, at best, healthy development or, at worst, survival. Although such considerations have a bearing on garden planning, where and how you position your herbs is a matter of personal preference, too.

Walk through any small town or village where people really care about their gardens, and you'll be struck by the variety of styles and approaches to garden planning. One garden may be laid out with neatly symmetrical beds, each planted with military precision. There may be meticulously straight rows of chives, sage, chamomile and lavender with never an intervening trail of orange-bright nasturtium to interrupt the geometry. Next door the garden may be planted with clumps and clusters of herbs and flowers, patches of bachelors' buttons, pot marigolds, lady's mantle, purple sage and variegated apple mint mingling with one another and, an added bonus, planted closely enough to deter weed growth.

Another garden may demonstrate a strong preference for roses, from wild shrub and rugosa types to large-flowered modern hybrids, planted in random-shaped beds and borders and interplanted with vigorous herbs such as woodruff, marjoram and borage: truly a scented garden. Inspired perhaps by one of the great formal estate gardens, a fourth plot may be given over to an all-white garden, using silver-foliaged plants as much for the characteristics they share as for those that separate them. There may be the brilliant yellow, tiny button-shaped flowers of lavender cotton next to the minute pink flowers of the wooly betony and the purple spikes of sage and lavender.

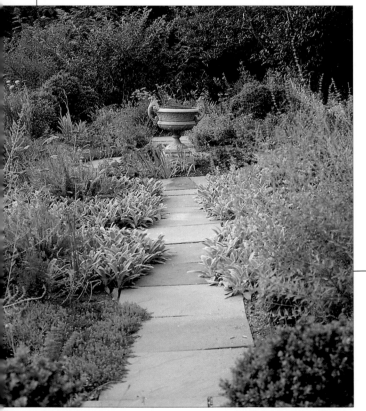

A LOOK OF FORMALITY

If your own image of an herb garden or an herb patch runs along formal and well-defined lines, it may be a case of going back to the drawing board, or at least to the graph paper, to plot the outlines. The size of the patch is immaterial, as "formal" is in no way synonymous with "grand." It is possible to achieve a look of complete formality in the smallest of plots, or to create a formal island, perhaps in the shape of a diamond or a series of concentric circles, in the midst of an otherwise undisciplined garden.

Once you have allocated the space you wish to plant, and taken note of the aspect and soil type, measure it accurately and draw the outlines on graph paper, allowing one quarter-inch for each foot. The more

The plants in this formal herb garden in Pennsylvania are well contrasted for height and leaf color, with the low-growing ones spilling over onto the stone pathway.

The fragrance of honeysuckle, fennel, rosemary and nicotiana mingles with hemerocallis lilies and a delicate pink rose in this scented border.

formal and stylized you want the garden to be, the more important it is to make sure that the measurements and subsequent subdivisions you intend to make are precise. Whatever the overall shape you favor, it is important not to lose sight of the practicalities. Easy access is essential. All flowerbeds and borders need tending from time to time. Weeding, watering, trimming and pruning are all necessary tasks. Culinary herbs will also have to be harvested. A large part of the *raison d'être* of an herb bed is that you can have seasoning at your fingertips: a sprig or two of mint to enhance the new season's potatoes and peas or a few stalks of parsley, thyme and rosemary

to tie into a *bouquet garni*.

Gathering herbs from your garden is always a pleasure, but somewhat less so if you have to put on boots to reach the back of a wide border on a rain-soaked day, or tread perilously close to tender plants. It is therefore important to plan the herb beds with picking in mind. Divide large patches into two or more smaller beds separated for the sake of convenience and appearance by narrow paths or stepping stones. As a general rule, to avoid having to step on to the beds, those that are accessible from only one side should be little more than 3 feet wide. (Such beds may be

Traditional patterns for a formal herb bed

Make rough drawings of some possible traditional designs within your proposed outline.

Divide the herb garden by criss-crossing paths.

Diamond bed with a tri-angular bed at each corner.

A square or rectangular bed of six triangles.

bordered on one side by a fence, a hedge, a screen or other structure which prevents all-round access.) Those that can be approached from all sides, an island bed for example, may be conveniently up to 5 feet wide.

PREFERENCE FOR PAVING

The choice of paving may be determined to a certain extent by local materials or simply by your own preference. Once the area has been thoroughly weeded, lay down dividing paths of bricks (laid in any one of a number of patterns, such as herringbone or circular), stone, gravel, granite chippings, wood chips or even thyme. The latter is soft underfoot and has the advantage of adding fragrance to the garden. Choose dwarf and creeping varieties that would provide complete ground cover, but remember thyme paths need more attention than those of other materials.

Whatever style of planting you envisage and whatever herbs you plan to plant it is important first to prepare the ground well to make sure that there is a hospitable balance between good drainage and adequate nutrients. If drainage is a problem, it may be necessary to dig out the designated area to a depth of about 12 inches and fork over the bottom. Then half fill the trench with rough stones, cover it with a 4 inch layer of good loamy soil enriched with plenty of well rotted manure or garden compost and level it off with a layer of gravel or stone chippings.

herringbone brick path

paving and gravel

granite chippings

chamomile

Dark grey brick paving makes a dramatic background for golden- and silver-leaved plants.

Formal herb gardens

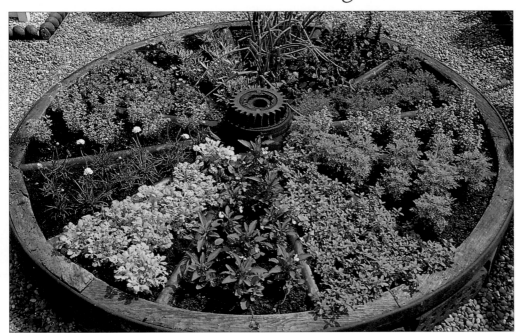

The red, weathered spokes of the cartwheel neatly divide low-growing herbs into wedge-shaped segments.

AN ATTRACTIVE WAY OF achieving a formal-looking herb garden without any structural work is to use an old cart wheel, which you may be able to buy from country antique shops or farm sales. After preparing the ground in the way described above, position the wheel and plant dwarf varieties in the segments between the spokes. Those herbs with a neat and easily-restrained habit such as chives, dwarf lavender, santolina and sweet violets would all be suitable. To maintain the visual effect of the wheel it is important to keep the plants in order by trimming and pruning them so that the spokes are not concealed beneath a mass of foliage.

A wheel garden will have its own built-in central feature, a well-turned and well-ground hub, but other symmetrical herb garden layouts can be enhanced by a well-planned focal point. It is never too early to start looking out for an old weathered sundial partially

covered with moss or a stylish birdbath. If beekeeping happens to be a hobby of yours, a traditional straw bee skep would be an appropriate choice. There is an environmental link between a well-used hive and the surrounding bee-attracting plants found in herb gardens. Such features not only draw the eye to that section of the garden, but provide an interesting contrast of texture and tone to that of the foliage.

Plants, too, can hold center stage in a similar way. Clip a standard bay tree to form a neat cone or characteristic ball shape; or train a weeping rose around

This Physick Garden, at the Botanic Gardens, University of British Columbia, Vancouver, emulates the traditional cartwheel design using brick as dividers between medicinal and ornamental planting.

Brick 'stepping stones' across the beds allow easy access to all the plants.

a sturdy pole. Morning glory or clematis can be allowed to ramble up and over trellis. Another equally colorful option would be a lead, stone, or terracotta urn, or one of their lookalikes, planted with trailing nasturtiums, purple and white-flowering thyme, and feverfew, cascading over the rim like a fragrant fountain.

CREATING AN EFFECT

With the garden planned in outline, and perhaps a central feature in mind, it is time to decide on the overall style of planting you want to achieve. A garden or a plot planned on symmetrical lines need not be planted in a formal way. Take, for example, a diamond bed subdivided into four triangles and a square. You could

plant each individual bed with neat clumps of herbs following the geometric outlines, or with rows of, say, compact lettuces, ornamental cabbages or other vegetables, each outlined with a different herb, a thyme edging one bed, chives or oregano another. Any of these options would look neat and orderly provided you keep the beds well weeded and the herbs well trimmed.

A different approach to the same geometric layout is to plant each individual bed with one herb variety, which in this context can be as wayward and straggly as a wild plant. In a small plot you could plant one section with mints, secure in the knowledge that the confines of the bed would restrict their root development and prevent the colonization that can be a problem when this species is planted in a mixed bed. Plant one triangular section of variegated apple mint, others of bergamot mint with its purplish flowers, plain-leaved apple mint with its rounded, wooly leaves and the fourth with the contrasting features of curly mint. The square bed in the center could be planted with pennyroyal covering the ground around, a birdbath, or simply with a tall herb such as a clump of feathery bronze fennel.

A different approach to planting may be preferable where larger herb beds are planned, when for example each one is around 5 feet across. This may be a case for the type of graduated planting that is popular for island beds planted with herbaceous plants, with the tallest in the center, those of medium height around them and low-growing ones at the front, forming an edging. More specific ideas and details of planting schemes are given later in this section.

Neat areas and clumps define a diamond bed.

Add definition with bright spikes of clary.

Informal herb gardens

SOMEWHERE BETWEEN THE DISCIPLINES of a geometric plan and the free-style planting of a cottage garden comes a checkerboard garden. This design, created by planting herbs between paving stones, is equally attractive in a town or a country setting. It is achieved by leaving squares of open soil between alternate paving stones. Each bed-in-miniature can be filled with a mixture of small herbs, or confined to a single plant type. Some squares can be left free for sowing annual herbs, or you can plant out nursery-grown ones, such as basil, borage and dill. Depending on your garden, you could plant larger herbs, such as fennel, caraway, sweet Cicely and horseradish, to form a screen from the prevailing wind, or where they would curtain off a utilitarian but unattractive corner of the garden, such as a compost bin.

From growing herbs between paving stones to growing them in gravel is a short visual step. In either case the plants can easily be tended and harvested, and are set off to good effect by a contrasting and sympathetic material. Herbs from the dry Mediterranean region will grow well in gravel and some will seed themselves freely. Make your selection from, among others, rosemary, sage, thyme, marjoram, summer and winter savory and pot marigolds.

Herbs tumbling over gravel, brick and stone paths conjure up images of country-style gardens, where herbs intermingle with other flowering plants and vegetables in a way that takes no account of horticultural demarcations. This concept of mixed planting has much to offer today, especially where a small plot is concerned. A clump of stately globe artichokes could grow alongside caraway and coriander, the yellowy green flowers of the herbs contrasting

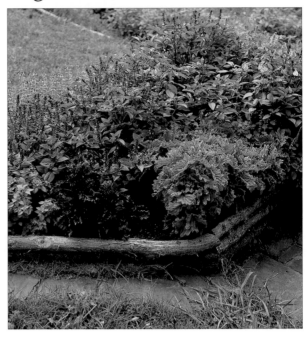

Raised herb beds edged with fallen logs make light work of tending the plants.

strikingly with the gray-green foliage of the vegetables. Plant green- and bronze-leaved fennel among hollyhocks and foxgloves – the feathery leaves will give pleasure long after the flower spikes have faded. Mounds of golden marjoram and thyme could cover the ground beneath sorrel and perpetual spinach, and purple sage interplanted with ornamental cabbage illustrates that this approach to planting recognizes no limitations.

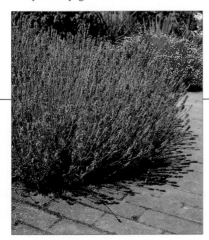

Lavender 'Twickle Purple' creates natural curves in the brick path.

Soften the lines and angles of square paving with clumps of low-growing herbs.

GROWING HERBS IN CONTAINERS

Where garden space is limited, or where your claim on the great outdoors begins and ends at the balcony or windowbox, you can create visual and literal feasts with herbs grown in troughs, pots, old stone sinks, barrels and wheelbarrows. In some Mediterranean countries, no doorstep or windowsill is complete without a flourish of basil, rosemary, oregano and thyme, and culinary herbs are proudly grown in used and often unpainted olive-oil cans; and no less decorative for that.

HERBS SUCH AS SWEET bay and rosemary are also at their most effective when planted on their own in a container. Then they can also be brought inside for winter. A pair of clipped bay trees in troughs on each side of a doorway or flight of steps is classic among decorations. For lesser formality, they could be underplanted with, for example, nasturtiums, lady's mantle, or thyme.

A tall, urn-shaped, terracotta strawberry pot, purpose-made for the cultivation of alpine strawberries, is a perfect container for a collection of herbs. Those with a trailing habit, such as thyme and nasturtiums, are well suited to planting in the cupped holes around the sides and in the top, allowing their stems to cascade gracefully. Reference to the *Directory of Herbs* will remind you of the variation of leaf and flower color, and of aroma, that could be achieved by planting such a container with various thymes.

Shallow containers such as stone sinks and terracotta

Create a bed in a strawberry pot if you are short of space.

troughs are suited to annual herbs such as sweet basil, dill, chervil and pot marigolds. In containers, as in open ground, it is advisable to separate annuals and perennials so that you do not disturb the long-term herbs when you plant or discard the annuals.

ARTIFICIAL ENVIRONMENT

Whatever type of container you use, the first essential is to check that it has adequate drainage holes in the base. Without these, and a layer of shards to cover them, plants will be in danger of becoming waterlogged and will soon perish. When planting a large container, cover the shards with some bulky organic material. Then fill with a soil-based potting soil, well firmed down to give the roots a good hold; peat-based soil, which dries out much more quickly, especially in terracotta pots, is not suitable.

Position pots of sun-loving plants where they will have at least five or six hours of strong light every day. If your balcony or windowbox makes this impossible, concentrate on growing herbs such as bay, lemon balm, mint, parsley, and thyme.

How often to apply water and how much to give container-grown herbs is a matter of fine judgment. The general rule is to water the pots when the top 1 inch of soil has dried out – which will happen more rapidly in strong sunlight or windy conditions. To check for dryness in a terracotta pot, tap the side of the container; when it sounds hollow, it needs water. However, this test will not work for containers made of other materials, so you will need to feel or test the soil below the surface. It may be that herbs will need light watering every day or two, or even twice a day in very hot or windy conditions. They will also need feeding. Apply a liquid fertilizer every two or three weeks. Alternatively use a slow-release fertilizer that will keep plants going all summer with one application.

Nasturtiums grown in a hanging planter (above) for an eye-level treat.

Container-grown herbs clustered together on a wooden deck are redolent of southern climes.

Plant a stone trough with dill, chervil and pot marigolds to make an herb corner on a patio.

GROWING HERBS INDOORS

Plants grown in containers on a balcony, patio or elsewhere may be brought indoors to create a special effect – perhaps a cluster of small pot-grown herbs to make an informal table decoration. A collection of scented geraniums can be used instead of potpourri in a bedroom or conservatory, a trough of annual herbs in a window recess forms a seasonal focal point, and a rosemary bush in a large planter can seem like a living sculpture in a conservatory.

WHETHER OR NOT YOU have a yard, growing herbs indoors has many practical and esthetic advantages. Pots of culinary herbs basking in the sun on a kitchen windowsill can be conveniently harvested, a leaf at a time, whatever the weather. They form a verdant and fragrant link with the world outside, serve as environmental air fresheners, and some, such as mint, may even deter insects.

Much of the advice given earlier for growing plants in containers applies to those cultivated indoors; only more so. If the herbs are not only to survive but flourish, they will need at least four to five hours' strong light each day or, if that is impractical, eight to ten hours of artificial light. Herbs do not take well to extreme temperature changes and should not be positioned near radiators or in strong drafts. Container-grown herbs may be arranged in a group but should never be crowded, as a free circulation of air between plants is essential and will help minimize the incidence of pests and diseases.

Good drainage is another essential requirement, which clay or plastic pots with drainage holes covered with shards or pebbles will provide. Such pots, acceptable in the yard, may not always complement the interior decoration, so they may be placed in a trough or tray, or in a ceramic, wicker, tin or other pot holder or *câchepot*. When herbs are planted directly in containers with no holes, for example in a ginger jar, a decorative bowl or a floor-standing urn, then special provisions for adequate drainage must be made. Before filling with soil, place a layer of gravel or pebbles in the base of the container – the depth of the layer will depend on the size of the pot – followed by a thin layer of broken charcoal to keep the soil "sweet." This will allow the soil to drain and avoid waterlogging.

GOOD GROWING MEDIUM

The choice of the growing medium will also have an effect on water retention. Soil taken from the garden, no matter what its composition, is wholly unsuitable, not least because it may contain disease organisms and

Pots of herbs fill the foreground in this indoor arrangement of shaped and clipped shrubs.

pests which would flourish in the warmer indoor environment. Two types of soil are suitable. The first, earth-based type, is composed of sterilized loam blended with fertilizer, lime and sand. The other, soilless compost, may be all-peat or a mixture of peat and sand. The latter is heavier and especially suited for use in large containers. Soilless composts also have fertilizer added. This is normally adequate to nourish the herbs for the first few weeks after planting.

Indoor herbs should be watered only when the top inch or so has dried out. The frequency will vary according to the temperature and humidity of the room. In a centrally-heated room kept at a high temperature watering could be necessary every day or two, and feeding every week or two after planting.

Indoor herbs will rarely be as vigorous or prolific as those grown in the open, so show restraint when harvesting since the plants will have more difficulty in restoring growth. Pluck off a few leaves or a small side shoot rather than denuding or cutting off the main stem. The herbs will produce over a longer period.

Herbs grown indoors should be placed near a window so that they receive direct light. For best effect, arrange a variety of herbs in attractive containers.

SELECTING YOUR HERBS

Before you start selecting the herbs you want to grow, first decide what purpose they are to serve. Do you want them primarily to enhance the appearance of your yard? Do you want large quantities for culinary, medicinal, and cosmetic preparations? Or perhaps you wish to grow plants to sweeten the air and improve the quality of the environment. The chances are that you will want to achieve all these aims, and with even a small selection of herbs it is possible to do so.

Traditionally some herbs have been grown with other plants to the benefit of one or all. Chives are said to prevent black spot on roses, and garlic to encourage more prolific flowering. Rosemary and sage are thought to be ideal companions and of mutual benefit. Some fragrant herbs such as chives, hyssop, marjoram, parsley, sage and thyme are believed to improve the production of vegetables. Tarragon is held to strengthen the growth of all the vegetables and flowering plants in its vicinity, which seems reason enough for its inclusion.

Many herbs have powerful bee- and butterfly-attracting properties, and a list of these plants is given right. Some have an especially strong fragrance. Choose from anise, lavender, lemon balm, lemon verbena, pineapple sage, rose, sweet violet and wormwood to create an open-air potpourri.

While the majority of herbs have relatively small flowers, some have blooms which are decidedly showy. Bright red bergamot, citrus yellow and orange pot marigolds and nasturtiums, deep golden tansy and yarrow and pale lemon evening primrose are fine examples of flowering herbs. Attractive companion plantings can be achieved by mixing and mingling these "extroverts" with others that are admired more for their foliage, and by contrasting neighboring foliage colors and shapes. Purple sage with its long spikes of deep mauve flowers emphasizes the fluffy delicacy of yellow-green lady's mantle; bee balm towers brilliantly above salad burnet; clumps of marjoram seem all the brighter when placed next to yellow-leaved feverfew.

Whenever space allows, it is a good plan to plant each herb type in small groups or rows so that its characteristics can be fully appreciated. In a formal setting this means spacing the plants so that they are seen to be separated by soil when they are fully grown. In an informal setting, on the other hand, herbs are planted so that at maturity they are closely blended without being overcrowded.

Select your plantings for foliage and color, contrast, shape and definition.

Bee- and butterfly-attracting herbs

The brilliant red flowers of bergamot (Monarda 'Lodden Crown') are among the showiest blooms in the herb garden.

Anise	*Pimpinella anisum*
Basil	*Ocimum basilicum*
Bee balm	*Monarda didyma*
Catnip	*Nepeta cataria*
Chicory	*Cichorium intybus*
Chives	*Allium schoenoprasum*
Comfrey	*Symphytum officinale*
Dandelion	*Taraxacum officinale*
Evening primrose	*Oenothera biennis*
Fennel	*Foeniculum vulgare*
Horehound	*Marrubium vulgare*
Hyssopus	*Hysoppus officinalis*
Lavender	*Lavandula*
Lemon balm	*Melissa officinalis*
Marjoram	*Origanum*
Marsh mallow	*Althaea officinalis*
Meadowsweet	*Filipendula ulmaria*
Peppermint	*Mentha × piperata*
Rosemary	*Rosmarinus officinalis*
Sage	*Salvia officinalis*
Thyme	*Thymus*
Valerian	*Valeriana officinalis*
Yarrow	*Achillea millefolium*

Butterflies cover the blossom of low-growing marjoram.

Lavender in flower is an important source of pollen for bees.

SEEDS VERSUS PLANTS

The stock of most herbs can be increased in more than one way. It is up to you to decide whether to take charge of the whole growing cycle and start from seed, or come in halfway through the operation. You can buy small plants from a nursery or other specialist grower, or you can propagate the new plants yourself by stem cuttings, layering, root cuttings or division. The methods suitable for each plant are given in the *Directory of Herbs*.

Pots of rosemary, bay and sage stand in moist gravel in a greenhouse.

For most gardeners, a mixture of the two approaches proves most suitable. Some herbs either do not set seed, or the seed does not grow reliably to type, and so starting from scratch is not an option. Foremost among such herbs, especially for the enthusiastic cook, is French tarragon which, unlike the inferior Russian tarragon, rarely produces seed. So if bottles of homemade tarragon vinegar and deliciously flavored fish dishes are in your sights, it will be necessary to buy plants, or propagate from cuttings or pieces of root provided by a friend. Other herbs best bought as plants include mints, most of which are hybrids, and the decorative forms of thymes and sages. These can also successfully be grown from cuttings or divisions.

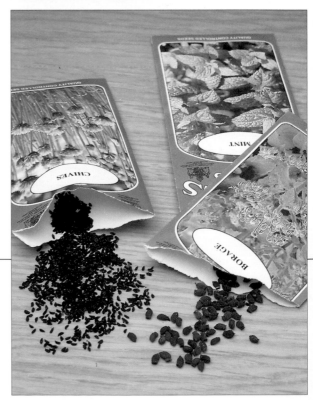

For best results, buy your seeds each year from a reputable supplier and follow the directions on the packet.

Growing from seed

PROPAGATING HERBS FROM SEED is what Nature does all the time. And so once you have an established herb garden, or some herbs intermingled with other plants, you can rely on the process of self-seeding to increase your stock. Many species, caraway, dandelion, lady's mantle and pot marigold among them, seed themselves prolifically, although not always just where you might have chosen. The tiny parachute-like seeds of dandelion, so readily borne on the wind, are likely to emerge as vigorous little plants far from the parent, and so frustrate the best-laid garden plans. But as self-sown plants are usually more rugged than those raised from collected seed, they can be transplanted while young to form a new colony elsewhere. However, some seedlings, like those of caraway, do not transplant successfully.

In order to germinate successfully, most seeds have certain basic requirements – the appropriate levels of moisture, warmth, air and light, although most seeds will germinate in the light or the dark. These conditions are usually best provided by sowing seed under glass or indoors, in trays or pots. Larger seeds may be successfully sown outside. Once germination has taken place light becomes essential for healthy growth.

Most seeds get off to the best start if they are sown in spring, when there is likely to be a steady rise in temperature and in daylight hours. However, some seed

Dandelion, with its wind-borne seedhead "clock."

needs to be sown as soon as it ripens. A few annual herbs, such as chervil, may be sown in the fall and can be overwintered. Seeds of biennial herbs like caraway are best sown in late spring to flower the following year. A few types, those which rely on extreme cold to break down their seed coats and end their period of dormancy, are better sown in the fall.

Sowing seed outdoors

Careful preparation of the seed bed is all-important when sowing seed outside. The soil should be free of large stones and all weeds, and raked until it is fine and crumbly, a texture known as fine tilth. In order to satisfy the temperature requirements for germination, it is essential to delay sowing until there is no longer any danger of frost and preferably to wait until the soil has been warmed by a few days of sunshine. You can bring forward the time of sowing by placing glass over the seed bed a week or two before planting, to trap all the available heat.

hoe to a fine tilth

cover seeds with cloches to protect

Sowing seed indoors

By sowing seed indoors or in a greenhouse or cold frame, you can advance the date of sowing by three weeks or more, thereby getting seedlings well established before planting out.

1 Sow seed in seed trays filled to within ½ inch of the top with a proprietary seed compost. Level the surface, firm it down with a block of wood.

2 Water thoroughly, using a watering can with a fine rose.

3 Sow the seeds thinly and sift over more compost to cover to the required depth of two to three times the seeds' diameter. Lightly water – never allow to become waterlogged.

4 Label the tray with the relevant details, the type of seed and, for future reference and comparisons, the date it was sown.

5 Place a piece of glass over the tray, cover with a sheet of paper and move to a shaded spot. Check the tray every day until germination begins.

6 Once the seedlings appear, remove the paper and the glass covering and move the tray to a lighter position, but out of full sun.

Pricking out

WHEN THE FIRST TRUE leaves appear after the seed leaves, it is time for the seedlings to be transferred, or transplanted, into pots containing soil-based compost. Lift each tiny seedling out gently with a round-bladed knife or a wooden popsicle stick eased under the roots. Hold the seedling carefully by a leaf tip between thumb and index finger and lower it into a hole in the soil made by a pointed wooden tool known as a dibber. Firm the soil around the stem with your fingers or the dibber, and give the soil a light watering. Check daily to make sure the seedlings do not dry out.

The seedlings can be left to develop in the pots until their root systems begin to grow through the bottom – a sure sign that it is time to move them on again. At this

Potting compost needs to be firmed around the stems of delicate seedlings.

stage, you can introduce the plants to outdoor conditions by opening the cold frame wide during the day, or by standing the pots in the yard, on a balcony, or in front of an open window during the day and either bringing them in or covering them at night and in bad weather.

After two or three weeks of "hardening off," or conditioning in this way, the herbs will be ready for planting out in their permanent site. This may be a pot or trough on the balcony, or a prepared site in the yard. Whatever the case, it is important to minimize the effect of the transition by transplanting when conditions are most favorable.

Herbs grown from seed and transferred to larger pots can be grown on under cover or planted outdoors.

Taking stem cuttings

MOST HERBS WITH WOODY or semi-woody stems, such as hyssop, lavender, rosemary, sage, scented-leaved geraniums, marjoram, thyme, and winter savory, can be readily propagated by taking stem cuttings, known as softwood cuttings, in late spring and early summer. This is when the new shoots are soft and the sap is still rising. Trim off about 2–4 inches of new growth just below a leaf node. Remove the lower leaves and stipules (present on the stems of geraniums), and dip the base of the cutting in a hormone rooting compound. Cuttings of some woody herbs, such as lavender and southernwood, give better results if they are pulled off

with a "heel" of older wood. This heel needs to be trimmed with a knife before the cutting is prepared as described above.

Fill a pot with potting soil or an equivalent that is low in nutrients, well drained and well aerated. Insert the cuttings around the edge of the pot, about 1 inch into the compost, and firm it in with your fingers. Lightly spray the soil with water and place the pots in a covered propagating case. Alternatively cover the individual pots with a plastic bag held in place with a rubber band around the rim, or with an upturned glass jar to keep the soil moist. Place the propagating case or pots in a shady place, taking care to avoid full sun. Once they start to root and show signs of growth give them regular foliar feeds.

When the cuttings are well rooted, transplant them on into small individual pots filled with a general-purpose potting compost. Then treat them as the young healthy plants they are, and condition or harden them off before planting them in their permanent site.

You can continue to take cuttings of semi-ripe wood of lavender and rosemary during the summer months. Treat them in a similar way to softwood cuttings, but leave them to overwinter in a cool greenhouse or unheated room, then transplant them in spring.

Layering

SOME HARDY PERENNIALS, subshrubs, and shrubs can be grown from layered stems, for example sage. In fact, some plants, like mint, spread naturally by means of runners, creeping stems that root at intervals to produce new plants.

You can encourage less vigorous subjects to form roots by selecting a leggy shoot, then without severing it from the parent plant, make slanting cuts at intervals along the length, using a sharp knife. Peg the shoots in the soil with pieces of bent wire or staples and cover with a thin layer of sifted soil. If the layered shoots are pegged out in a wheel formation around the parent plant a healthy clump of herbs will soon be established. Once new young plants with well-developed root systems have formed along the cut stem, they can, if you wish, be cut from the parent and transplanted.

For layering, pin down a vigorous shoot and cover. Separate from the parent plant when well rooted.

Root cuttings

Propagation by root cuttings (left). Dandelion roots forced in winter will provide early salad leaves in spring.

MINT AND LICORICE CAN be raised from root cuttings taken at the end of the growing season to produce new young plants and fresh leaves throughout the winter. Expose some roots and cut them into 4 inch lengths. Lay them in a box of general-purpose potting soil, cover them lightly with more soil, water them and bring them indoors. They will soon send out shoots and provide new leaf growth.

Fleshy roots such as horseradish and orris root can also be propagated from sections of root, or rhizome in the case of orris. Lift a section of root/rhizome carefully and cut it into short sections – a straight cut across the top, a slanting cut across the bottom. Plant these the correct way in a large pot or into prepared ground.

Division

CLUMP-FORMING PERENNIALS THAT that have been established for at least two years can be propagated by division. Indeed, most will benefit from the procedure.

Divide the plants in spring or fall, using a knife or a spade blade to cut through the center of the clump. Carefully ease the individual plants apart and replant them, or a small part of the clump, in prepared ground.

CARING FOR YOUR HERBS

Maintaining a herb garden should be a pleasurable hobby: pulling up any weeds that threaten to overcome young plants; watering and feeding the plants from time to time; staking up any herbs that are becoming straggly, and pruning unruly shoots at the end of the growing season. Sounds like hard work? Not when you consider that every time you brush against a plant, or spray it lightly with water, you will release and savor the fragrance for which you chose it in the first place.

Watering and feeding

THE MANY HERBS THAT originate in hot, dry Mediterranean regions do not need a rigorous watering routine. Indeed, they can survive long, dry spells with no water at all. However, regular, light watering is beneficial. It not only helps to keep the plants, annuals especially, fresh-looking, but helps to maintain their fragrance. It is important not to overwater, particularly those plants with soft stems. These cannot readily dry out, and excessive moisture can lead to fungus growth. In a region where heavy rainfall is likely to be a problem, giving the plants space for air to circulate around them is essential.

However, other herbs, particularly those with fleshy roots like marsh mallow and meadowsweet, require a moist spot and benefit from watering in dry summers.

Herbs growing in open ground make few demands in terms of nourishment. Well-rotted garden compost dug into the soil before planting, and at the end of every growing season, will provide most of the nutrients the plants need. An occasional dressing of an organic fertilizer may be applied, particularly if plants begin to look sickly.

Herbs growing in containers benefit from feeding.

Pest and disease control

Pennyroyal and nasturtiums are known to repel ants, rosemary to repel carrot fly, and basil, sage, and chamomile (which is known as "the plant's physician") to keep harmful insects at bay. Mint discourages flies, and chives will help prevent scab on apple trees and black spot on roses. Thyme plants will lure slugs away from other species, causing the pests to congregate in specific locations, for easy eradication each evening.

Aphids tend to be the main pest problem on herbs. To keep them at bay, clean the garden regularly. If you

have an inadequate colony of ladybugs, which eat aphids, spray the plants with an organic pesticide made from an infusion of elder leaves. Rust on mint, another unsightly problem, takes more perseverance to overcome. If, as is often the case, you have a surfeit of plants, pull up the affected ones and use a flame gun on the soil to kill the spores. Otherwise, pull off the damaged leaves and cut back the stems, disposing of the affected parts by burning or some other method. Never put them in the compost bin. Then dig up the plants.

Soak the roots in hot water, then replant them in a different, uncontaminated situation.

PLANNING AHEAD
At the end of the growing cycle it is time to start planning the following year's planting. Make a note to include more of the herbs which are bee-attracting — borage, coriander, lemon balm and summer savory among them — to be sure of a high pollination level.

Pruning

TAKE STOCK OF YOUR herbs at the end of the growing season. When it is time to pull out and discard the annuals (having first saved the seed), the time is right to see how the perennials are shaping up.

Use sharp pruning shears to cut back any dead stems,

Lavender before pruning　　*After pruning*

and to cut off long, straggly growth. Vigorous and woody plants, like lavender, rue, sage, and thyme, should be cut back hard (but in the case of lavender not back to the old wood) to reshape the plant and encourage fresh, neat growth. With the exception of rue, do not consign the clippings to the compost bin, but throw them on a wood fire or a bonfire to enjoy the last of their fragrance. Such plants are perennial but not everlasting, and there will come a time when they will no longer regain or retain an attractive shape and a concentration of growth. That is when to propagate.

Lemon verbena is pruned in the growing season to remove the dead flowers and straggly or woody stems.

Staking

MANY HERBS HAVE A naturally dwarfing habit, and others are bred specially to form low-growing mounds. Even the tallest herbs, like angelica, evening primrose, and fennel, are usually able to stand their ground, even in high winds, especially if you have taken the precaution of planting them in a reasonably sheltered part of the garden.

If plants do start to flop and sprawl, then help them to stay upright by inserting stout bamboo stakes, positioning three at intervals around a clump, and tying with green twine.

Stake tall plants as they grow to prevent damage to the long stems and flowers.

HERBS IN

ACTION

PRESERVING HERBS

Timing is everything when you are harvesting herbs for preserving and storing. Whether you intend to use herbs for medicinal purposes or for cooking, it is important to gather them at the point in their growing cycle when their volatile oils are most concentrated, and at the time of day when there is no unnecessary moisture on them. To obtain maximum benefit from herbs, treat them with great care, preserve them without delay, and store them away from the light.

Gathering herbs

Leaves are at their most fragrant, and richest in volatile oils, before any flowers have opened. Flowers are harvested as soon as they have fully opened. Seeds should be captured as soon as they are ripe, while roots need to be left in the ground until the end of the growing season, when they will have the greatest concentration of stored nutrients.

Exposed parts of the plants –

flowers, leaves, seeds, and stems – should be harvested early on a dry day, as soon as the dew has dried. By noon, when the sun is at its height, the volatile oils will have dissipated. Always use sharp pruning shears or scissors to cut stems, to avoid damaging the plants. Shake off any insects, pick off damaged or discolored leaves and flowers, and put straight into water. Keep the plant material

away from strong light, which will draw out the volatile oils.

Harvest seedheads each day, as they ripen, tying a piece of cheesecloth over them to catch any seeds as they fall. Do not use a plastic bag as condensation could cause the seeds to rot.

Drying herbs

Drying requires free circulation of warm, dry air and the absence of strong light, especially sunlight. Herbs can be dried over several days in a cool room, more quickly in a warm atmosphere, but never hang them in a steamy kitchen or bathroom. Leaves are best dried on the stem, though large ones, such as borage, may be separated and

dried on a rack. Seedheads should be hung to dry inside a paper bag to collect the seeds as they fall. Flowers for drying should be cut from their stems. Roots must be brushed clean and then cut into 1 in slices.

Separate stems into small bunches to allow the warm air to circulate freely around them, and

hang bunches at a good distance from the wall. Spread loose plant material in a single layer on a suitable drying rack, or place on baking trays and dry in a cool oven with the door slightly ajar to allow the moisture to escape. Flowers and leaves are dry when they are crisp and rattly; roots when they are hard and woody.

Peppermint

Chamomile

Meadowsweet

Storing dried herbs

Gradually strip leaves from their stems and crumble them lightly between your fingers. Pull marigold petals from the flower centers. Untie the bags covering seedheads and carefully collect the fallen seeds.

Store dried herbs separately in lidded glass or ceramic (not plastic) jars, and label. Dark-colored jars or pots are ideal since they keep out the light, or store clear glass jars in a dark, cool place. Keep a small "working jar" handy in the kitchen, replenishing it from time to time, which saves exposing a large jar of herbs to the air and light.

Freezing herbs

You can freeze herbs on the stem, or strip off the leaves and freeze them whole. In either case, spread the herbs in a single layer on a baking tray or large plate and freeze them uncovered. Once they are frozen, pack them into lidded containers – they will be too fragile and brittle to hold their shape in plastic freezer bags. Alternatively, crumble them lightly between your fingers to obtain the frozen equivalent of chopped herbs. The crumbled herbs are best stored in small, lidded containers. Be sure to label each herb.

Another method is to pack chopped herbs into ice cube trays and fill with water. When frozen, turn out into labeled plastic bags. These herbed ice cubes can be added to soups and casseroles straight from the freezer.

Small sprays of herbs or edible flowers can be frozen in ice cubes, or in fancy-shaped cookie cutters wrapped with foil and filled with water. Match the herb fragrance to the drink – lemon verbena with lemonade – or choose flavor contrasts – scented geranium-leaf cubes in a tall glass of iced chamomile tea.

Coriander

Pot marigold

Comfrey

COOKING

Although these days we tend to think that the herbs added to our meals are there purely to provide flavor, in the past they were regarded as far more functional. Many are good gastric stimulants, making it easier to digest strong, rich meats like pork or game. Others were used to balance the meal and prevent illness: Culpeper tells us that in the 17th century all housewives cooked fish with fennel because fish – coming from the sea – were damp and so could cause stomach upsets, while fennel was a dry, hot herb to provide balance. Herbs are also ideal to add flavors to replace over-dependence on salt or sugar.

FOOD TYPE	HERB	SERVING SUGGESTIONS
Soups		
Clear/light	Chervil	Enhances consommés
	Tarragon	Good with chicken broth soups
Fish	Dill	Use seeds with strong fish; leaves with lighter varieties
	Lemon balm	Can replace grated lemon rind
	Tarragon	Good with strong-flavored fish
Lentil	Caraway/Dill seed/Fennel	Use ground seeds
Rich/meaty	Coriander seeds	Use ground early in cooking
	Lovage	Chopped stems can thicken soups and broths
Vegetable	Chervil	Enhances flavors
	Dill seed	Use ground seeds
	Fennel	Use ground seeds or finely sliced bulb of Florence fennel
	Lovage	Stems can replace celery
	Oregano	Adds Mediterranean flavor
	Sage	Use sparingly as quite strong
Pea	Coriander	Use ground seeds
	Cumin/ Fenugreek	Ground seeds add spicy flavor
	Ginger	Use fresh chopped root
	Turmeric	Use ground and sparingly
Starters		
Rich pâtés	Bay	Good with all game dishes
	Parsley	Italian/flat-leaved has a stronger flavor
	Sage	Good in pork/rabbit dishes
Main dishes		
Fish-fat/rich	Basil	Use with mackerel/shellfish
	Dill seeds	Ideal for salmon
	Tarragon	Use in rich cream sauces
	Thyme	Good with strong-flavored fish

FOOD TYPE	HERB	SERVING SUGGESTIONS
Fish – white	Chervil	Combine with lemon balm in light fish dishes
	Dill weed/ Fennel	Use young sprigs finely chopped
	Lemon balm	Can replace lemon
Beef	Coriander	Use for an oriental flavor
	Dill seeds	Good with veal
	Hyssop	Good in casseroles
	Lovage	Adds celery flavor, thickens
	Marjoram/ Thyme	Use in stews and casseroles
Lamb	Garlic	Combine with lavender for young baked lamb
	Rosemary	Classic for baked lamb and lamb casseroles
Pork	Chervil/ Marjoram	Use in stuffings and sauces for roasts
	Fennel	Good in casseroles/pâtés
	Sage	Use for stuffings
	Summer savory	Good with ham dishes
Chicken/ poultry	Coriander	Adds oriental flavor
	Lemon balm	Rub with leaves before stir-frying or roasting
	Sage/Summer savory	Add to casseroles and stir-fried dishes
	Tarragon	Ideal with baked chicken and light casseroles
Cheese dishes	Chervil	Chop into omelets and quiches
	Dill weed/ Marjoram	Add freshly chopped to cream cheese
	Mint	Add freshly chopped to cream or cottage cheese
	Oregano	Ideal for vegetarian dishes
	Sage	Add to cooked sauces or cheese and potato dishes

Classic fresh herb mixtures

The right combinations of herbs complement each other and enhance the foods they season.

FINES HERBES
equal amounts of chevril, chives, parsley and tarragon

BOUQUET GARNI
3 stalks parsley, 1 bay leaf and 1 sprig thyme

HERBES DE PROVENCE
oregano, rosemary, thyme, savory, majoram and French lavender

BEEF MIX
equal amounts of rosemary, thyme savory, orange peel and parsley

LAMB MIX
equal amounts of rosemary, thyme, savory, mint and parsley

PORK MIX
equal amounts of sage, thyme, and majoram

POULTRY MIX
equal amounts of parsley, thyme, majoram, tarragon and bay leaf (juniper berries for game birds)

SEAFOOD MIX
equal amounts of dill, tarragon and lemon peel

Food type	Herb	Serving suggestions
Egg dishes	Basil/Chervil/ Dill weed/ Thyme	Add chopped to omelets and other dishes
	Tansy	Use for sweet puddings
Pasta	Basil	Use fresh with tomato sauces
	Marjoram/ Oregano	Tends to taste stronger when dried
	Nutmeg	Use grated with Parmesan
Salads	Basil	Use chopped leaves from different colored varieties
	Borage/ Marigold	Sprinkle flowers/petals on salads as a garnish
	Chives	Chop finely for a mild onion flavor
	Coriander/ Lemon balm	Add two or three leaves to green salads
	Nasturtium	Use both flowers and leaves
	Salad burnet	Gives a taste of cucumber
	Sorrel	A little perks up lettuce
Vegetables Tomatoes	Basil	Gives all tomato dishes the classic taste of Italy
	Oregano	Use fresh in Greek salads
Rice	Fennel	Add a bag of seeds to boiling rice or use finely sliced Florence fennel
	Saffron	Classic for oriental dishes
Beans/peas	Chervil/ Summer savory	Great flavor enhancers
	Dill seeds	Add to broad beans/peas
	Mint	Add fresh to young peas
Cabbage family	Caraway seeds	Good with all cabbage dishes and sauerkraut
	Fennel seeds	Add to Brussels sprouts
	Marjoram	Good with broccoli
	Thyme	Add a sprig to boiled/ steamed cabbage

Food type	Herb	Serving suggestions
Root	Dill seeds	Cook whole with carrots and parsnips
	Fenugreek	Good with carrots
	Garlic	Add to baked potato dishes
	Paprika	Enhances carrots/turnips
	Sage	Add a sprig to boiling carrots/potatoes
Lentils/pulses	Caraway/ Fennel seeds	Use ground
	Ginger	Adds spice to lentil loaf
	Hyssop	Good with quick dishes
	Marjoram	Add to lentil loaf and casseroles
Onions	Caraway	Add to tarts
	Oregano	Use in quiches and soups
Desserts	Bergamot	Add flowers to fruit salads
	Mint	Use chopped in fruit salads and stewed pears/apples
	Rose petals	Use to flavor ice cream, junkets, or crystallize
	Scented geraniums	Use to flavor ice cream or sherberts, or as a garnish
	Sweet Cicely	Cook with rhubarb/apples to replace sugar
	Sweet violets	Crystallize for decoration
Cakes & Beads	Caraway seeds	Sprinkle onto breads and crackers
	Dill seeds	Use ground in crackers
	Fennel seeds	Use ground to flavor bread
	Ginger	For spicy cookies and shortbread
	Mint	Add to white cakes
	Tansy	Use in Easter cakes
Pickles & relishes	Dill	Use for pickles and to accompany fish
	Mint	Ideal with lamb/cold cuts
	Mustard seed	Use with gravad lax and strong-flavored dishes

SOUPS & STARTERS

Fresh green herbs and pungent spices demonstrate a variety of ways to begin a meal, from tangy sorrel soup or creamy garlic soup to a robust pâté. Accompanied by herb rolls or breads, any one of these dishes would make a delicious light lunch.

Rabbit pâté

If you prefer a less rich mixture, use chicken in place of the rabbit in this country pâté.

2¼ lb rabbit pieces
1 lb pork neck meat
1 onion, coarsely chopped
2 cloves garlic, roughly chopped
3 tbsp chopped parsley
2 tsp chopped sage
salt and black pepper
½ cup red wine
3 tbsp butter, melted
3 bay leaves

Remove the meat from the bones and cut it into pieces. Trim the pork and cut it into cubes. Combine the rabbit, pork, onion, and garlic in a food processor and process to make a smooth paste. Stir in the parsley and sage, season with salt and pepper, and stir in the wine.

Pack the mixture into a 5-cup loaf pan or terrine mold and level the top. Cover securely with foil, place the dish in a roasting pan and add enough water to come halfway up the sides of the dish. Bake in the oven at 325°F for one and a half hours.

Pour off any excess fat and allow the pâté to cool. Arrange the bay leaves on top and pour over the melted butter to cover. Chill until the pâté is set.

To serve 6 to 8

Chilled garlic soup

This elegant soup has a subtle flavor with no more than a hint of garlic.

12 blanched almonds
6 cloves garlic, peeled
2 tbsp olive oil
2 thick slices white bread, crusts removed, cut into small cubes
2½ cups chicken broth
⅔ cup dry white wine
salt and white pepper
2 tbsp chives, snipped

Process the almonds and garlic to a paste in a blender or food processor, or pound them with a pestle and mortar. Heat the oil in a small pan and fry the garlic paste and bread cubes over medium heat until the bread is golden brown.

Pour the chicken broth and wine into a blender or food processor, add the garlic and bread mixture, and season with salt and pepper. Process until the soup is smooth.

Stir in the chives, then chill for at least one hour. Before serving, taste and adjust seasoning if necessary. Garnish with croutons.

To serve 4

Garlic

Sage

Sweet bay

Sorrel

Sorrel soup

Deep, deep green with a sharp lemony tang, this soup can be served hot or cold.

1 lb sorrel
5 tbsp butter
1 onion, coarsly chopped
2½ cups chicken stock
salt and black pepper
1 tbsp lemon juice
1 tbsp flour
4 tbsp cream
1 tsp grated lemon rind, to garnish

Wash and drain the sorrel and tear off and discard the stalks. Melt 1 oz of the butter in a large pan and sauté the onion over medium heat until translucent but not colored. Add the sorrel and stir until it has wilted. Add the broth, season with salt and pepper, cover, and simmer for 15 minutes. Purée in a blender or food processor. Rinse out the pan.

Melt the remaining butter and stir in the flour to make a roux. Gradually pour on the sorrel purée, stirring all the time. Add the lemon juice, taste the soup, and adjust the seasoning if necessary. Reheat the soup to serve it hot. If you prefer to serve it cold, allow it to cool, then chill it for at least one hour.

To serve, swirl one tablespoonful cream over each portion and sprinkle on the grated lemon rind.

To serve 4

Spiced pea soup

Fragrant with the aroma of a medley of ground spices, this golden soup is garnished with glistening raisins.

¾ cup dried yellow split peas, soaked for at least one hour
2½ cups chicken broth
2 tbsp butter
1 tsp ground cumin
1 tsp ground coriander
½ tsp ground ginger
½ tsp ground turmeric
large pinch of ground fenugreek
pinch of sugar
salt
2 tbsp seedless raisins, to garnish
coriander leaves, to garnish

Bring the split peas to a boil in a large pan of unsalted water and cook, covered, for 30 to 45 minutes, until they are tender. Drain them and discard the liquid. Reserving two tablespoons of the cooked peas, purée the remainder with the broth in a blender or food processor.

Melt the butter in a large pan and cook the ground spices over medium heat for two minutes, stirring. Add the reserved peas, the pea purée, and sugar. Season with salt and heat until just simmering.

To serve, stir in the raisins and garnish with the coriander leaves.

To serve 4

VARIATION
For an even more pungent flavor, you can use whole cumin, coriander, and fenugreek seeds, pounding them in a pestle and mortar.

Cumin

HERB SAUCES, OILS, & VINEGARS

Salmon steaks brushed before broiling with tarragon oil; beef for pot roasting marinated in oregano oil and vinegar; baby vegetables tossed in aromatic herb butter, and fish pan-fried and served with a spoonful of green salsa – such herb flavorings and sauces can lift the plainest of dishes into the gourmet class, and keep alive the fragrance of the herb garden in spring.

Aromatic herb butter

Serve this butter as a dressing for broiled chops, steak and fish, toss with plain or green pasta, or drizzle over young spring vegetables.

7 tbsp unsalted butter,
at room temperature
1 clove garlic, finely chopped
4 tbsp chopped parsley
1 tbsp chopped chives
salt and black pepper
1 tsp lemon juice

Beat the butter with the garlic, parsley, and chives. Season with salt and pepper and gradually beat in the lemon juice, a few drops at a time. Shape the butter into a roll, wrap it in foil or plastic wrap, and refrigerate until firm. Cut it in slices, or pats, to serve.

To make ½ cup

VARIATIONS
For watercress butter, especially good with broiled or poached salmon, use one small bunch of finely chopped watercress leaves in the place of the parsley and chives. For chopped fennel, lemon balm, mint, summer, savory, or wild marjoram.

Green salsa

This piquant sauce is best served with pan-fried or broiled fish. To preserve the freshness of the herbs, make just before serving.

2 cloves garlic, crushed
2 tbsp capers, rinsed and drained
4 anchovy fillets, finely chopped
1 tbsp chopped basil
3 tbsp chopped flat-leaved parsley
1 tsp whole-grain mustard
3 tbsp lemon juice
3 tbsp olive oil
black pepper

Beat all the ingredients together until they are well blended. Taste the sauce and adjust the seasoning if necessary. If you find it a little too strong or salty, add one or two teaspoonfuls of heavy cream or plain yoghurt.

To serve 4

French tarragon

Herb oils

Use these fragrant oils to dress salads, in sauces and marinades, or brush on meat and fish for broiling. They are also good in casseroles and soups.

6 tbsp chopped herb such as basil, mint, oregano, tarragon, thyme or wild marjoram
2½ cups olive oil
1–2 sprigs of the herb

Pound the herb to a paste in a pestle and mortar or mixing bowl. Stir in a few drops of the oil, mix until it is well blended, then add the remainder. Pour the mixture into a dry, sterilized jar, cover, and set aside for two weeks, shaking or stirring once or twice a day. Strain the oil into sterilized bottles, add the herb sprigs, seal, and store in a cool dark place.

To make 2½ cups

Herb vinegars

Add piquancy to salads, sauces, marinades, and casseroles.

10 tbsp chopped herb, such as basil, mint, oregano, tarragon or thyme
2½ cups white wine vinegar
1–2 sprigs of the herb

Pound the herb to a paste and transfer it to a heatproof container. Pour the vinegar into a nonreactive pan, bring it to a boil, and pour it over the herb. Stir well and leave to cool. Pour the herb and vinegar into a sterilized jar, cover, and set aside for three weeks, shaking or stirring once or twice a day. Strain the vinegar into sterilized bottles. Add the herb sprigs, seal, and store in a cool, dark place.

To make 2½ cups

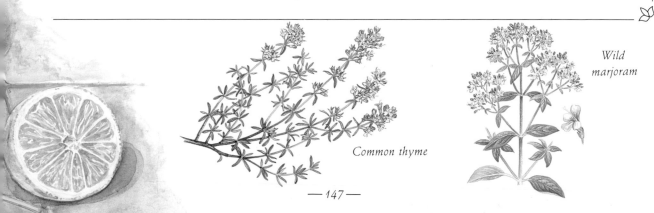

Common thyme

Wild marjoram

MEAT & FISH DISHES

The use of herbs to flavor and enhance the richness of meat and fish has its origins in ancient times, and cultures all around the world have absorbed classic combinations into their cultural heritage. Lamb studded with slivers of garlic and baked with rosemary sprigs; raw salmon wrapped in dill leaves before being marinated in salt and preserving spices for gravad lax; cubes of lamb, pork, or beef tossed in cumin, fennel, and coriander seeds for Malaysian satay. These and the recipes that follow illustrate some of the culinary bonds between aromatic plants and protein foods.

Meatballs in dill sauce

A traditional Greek egg and lemon sauce is flavored with dill to complement these meatballs, which are poached in herb-flavored broth.

12 oz lean pork, cut into cubes
1 small onion, coarsely chopped
6 tbsp fresh white bread crumbs
2 tbsp chopped chervil (or you can use parsley)
salt and black pepper
large pinch of grated nutmeg
1 egg, lightly beaten
flour, for dusting
3¾ cups chicken broth
5 or 6 parsley stalks
2 egg yolks
4 tbsp lemon juice
2 tbsp chopped dill
dill leaves, to garnish
lemon wedges, to serve

Process the meat and onion in a food processor or blender until it forms a smooth paste. Stir in the bread crumbs and chervil, and season with salt, pepper and nutmeg. Stir in the egg and mix until well blended. Cover and chill for at least one hour.

Dust your hands with flour and shape the mixture into walnut-sized balls.

Pour the broth into a large saucepan, and add the parsley stalks. When it is boiling, add the meatballs. Return the broth to a simmer, half cover the pan, and simmer for 10–15 minutes. Remove the meatballs with a spoon and arrange them on a heated serving dish. Keep them warm while you make the sauce.

Strain the broth and measure 1¼ cups into a clean pan. Bring to just

below simmering over medium heat. Beat the egg yolks with the lemon juice, stir in the dill, and season with salt and pepper. Pour a few spoonfuls of the hot broth into the egg and lemon mixture and stir well. (Do not allow the broth to come to a boil or the mixture will curdle.)

Return the sauce mixture to the pan and warm it gently over low heat, stirring constantly. As soon as the sauce thickens, remove it from the heat, taste, and adjust the seasoning.

Pour the sauce over the meatballs, garnish the dish with dill leaves, and serve with lemon wedges. Green salad and pasta shapes tossed in cream and chopped fresh herbs go well with this dish.

To serve 4

Chervil

Mediterranean baked fish

*The fish is cooked in a rich, colorful and aromatic sauce and can be
served "fisherman style," straight from the cooking dish.*

Whole fish, such as red snapper or striped
bass, cleaned, weighing about 3½ lb
juice of 1 lemon
salt and black pepper
3 bay leaves
6 tbsp olive oil
1 medium onion, sliced
2 cloves garlic, chopped
⅔ cup dry white wine
1 tbsp white wine vinegar
8 oz tomatoes, chopped
2 tbsp tomato paste
5 tbsp chopped Italian parsley
8 tbsp dry white bread crumbs
3 oz feta cheese, crumbled
12 black olives, to garnish

Wash the fish, pat dry, sprinkle it
inside with lemon juice, and season
with salt and pepper. Tuck the bay
leaves inside. Heat the oil in a pan
and cook the onion over medium
heat until it is transparent. Cook
the garlic for one minute, then add
the wine, wine vinegar, chopped
tomatoes, tomato paste and
parsley. Season with salt and
pepper. Stir well and bring to a
boil.

Pour half the sauce into a
shallow baking dish – a cast iron
one is traditional – and place the
fish on top. Pour on the remaining
sauce and scatter over the bread
crumbs. Bake the fish, uncovered,
in a preheated oven at 375°F for
35–40 minutes, until it is firm.
Sprinkle over the crumbled cheese,
garnish with the olives, and serve.

To serve 6

Herb-coated chicken

*Chicken breasts, marinated in a spicy mixture, are sautéed to give a
delicious crispy coating.*

4 small boneless, skinless chicken
breasts
2 tbsp Dijon mustard
1 tbsp whole-grain mustard
2 egg yolks, lightly beaten
3 tbsp cream
salt and black pepper
1 cup dry white bread crumbs
3 tbsp chopped French tarragon (or
coriander or Italian parsley)
flour, for dusting
oil, for cooking

Pat the chicken breasts dry. Mix the
mustards, egg yolks, and cream in a
shallow bowl, season with salt and
pepper. Combine bread crumbs
and chopped herb on a large plate
or a piece of wax paper.

Dip each chicken breast in flour
to coat it on all sides, then in the
mustard mixture, turning it to coat
it evenly. Drain off any excess, then
turn the chicken in the crumb
mixture until it is well coated.

Cover the coated chicken breasts
and place them in the refrigerator
for at least four hours. During this
time, the flavors will penetrate the
meat and the coating will set.

Heat oil in a large, heavy frying-
pan. Cook the chicken joints for
about 10 minutes on each side,
until golden brown. To test that the
meat is cooked, pierce the thickest
part with a fine skewer; the juice
should run clear.

To serve 4

Sweet bay

*Flat-leaved
parsley*

French tarragon

VEGETARIAN DISHES

Cooking for vegetarians has never been more imaginative or exciting, and using a wide range of herbs increases the possibilities. A rich whole wheat pastry with the aroma of caraway seeds, a vegetable crisp pepped up with a hint of ground ginger, pasta tossed in a fresh green parsley sauce. These recipes will appeal to a much wider audience than convinced vegetarians.

Carrot and lima bean crisp

Fresh spring vegetables complemented by the fragrance of herbs make a delicious lunch or supper dish.

1 lb carrots, trimmed and sliced
8 oz lima beans, fresh or frozen and thawed
1 tbsp butter
1 tbsp chopped marjoram
1 tsp honey
½ tsp ground ginger
3 tbsp reserved vegetable broth

FOR THE CRISP
3 tbsp whole wheat flour
¼ cup whole wheat bread crumbs
½ tsp ground ginger
1 tbsp sunflower seeds
1 tbsp sesame seeds
salt and white pepper
5 tbsp vegetable oil

Steam the carrots and lima beans until they are just tender. Reserve the broth. Toss the vegetables in the butter and stir in the marjoram, honey, and ginger. Turn the mixture into a baking dish and drizzle over the three tablespoons of reserved vegetable broth.

To make the crisp, mix together the flour, bread crumbs, ground ginger, sunflower, and sesame seeds, and season to taste with salt and pepper. Stir in the oil and spread the mixture evenly over the vegetables.

Bake in the oven (375°F) for 20 to 25 minutes, until the topping is golden brown.

To serve 4

Onion and caraway tart

*A hint of caraway in both the pastry and the filling gives this
vegetable tart an unusual piquancy.*

1 cup whole wheat flour
7 tbsp butter, diced
1 tsp caraway seeds, lightly crushed
salt
1 egg yolk mixed with 2 tbsp water

FOR THE FILLING
3 tbsp butter
1½ lb onions, thinly sliced
1 tbsp olive oil
2 eggs
2 egg yolks
⅔ cup cream
1 tsp caraway seeds
salt and black pepper

To make the pastry, mix together the flour and the butter and rub in the fat with your fingers. Stir in the caraway seeds and salt. Stir in the egg yolk and water and mix to a stiff dough. Wrap and chill for at least 30 minutes.

Roll out the pastry to line an 8-in tart pan. Trim the edges and prick the base. Cover the base with foil or parchment paper and weight with dried beans. Bake the pastry "blind" in the oven at 400°F for ten minutes. Remove the beans and foil or paper, and bake the pastry crust for five minutes more. Reduce the oven heat to 350°F.

To make the filling, melt the butter and oil in a pan and cook the onions over low heat until they are soft and just beginning to color. Remove from the heat.

Beat together the eggs, egg yolks, and cream. Stir in the caraway seeds and season with salt and pepper. Pour over the onions and stir with a wooden spoon. Pour the mixture into the partly-baked pastry crust and bake in the oven for 25 minutes, until the filling has set. Serve hot or cold.

To serve 4 to 6

Tagliatelle with parsley sauce

*Serve with a colorful salad of roasted red and yellow peppers, or
tomatoes sprinkled with chopped basil and sunflower seeds.*

1 lb fresh spinach tagliatelle
3 tbsp olive oil
6 scallions, thinly sliced
4 cloves garlic, finely chopped
*12 oz button mushrooms,
thinly sliced*
1 cup chopped curly-leaved parsley
salt and black pepper
pinch of grated nutmeg
⅔ cup heavy cream
8 oz feta cheese, crumbled

Cook the tagliatelle in boiling, salted water until it is just tender. Drain and keep warm.

Meanwhile, heat the oil in a pan and cook the onions over medium heat until translucent. Add the garlic and cook for one minute more. Add the mushrooms, stir well, cover, and simmer over a low heat for five minutes. Stir in the parsley carefully to avoid breaking up the mushrooms, and season with salt and pepper and nutmeg. Add the cream and heat through.

Turn the tagliatelle into a warm serving dish, pour on the sauce and toss well. Sprinkle on the cheese. Serve with crusty bread.

To serve 4

Caraway

Garlic

*Curled
parsley*

VEGETABLES & SALADS

Vegetables and lettuces that grow side-by-side with herbs in the garden have a natural affinity with them at the table, too. Add a sprig or two of herbs to the water when steaming vegetables. If you deep-fry vegetables in a crisp batter, toss them in chopped herbs before serving, and pep up a "plain" green salad with a sprinkling of mixed herb leaves.

Apple and mint relish

Ready in no time, this sharp, crunchy fruit dish is good served ice-cold, with broiled meat or fish.

2 lemons
4 large apples, cored
and thinly sliced
4 tbsp chopped mint
salt

Halve the lemons and cut two very thin slices. Reserve. Grate the rind and squeeze the juice from the remainder.

Put the apples in a bowl and immediately (to prevent them from discoloring) add the lemon juice and grated rind. Just before serving, stir in the mint and season with salt. Serve chilled, decorated with the lemon slices, cut in half.

To serve 4

Fenugreek carrots

This is a quick and easy way to add a little zest to carrots served as a vegetable side dish.

1½ lb small carrots, trimmed
4 tbsp olive oil
1 onion, finely chopped
1 clove garlic, finely chopped
1 tsp ground fenugreek seeds
1 tbsp red wine vinegar
2 tbsp orange juice
4 tbsp water
large pinch of paprika
salt and black pepper
1 tbsp orange rind
1 tsp chopped chervil

If small carrots are unavailable, cut the vegetable into 3 in slices. Heat the oil in a pan and cook the onion over medium heat until translucent. Stir in the garlic and fenugreek seeds, add the carrots, and cook for two minutes more. Add the wine vinegar, orange juice and water, and season with salt and pepper. Cover the pan and simmer very gently for 15 minutes, until the carrots are just tender. Shake the pan occasionally and make sure they are not drying out.

Sprinkle with the orange rind and chopped chervil, and serve hot.

To serve 4

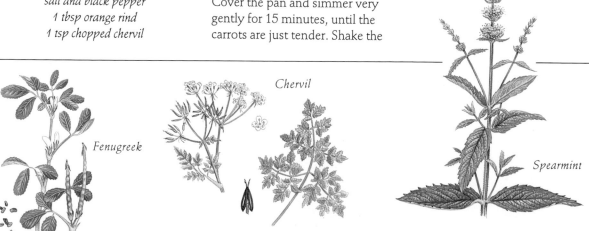

Chervil

Fenugreek

Spearmint

Nasturtium-flower salad

Use dramatic red, yellow and orange nasturtium flowers as "containers" for a creamy salad.

8 oz cream cheese
6 tbsp heavy cream
2 tbsp red lumpfish roe
1 tsp grated orange rind
1 tbsp orange juice

2 tbsp chopped lemon balm
1 tbsp snipped chives
12 nasturtium flowers, washed and dried, stamens removed
lettuce leaves, to serve

Beat together the cream cheese and cream. Fold in the lumpfish roe, orange rind, orange juice, and herbs. Spoon into the flowers.

To serve 4

Couscous and coriander salad

The couscous grains absorb the flavor of the herb dressing and form the base for the other principal ingredients.

¾ cup precooked couscous
juice of ½ orange
3 tbsp olive oil
3 tbsp chopped coriander leaves
salt and black pepper
1¼ cups boiling water
2 oranges
3 in piece of cucumber
4 tomatoes, quartered
3 eggs, hard-boiled and quartered
can of anchovy fillets, drained and halved lengthwise
12 black olives
1 tbsp pine nuts
coriander sprigs, to garnish

FOR THE SAUCE
⅔ cup plain yogurt
juice of ½ orange
2 cloves garlic, crushed
3 tbsp olive oil
2 tbsp chopped coriander leaves
large pinch of ground coriander seed
salt and black pepper

Line a strainer with cheesecloth, add the couscous and rinse with cold water. Drain well and transfer to a large bowl.

Mix together the juice of ½ orange, the olive oil, and chopped coriander and season well with salt and pepper. Pour the dressing over the grains and mix well. Pour on the boiling water and stir gently as the grains swell. Stir frequently as the grains double in size. Transfer the couscous to a large serving dish.

Peel and slice the oranges. Thinly slice the cucumber and arrange the cucumber and orange over the couscous, then arrange the tomato and egg wedges, the anchovies, and the olives. Sprinkle with the pine nuts, cover, and chill.

To make the sauce, mix together the yogurt, orange juice, garlic, oil, chopped coriander leaves and ground coriander seed and season to taste with salt and pepper.

To serve, garnish the salad with coriander sprigs and serve the sauce separately.

To serve 6 to 8

Nasturtium

DESSERTS & SWEET TREATS

Take a basket into the backyard or reach out to the windowbox and gather the youngest, freshest herbs to flavor creamy desserts and syrups. Pick the most perfect flower specimens of sweet violets, marjoram, and borage to turn into edible sugar-frosted decorations.

Rose-petal pudding

This light, summery recipe is based on a traditional 18th-century English dessert called Junket, or "swaying cream."

*2½ cups whole milk
1 tbsp rose-petal superfine sugar (see page 159)
1 teaspoon gelatin, powdered
2 tbsp triple rosewater
1 cup heavy cream
crystallized rose petals, to decorate (see page 156)*

Heat the milk and sugar to boiling point stirring once or twice. Remove from the heat and stir in the powdered gelatin and the rosewater. Pour into a decorative glass dish and leave, uncovered, for about 30 minutes, until the dessert is just set. Once the pudding is set, whip the cream and spread over the top and decorate with crystallized rose petals.

The dessert is delicious served with fresh raspberries or strawberries, or with lightly cooked and sweetened black currants.

To serve 4

Bee balm fruit salad

The fragrant leaves of this versatile herb flavor the syrup and the bright red, shaggy flowers decorate the dish.

*6 tbsp superfine sugar
¾ cup water
juice of 2 oranges
4–6 bee balm leaves
1 cup black currants,
stripped from stalks, or blackberries
2 cups strawberries, hulled
2 cups raspberries, hulled
2–3 bee balm flowers, to decorate
scented geranium leaves, to decorate*

Put the sugar, water, orange juice, and bee balm leaves in a pan over low heat. Stir occasionally until the sugar has dissolved, then bring to a boil for five minutes to reduce the syrup. Discard the bee balm leaves, add the black currants, and return to a boil. Simmer for 5 minutes. Remove from the heat and set aside to cool.

Stir in the strawberries and raspberries, pour into a decorative glass dish, and decorate with the bee balm flowers and scented geranium leaves.

To serve 4–6

Wild marjoram

Sweet violet

Bergamot

Frozen citrus dessert

Lemon-scented geranium leaves add a subtle flavor and fragrance to this quick and easy dessert, which may be served frozen or chilled.

grated zest and juice of 2 oranges
grated zest and juice of 1 lemon
3–4 lemon-scented geranium leaves
12 tbsp unsalted butter, at room
temperature
¾ cup superfine sugar
3 eggs, separated
16 ladyfingers' cakes

Line a 1-lb loaf pan. Infuse the zest and juice of the oranges and lemon in a bowl with the geranium leaves for 30 minutes.

Beat the butter and sugar until thick and pale lemony; beat the egg yolks in one at a time. Discard the herb leaves and gradually beat the fruit juice into the egg mixture. Whisk the egg whites until stiff, then fold them into the mixture.

Arrange alternating layers of ladyfingers and fruit mixture in the pan, finishing with ladyfingers. Wrap in foil and freeze for at least 3 hours. Serve the dessert frozen, or transfer it to the refrigerator for 1 hour and serve it chilled. Decorate the top with scented geranium leaves.

To serve 6

Scented-leaved geraniums

Apothecary's rose

BAKING DAY

Chopped fresh herbs and pungent seeds impart their fragrance to baked goods – from whole wheat bread and scones to crisp, crunchy savory cookies. And for a delectable breakfast treat, try rose-petal preserves. These are a few of the many ways herbs can add interest to baking day.

Ginger shortbread

Chopped crystallized ginger in melt-in-the-mouth shortbread creates a delicious addition to the holiday cookie repertoire.

*3½ cups flour, plus extra
for dusting
1 tsp ground ginger
salt
12 tbsp butter
½ cup confectioners' sugar
3 rounded tbsp set honey
¾ cup crystallized
ginger, finely chopped
raw sugar, for dusting*

Sift together the flour, ground ginger, and salt. Rub in the butter and stir in the sugar. Mix in the honey and chopped crystallized ginger and form it into a stiff dough. Knead lightly in the bowl.

Halve the dough and roll out each piece on a lightly floured board to make an 8-in circle. Transfer the rounds to baking sheets, mark each one into eight wedges with a sharp knife, and prick the top with a fork.

Bake at 325°F for 15 to 20 minutes, until crisp and golden brown around the edges. Sprinkle with raw sugar and leave to cool slightly. Transfer to a wire rack to cool completely.

To make 16 slices

Crystallizing flowers, petals, and leaves

Select only flowers that you know are edible – borage, pot marigold, sweet marjoram, thyme, sweet Cicely, lavender, sweet violet and rose are examples – and decorative herb leaves such as lemon balm, mints, lemon verbena, and sweet Cicely.

Cut clustered flowers, such as those of marjoram, into small sprays. Pull off each rose petal separately and cut all individual flowers from their stalks. Cut herbs into small sprays or pull off individual leaves. Whip an egg white until it is just frothy and, with a small camel hair paintbrush, paint every part of every surface of the plant material to cover it completely and exclude the air. Lightly sprinkle on superfine sugar, again to cover the surface completely.

Spread the sugared flowers, petals, and leaves on wax or parchment paper and leave to dry for at least two hours. Store in single layers between paper in an airtight container.

Dill-seed crackers

*To make these crackers even more spicy, substitute cumin seed or
caraway seeds for the milder dill.*

*6 tbsp flour, plus extra for dusting
2 tbsp butter, plus extra for greasing
salt
pinch of cayenne pepper
1 tsp dill seeds
1 cup shredded Cheddar cheese
1 egg yolk, lightly beaten
1 tbsp ice water*

Sift the flour into a bowl and rub in the butter. Stir in the salt, cayenne, dill seeds, and shredded cheese. Stir in the egg yolk and mix to a soft but firm dough with the water. Wrap in foil or plastic wrap and chill for at least one hour.

Roll out the dough on a lightly floured board to a thickness of about ⅛ in and cut into rounds with a 1½ in pastry cutter or small glass. Gather up the trimmings, roll out again, and cut out more rounds. Place well apart on a greased baking sheet and bake at 400°F for seven minutes, until golden brown. Leave to cool slightly on the baking sheet, then transfer to a wire rack to cool.

To make about 20 crackers

Fennel bread

*There is nothing that beats the smell of freshly baked bread, except
when the bread has the added fragrance of herbs.*

*4 cups lukewarm water
1 tbsp active dry yeast
9 cups whole wheat flour, plus extra for
dusting
3 tbsp salt
3 tbsp butter, plus extra
for greasing
3 tbsp chopped fennel
milk, for brushing
3 tbsp fennel seeds, for topping*

Pour 1¼ cups of the water into a bowl and sprinkle on the yeast. Leave in a warm place for about ten minutes, until it is frothy.

Sift the flour and salt into a large mixing bowl and add in any bran remaining in the strainer. Rub in the butter until the mixture resembles coarse crumbs, then stir in the chopped fennel. Gradually pour in the yeast liquid and the remainder of the warm water, stirring constantly, and mix until the dough comes away from the sides of the bowl. Transfer to a floured board and knead until smooth and elastic; or use the dough hook of an electric mixer.

Divide the dough into three equal parts. Press it into three greased 2¼ lb bread pans and cover with greased foil or plastic wrap. Leave in a warm place for 60 to 90 minutes, until the dough has risen to the tops of the pans.

Brush the tops of the loaves with milk and sprinkle with the fennel seeds. Bake in the oven at 425°F for 40 minutes, until the bread is brown and thoroughly cooked. It should sound hollow when the pans are tapped on the bottoms.

Turn the bread out of the tins and cool on a wire rack.

To make three 2¼ lb loaves

Dill

Borage

AROMATIC PRESERVES

This selection of the many jams and jellies, syrups and cordials, pickles and other preserves that capture the characteristics of both sweet and pungent herbs includes flavored sugars and a Victorian favorite, violet honey.

Dill pickles

Serve these sweet-and-sour pickled cucumbers with broiled fish such as mullet and bluefish, or with bread and cheese, or pâté.

2 pickling cucumbers
1½ cups cider vinegar
6 tbsp sugar
½ tsp salt
6 black peppercorns
4 cloves
½ tsp mustard seeds
1 tsp dill seeds
2 sprigs dill leaves

For the spiced vinegar, put vinegar, sugar, salt, peppercorns, cloves, mustard, and dill seeds in a nonreactive pan, bring slowly to a boil and boil two to three minutes. Cover, set aside for two hours.

Trim the cucumbers and cut them into ¼ in slices. Pack into cooled, sterilized jars.

Return the pan to the heat, bring the vinegar to a boil, cool it slightly, then strain it over the cucumbers. Put one sprig of dill into each jar. Close the jars with vinegar-proof lids, label, and store in a cool place. The pickles will be ready to eat after about seven days.

To make 2 lb

Violet honey

Flower-scented honey was popular in Victorian England. You can use it as a spread, to flavor sauces, or stir into yogurt.

1 cup clear honey
½ cup sweet violet petals

Pour the honey into the top of a double boiler, or a bowl set over a pan of simmering water. Stir in the violet petals, cover, and heat for 30 minutes. Remove from the heat and leave to infuse for seven days.

Reheat the flavored honey – it will be easier to pour – and strain it back into the jar.

To make 1 cup

VARIATION
Rosemary honey, made in a similar way, by infusing three or four sprigs of rosemary leaves, makes a delicious breakfast preserve.

Rosemary

Sage and cider jelly

*Brush this sweet-and-sour jelly on ham, pork or duck to glaze the
meat before cooking, or serve it as an accompaniment to roast or broiled meats.*

2¼ lb apples, sliced
juice of 1 lemon
3⅔ cups water
3⅔ cups hard cider, medium sweet
6 sprigs sage leaves
3 cups sugar approximately (see method)
5 tbsp chopped sage

Put the apples, lemon juice, water, and cider into a large pan, add the sage sprigs and bring slowly to a boil, stirring occasionally, until the sugar has dissolved. Boil for 25 minutes or until the apples are tender. Strain the fruit and liquid through a jelly bag and leave it to drain for several hours. Do not squeeze the bag to hasten the process, or the jelly may be cloudy.

Measure the strained fruit juice and weigh 1½ lb of sugar to each 4 cups of liquid. Pour the fruit juice back into the pan, add the sugar, and stir occasionally over low heat until it dissolves. Increase the heat, bring to a boil and boil vigorously for ten minutes. Skim off any scum that rises to the top.

To test for set, put a little of the jelly on a saucer and leave it to cool. It should wrinkle when pushed with a finger. When the jelly has reached setting point, remove the pan from the heat, stir in the chopped sage, and leave for about five minutes. Stir the jelly again and pour it into warm, sterilized jars. Cover with wax and transparent paper covers, or with screw or clip-on lids, label, and store in a cool, dry place.

To make about 3¼ lb

VARIATIONS
Using apple jelly as the "carrier" you can make a variety of herb jellies in a similar way. You can, if you wish, replace some of the hard cider with water.

Flavored sugars

Keep a range of superfine and confectioners' sugars in small, lidded jars and flavor them with mint, rose petals, rosemary sprigs, bay leaves, lavender flowers, scented geranium leaves, and sprigs of thyme. The amount of herbs you use will depend on the quantity of sugar, and the intensity of flavor you require. Experimenting to "find your level" is one of the joys of the kitchen!

Before use strain sugar that may contain stray petals, such as lavender or geranium.

Lavender
'Munstead'

Sage

COSMETICS

In the 17th and 18th centuries, every large household had its still-room for making perfumes and potions, scents and soaps, scented washballs and skin lotions. Many of these recipes gained world renown – like the famous Hungary water for whitening and cleansing the skin. Herbal cosmetics are simple to make at home and can be just as effective as and cheaper than commercial products.

An infusion of marigold petals used as a hair rinse can lighten fair hair.

Store herbal cosmetics in dark containers or away from damaging light.

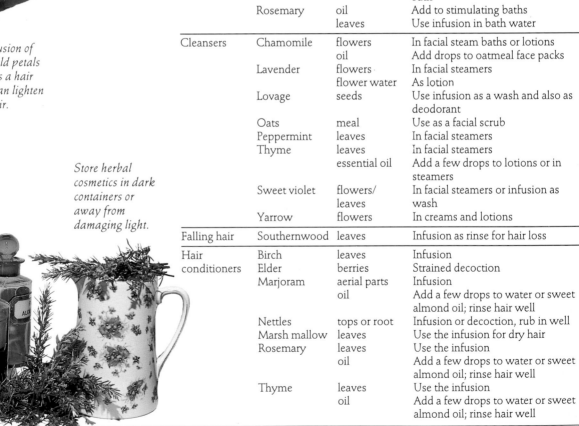

APPLICATION	HERB	PART USED	HOW TO USE
Baths	Chamomile	flowers	Relaxing – add an infusion
		oil	Add a few drops
	Dandelion	leaves	Cleansing – add an infusion
	Eucalyptus	oil	Add a few drops for muscle aches
	Jasmine	oil	Add a few drops for stimulating baths
	Lavender/	oil	Add a few drops for relaxing baths
	Marjoram	flowers	Use in tincture as body splash
	Lemon balm	leaves	Add an infusion for a relaxing bath
	Marigold	petals	A cleansing and astringent infusion
	Oats	meal	Add a satchet filled with oatmeal
	Peppermint	leaves	Add an infusion for a stimulating bath
	Rosemary	oil	Add to stimulating baths
		leaves	Use infusion in bath water
Cleansers	Chamomile	flowers	In facial steam baths or lotions
		oil	Add drops to oatmeal face packs
	Lavender	flowers	In facial steamers
		flower water	As lotion
	Lovage	seeds	Use infusion as a wash and also as deodorant
	Oats	meal	Use as a facial scrub
	Peppermint	leaves	In facial steamers
	Thyme	leaves	In facial steamers
		essential oil	Add a few drops to lotions or in steamers
	Sweet violet	flowers/leaves	In facial steamers or infusion as wash
	Yarrow	flowers	In creams and lotions
Falling hair	Southernwood	leaves	Infusion as rinse for hair loss
Hair conditioners	Birch	leaves	Infusion
	Elder	berries	Strained decoction
	Marjoram	aerial parts	Infusion
		oil	Add a few drops to water or sweet almond oil; rinse hair well
	Nettles	tops or root	Infusion or decoction, rub in well
	Marsh mallow	leaves	Use the infusion for dry hair
	Rosemary	leaves	Use the infusion
		oil	Add a few drops to water or sweet almond oil; rinse hair well
	Thyme	leaves	Use the infusion
		oil	Add a few drops to water or sweet almond oil; rinse hair well

Application	Herb	Part used	How to use
Hair rinse	Chamomile	flowers	Use the infusion for fair hair
	Lavender	rinse	Use the infusion for greasy hair
	Lemon	juice	Use the infusion for fair hair
	Nettles	leaves/tops	Use the infusion for dandruff
	Peppermint	leaves	Use the infusion or decoction with vinegar for greasy hair
	Rosemary/ Sage	leaves	Use the infusion for dark hair and dandruff
Hand cream	Chamomile/ Elder/Lavender	flowers	Use for creams and lotions
Herbs for dry skin	Chamomile	flowers	Use in creams
		oil	Add to creams
	Comfrey	leaves	Use in creams and infused oils
	Marigold	petals	Use in creams and infused oils
Herbs for oily skin	Agrimony	leaves	Use infusion as lotion
	Fennel	seeds	Use infusion as lotion with witch hazel
	Lady's mantle	leaves	Use infusion as lotion with witch hazel
	Marigold	petals	Use infusion as lotion
Moisturisers	Chamomile	flowers	Combine infusion with almond oil to make emulsion
		oil	Add a few drops to almond oil and cocoa butter base
	Rose	petals	Use in creams
		flower water	Mix with almond oil or glycerin
Scented water cologne	Lemon balm	leaves	Use the tincture or infusion
	Orange	rind	Use the infusion
		flower water	Use undiluted or combine with other scented oils
	Rose	petals	Use the infusion
		flower water	Use undiluted or combine with other scented oils
		oil	Add a few drops to water or alcohol
	Rosemary	leaves	Use the infusion
		oil	Add to water or alcohol
Shampoo	Nettle	leaves	Add to any shampoo to treat dandruff
	Rosemary	leaves	Add to any shampoo
	Soapwort	leaves	For dry hair or as a basis for soap mixtures
Toners	Agrimony	leaves	Use the infusion as a face wash
	Fennel	seeds	Use the infusion as a face wash
		essential oil	Add a few drops to skin lotions
	Lady's mantle	aerial parts	Infusion as face wash
	Lavender	flower water	Combine with witch hazel
	Marigold	petals	Use the infusion as a face wash
	Mint	leaves	In vinegars/infusions as face wash
	Peppermint	oil	Add drops to face wash
	Witch hazel	distilled extract	Combine with rose- or lavender-water
	Yarrow	flowers	Combine infusion with distilled witch hazel
Anti-wrinkle	Comfrey	leaves	In creams or infused oils

Cucumber slices can revitalize tired eyes.

A pestle and mortar are as useful in the bathroom as they are in the kitchen.

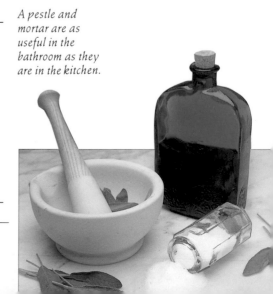

BATH PREPARATIONS

Taking a bath can be all things to all people. Depending on your choice of herbs, a bath or shower can help you face the rigors of the day or relax afterwards. Not only that, a bath can help soften the skin and replenish the body's natural oils.

By making your own bath products, you can be sure of using only pure ingredients, and also match the herbs to your needs. Keep a variety of bath oils and gels, soap and sachets in the bathroom cabinet and make your selection day by day.

Herbal bath splash

Somewhere between a bath oil and a soap, splashes are made by blending a herbal infusion with grated pure castile soap.

1 handful of blackberry or eucalyptus leaves
2 pints soft water, rainwater if possible
5 tbsp grated castile soap

Put the leaves in a pan, pour in the water, bring to a boil, cover, and simmer for 15 minutes. Remove the pan from the heat and leave to infuse for two hours.

Strain the infusion, discard the leaves, and return the liquid to the pan. Bring to a boil and beat in the grated soap. Beat until it has dissolved, then remove from the heat and set aside to cool.

Pour into bottles, cover, label, and store in the refrigerator. Use as a soft soap.

To make about 2 pints

Floral bath gels

These are made with fresh or dried flowers such as lavender, thyme, and chamomile ground to a paste or powder.

3 tbsp fresh or dried flowers, picked from the stalks
½ cup water
12 tbsp grated castile soap
3–4 drops oil of lavender or thyme (optional)

Pound the flowers with a pestle and mortar until they form a paste or powder. Put the water into a small pan, bring to a boil, and beat in the grated soap until it has dissolved, then remove pan from the heat. Stir in the flowers and, if you wish, the oil.

Leave to cool, then pour into bottles, cover, label, and store in the refrigerator. Use as a soft soap.

To make about 1 cup

Lavender
'stoechas'

Lavender
'Twickle Purple'

Common
thyme

Frothy bath oil

This is the ultimate in bath preparations which will feed, soothe, and moisturize the skin.

2 eggs
1 cup olive oil
½ cup corn oil
½ cup almond oil
2 tbsp clear honey
1 cup milk
½ cup vodka
1 tbsp mild soap flakes
3 drops essential oil, to choice

Beat together the eggs, vegetable oils, and honey. Add the milk, vodka, soap flakes, and essential oil, still beating. Pour into bottles, cover, label, and store in the refrigerator.

Add one tablespoonful under the faucet when running the water for a warm bath.

To make about 4½ cups

BATH OILS AND VINEGARS
Herbal oils and vinegars can usefully travel between kitchen and bathroom. Add about one tablespoonful of oil or up to half a cupful of vinegar flavored with mint, thyme, wild marjoram, or what you will, to a warm bath. Then luxuriate in its toning and restorative effect.

Bowles mint

Variegated apple mint

Wild marjoram

Honey and herb soap

*If you don't want to make your own soap – a messy procedure – add
your individual choice of herbal oils to pure castile soap.*

*10 tbsp grated castile soap
½ tsp olive oil
2 tsp clear honey
2–3 drops essential oil, such as
rosemary*

Put the grated soap in the top of a
double boiler or a bowl in the
microwave set on low power. Melt
the soap. Stir in the olive oil, a drop
or two at a time. Stir in the honey
and essential oil, then remove from
the heat. Continue to stir until the
mixture is well blended.

Pour into molds such as wax-
paper cupcake papers, cover and
leave undisturbed to become hard
– this may take up to two weeks.
Unmold and wrap in wax paper to
store.

To make 1 bar of soap

Elizabethan washballs

*Surely one of our most evocative links with the past, individual
soaps perfumed with roses.*

*6 oz grated pure castile soap
½ cup rosewater, plus extra for brushing*

Melt the soap over simmering
water (*see Honey and herb soap*) and
stir in the rosewater. Beat until the
mixture is well blended. Remove
from the heat, cool slightly, and
using a teaspoon, form into small

balls. Dry on wax paper in a warm
place.

Moisten a cotton ball with
rosewater and polish the soap balls
once they are hard.

To make about 10 oz

Rosemary

Apothecary's rose

Dandelion

Herbs to use in the bath

Infuse a handful of leaves or flowers in 2 pints boiling water, then add to a warm bath.

PLANT	PART OF PLANT	EFFECT
Blackberry	Infusion of leaves	Soothing to the skin
Chamomile	Infusion of leaves and flowers	Soothing
Comfrey	Infusion of leaves or decoction of root	Healing
Dandelion	Infusion of leaves	Cleansing
Elder	Infusion of leaves	Healing and stimulating
Eucalyptus	Infusion of leaves	Cleansing and soothing
Horsetail	Infusion of stems	Healing
Lady's mantle	Infusion of leaves	Soothing
Lavender	Infusion of flowers	Cleansing and deodorizing
Lemon verbena	Infusion of leaves	Stimulating
Lovage	Infusion of leaves	Cleansing and deodorizing
Mint	Infusion of leaves	Healing and cleansing
Pot marigold	Infusion of leaves	Healing, especially thread veins and varicose veins
Rosemary	Infusion of leaves	Stimulating
Thyme	Infusion of leaves and flowers	Stimulating and cleansing
Yarrow	Infusion of leaves	Astringent and cleansing

Bath sachets

Resist the temptation to toss a handful of aromatic herbs into the bath tub. You will emerge with bits and pieces clinging to your body.

If you like the hands-on approach of using fresh or dried herbs, rather than an infusion, it is better to tie the leaves or flowers into a piece of cheesecloth and suspend the sachet below the hot-water faucet.

Another way, a development of the medieval pomander principle, is to pack the herbs into a perforated tea infuser and swish under the hot faucet.

Lady's mantle

Lovage

COSMETIC TREATMENTS

Making your own skin preparations is itself a pleasurable pastime. Just to stir a handful of pot marigold petals into a bowl of steaming water is both invigorating and calming, an indirect form of aromatherapy. You may wish to scent cleansing, moisturizing, and nourishing creams with a herbal infusion or oil, to pamper and soothe your skin. This section suggests many cosmetic and therapeutic recipes using a blend of aromatic herbs to help you care for your skin, or just to allow a little self-indulgence.

Lavender cleansing cream

Lavender refreshes and feeds the skin. Suitable for dry skin, this rich cleansing cream helps replenish natural oils.

6 tbsp almond oil
10 tbsp grated white wax
3 tbsp lavender water
½ tsp cider vinegar
1 drop oil of lavender (optional)

Melt the oil and wax in the top of a double boiler. Remove from the heat, cool slightly, then beat in the lavender water, cider vinegar, and oil of lavender if you use it. Pour the cream into a lidded jar. Do not refrigerate.

Smooth the fragrant milk over your face and neck, avoiding the area around the eyes, and remove with cotton balls.

To make about 1 cup

Chamomile cleansing milk

With its lemon juice content, this preparation is especially suitable for normal and oily skins.

½ cup buttermilk
2 tbsp lemon juice
3 tbsp chamomile tisane

Beat the ingredients together until well blended. Pour into jars and store in the refrigerator.

Soak a pad of absorbent cotton in the preparation and wipe it lightly over your face and neck, avoiding the area around the eyes.

To make a scent cup

Chamomile

Lavender
'stoechas'

Rose-petal cold cream

Use this as a moisturizing night cream. It is suitable for all skin types.

*1½ cups approximately of damask or
other scented rose petals
6 tbsp olive oil
1½ tbsp purified beeswax
about 1 tsp distilled water*

Check the rose petals and discard any blemished ones. Put the olive oil in the top of a double boiler and heat gently. Stir in as many rose petals as the oil can take up. Remove from the heat. Cover and infuse for seven days.

Strain the oil through a non-metallic strainer, pressing the petals against the sides to extract as much of the oil as possible.

Melt the beeswax in a bowl over simmering water, then gradually stir in the fragrant oil. Remove from the heat and add the water, drop by drop, until the cream has the consistency you like. Pour the cream into a jar, cover, and label.

To make ½ cup

Floral hand gel

*Lavender flowers and chamomile flowers have similar and beneficial
properties, to cleanse, soothe, and soften the skin. Apply this hand
gel sparingly, rubbing it well into the skin.*

*½ cup petroleum jelly
2 tbsp lavender flowers,
stripped from the stalks
1 cup chamomile flowers,
approximately*

Heat the petroleum jelly in a double boiler. Stir in as many flowers as the jelly can take up. Cover and simmer for one hour, stirring occasionally. Remove from the heat, and leave to cool. Strain through a non-metallic strainer, pressing the flowers against the sides to extract as much of the volatile oils as possible.

Pour the fragrant jelly into jars, cover, and label.

To make 1 cup

Massaging oils

*Create your own scented oils using a
combination of these vegetable oils and other
herbal products.*

Almond oil
Apricot oil
Avocado oil
Beeswax, purified
Cocoa butter, melted
Coconut oil (a
  saturated oil
  which sets hard)
Corn oil
Glycerin
Lanolin
Peach oil
Peanut oil

Safflower oil
Soyabean oil
Sunflower oil
Wheatgerm oil

Lavender-flower lotion

Splash on this gentle toning lotion to tighten and refresh the skin.

5 tbsp lavender water
5 tbsp witch hazel
5 tbsp lemon juice, strained
2–3 drops oil of lavender

Pour all the ingredients into a bottle, close it with a cap or cork, and shake it vigorously. Shake well before use.

To make ¾ cup

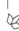

Mint astringent

This gentle astringent soothes the skin and helps improve the complexion.

2 tbsp chopped mint
4 tbsp cider vinegar
2½ cups distilled water

Put the mint and vinegar in a lidded jar, cover and leave to infuse for seven days. Strain and pour in the distilled water. Mix well.

Bottle the astringent, cover, and label. Shake well before using.

To make 2½ cups

Dandelion oil

This old country recipe uses the volatile oils in dandelion leaves to bleach freckles and other skin blotches. Use no more than twice a day.

6 young dandelion leaves, chopped
6 tbsp castor oil

Place chopped leaves and oil in a small glass or enamel pan over low heat, bring to simmering point, and simmer for 15 minutes. Remove from heat, cover, and infuse for

four or five hours. Strain through a non-metallic strainer, pressing the leaves against the sides to extract as much oil as possible. Bottle, cover, and label.

To make 6 tbsp

Herbs for the skin

This chart will help you to select the most beneficial herbs to use in lotions.

Herb	Effect
Chamomile	Cleansing, cooling, soothing
Comfrey	Emollient
Dandelion	Bleaching, drying
Fennel	Astringent
Horseradish	Bleaching, drying
Horsetail	Astringent
Lady's mantle	Astringent
Lavender	Antiseptic, stimulating, toning
Marigold	Astringent, cleansing, toning, healing

Herb	Effect
Marsh mallow	Emollient
Mint	Astringent, cleansing, soothing
Parsley	Lightening
Rosemary	Cleansing, stimulating
Thyme	Cleansing, antiseptic, toning
Violet	Cleansing, emollient
Witch hazel	Astringent, healing
Yarrow	Cleansing, toning

Facial steam

Choose the herb according to your skin type. This fragrant steam will be helpful in cleansing both dry and greasy skins.

2 cups fresh herb or 1 cup dried herb, such as lavender, peppermint, or thyme hot water (not boiling)

Place the herbs in a bowl, pour in the hot water, and stir well. Drape a towel over your head to trap the steam, and steam your face for five minutes.

If your skin is dry, nourish it by massaging in a little moisturizing cream after steaming.

To make one facial steam

Herbal face pack

Spread this soothing face pack over the skin, avoiding the area around the eyes and mouth. Place a slice of cucumber over each eye and rest for ten minutes. Wash off with warm water, or a herbal infusion.

*2 tbsp plain yogurt
2 tbsp finely chopped herb leaves or flowers, selected according to skin type
1–2 tbsp fine oatmeal*

Stir the yogurt and herbs together until they are well blended. Stir in just enough oatmeal to form a soft paste and mix well.

If you need to store the paste,

spoon it into a jar, cover, label, and store in the refrigerator.

To make about 5 tbsp

Lavender 'Twickle Purple'

Bowles mint

Peppermint

Dandelion

FLORAL WATERS & COLOGNES

The image of the "mistress of the potpourri," familiar to us through paintings and engravings, is one of daylight hours spent in the still-rooms of great European estates, where exotic and alluring fragrances were created.

Although our modern kitchens may lack the specialist equipment used in those days, our gardens are a rich source of fragrant leaves and flowers, and herbalists' shelves are well stocked with essential oils to add more concentrated aromas.

Lavender water

This reviving floral water can be used as a body splash after bathing or – as it was in the nineteenth century – sprinkled on a handkerchief and inhaled.

2 cups lavender flowers
2 pints distilled water, boiling
2 tbsp vodka

Put the lavender flowers into a flameproof container, pour on the boiling water, and stir well. Cover and leave to infuse for about 48 hours, stirring occasionally.

Strain the liquid through a non-metallic strainer pressing the flowers against the sides to extract the maximum fragrance. Stir in the alcohol, pour into bottles, cover, and label.

To make 2 pints

Floral splash

This "splash" has a pungent, heady aroma. You can vary the fragrance by substituting other essential oils.

4 drops rosemary oil
4 drops bergamot oil
2 tbsp rosewater
1 cup vodka

Stir all the ingredients together, pour into a bottle, cover and set aside for at least six weeks, shaking every day if possible.

To make about 1 cup

Rosemary

Lavender
'Hidcote'

Floral toilet fragrance

Create the fragrance of your choice by using a single flower type or blending two or more.

4 cups fragrant flowers or petals, such as chamomile, lavender, pot marigold, rose, and violet
2½ cups white wine vinegar
1¼ cups distilled water

Place the flowers or petals in a flameproof container. Heat the vinegar and water to boiling point, pour onto the flowers, and stir well. Cover and leave in a warm place for three weeks, stirring at least once a day if possible.

Strain through a non-metallic strainer, pressing the flowers against the sides to release the maximum fragrance. Pour into bottles, cover, label, and store.

To make about 4 cups

Lemon balm and rosemary cologne

Fresh herbs add a contrasting fragrance to the rosewater and alcohol in this refreshing splash cologne.

3 tbsp lemon balm
3 tbsp rosemary
strip of thinly pared orange rind
1 cup rosewater
6 tbsp vodka

Put all the ingredients into a jar, cover, and shake vigorously. Leave to infuse for two weeks, shaking at least once a day.
Strain through a non-metallic

strainer, pressing the herbs against the sides to extract the maximum fragrance. Pour into a bottle, cover, and label. Store in a cool, dark place.

To make about 2 cups

Rosewater

True rosewater is the delightfully fragrant byproduct of distilling roses, the process by which rose oil, or attar of roses, is extracted.

10 cups fragrant rose petals, traditionally those of damask roses
2½ cups distilled water
1 tsp liquid storax
1 tsp tincture of benzoin

Put the rose petals and water into a pan which has a tight-fitting lid, or cover the pan tightly with foil. Bring the water slowly to a boil, reduce the heat, and simmer very slowly for two hours. Remove from the heat and leave to infuse for about 48 hours.
Bring the water and the petals to

a boil again, simmer for a further hour, and leave to cool. Strain through a non-metallic strainer, pressing the petals against the sides to extract the maximum fragrance. Stir in the storax and tincture of benzoin. Pour into bottles, cover and label.

To make about 2½ cups

Chamomile

Pot marigold

Sweet violet

HAIR CARE

A glance along the hair-care counter in a drugstore will confirm that the practice of using herbs in shampoos, conditioners, and tonics is as alive and well today as it has ever been. Folklore abounds with herbal recommendations for hair lighteners and darkeners, strengtheners and improvers; chamomile rinse for fair hair and rosemary for dark tresses are probably among the best known of the country-lore prescriptions. The following recipes use different herbs to suit varying hair types and conditions.

Horsetail shampoo

This all-in-one shampoo and conditioner combines the cleansing properties of soapwort root and the conditioning ability of horsetail, sometimes known as the "hair gloss herb."

7 tbsp snipped horsetail stems
7 tbsp grated dried soapwort root, soaked overnight and drained
1 gal soft water

Put the horsetail and soapwort into a pan, pour in the water, and stir well. Bring to a boil. Cover and boil for 15 minutes. Remove from the heat and leave the mixture to infuse for one hour.

Strain the liquid into bottles, cover, and label. Use about 1 cup of the shampoo each time.

To make 1 gal

Herbs for the hair

HAIR TYPE	HERB
Dry	Comfrey, marsh mallow
Greasy	Lavender, peppermint
Dull and lifeless	Fennel, parsley, rosemary, garlic
Fair	Chamomile flowers
Dark	Comfrey, rosemary, sage, thyme
Auburn	Pot marigold petals
To treat dandruff	Bergamot, mint, parsley, sage, southernwood, thyme
General conditioners	Birch leaves, horsetail stems, marjoram, rosemary, thyme

---

Soapwort

Parsley

Chamomile

Controlling lotion

This solution may be just what is needed for all those who say they
can't do a thing with their hair.

10 tbsp herbal tisane (chosen from chart
according to hair type)
1 tbsp eau de Cologne
1 tbsp glycerin

Pour the herbal infusion and eau de Cologne into a bowl and add the glycerin drop by drop, beating all the time. Pour the lotion into a ·bottle, cover, and label.

Rub a little into the scalp, or comb it through the hair.

To make about ¾ cup

Garlic conditioner

With its strong antiseptic properties, garlic is a useful aid to healing
scalp conditions and can put the sheen back into dull, lifeless hair.
Shampoo your hair with your favorite fragrance after this treatment!

10 large cloves of garlic, crushed
½ cup castor oil, hot

Stir the garlic and castor oil thoroughly, cover and infuse for two days. Strain into a bottle, cover, and label.
　　Massage the oil into the scalp,

wrap the head in a towel, and leave it for about an hour, then shampoo thoroughly.

To make about ½ cup

Peppermint rinse

This aromatic hair rinse is especially beneficial for greasy hair.

10 tbsp chopped peppermint leaves
2 pints soft water
2 pints cider vinegar

Put the peppermint leaves in a pan, pour in the water, and bring slowly to a boil. Simmer for 15 minutes, remove from the heat and infuse for one hour. Strain the infusion and stir in the vinegar. Pour into bottles, cover, and label.
　　Use about ½ pt of the rinse after shampooing.

To make about ½ gal

Garlic

Peppermint

REMEDIES

For many of the world's people, herbs are – even today – the only available medicine, and folk healers still prepare their remedies following centuries-old traditions. In the West, we are more likely to use herbal medicines in the form of chemical extracts – like aspirin, which was originally derived from willow bark, or ephedrine, originally found in the Chinese plant *Ma-huang*. Whole plants can, however, be just as effective as many of these patented extracts: they're gentler, too, with fewer side effects, though caution must be observed.

Marsh mallow's medicinal uses date from ancient times.

Ailment	Herb	Application
Blackheads	Comfrey	Root poultice mixed with marigold infusion; leaf infusion as face wash
	Marigold	Diluted tincture from petals in compress
Breath fresheners	Caraway/ Cumin/ Fennel/ Fenugreek/ Lovage	Chew the seeds fresh or dry
	Mint/Parsley	Chew the fresh leaves
Bruises	Comfrey	Leaf infusion in compress
	Witch hazel	Distilled extract in compress
Burns	Marigold	Dilute petal tincture in compress
	Lavender	Use essential oil diluted in compress or add to St. John's wort infused oil
	St. John's wort	Made from flowering tops, use dilute tincture in compress; apply infused oil directly
Colds & flus	Eucalyptus/ Hyssop/ Thyme	Use the essential oil in chest rub/steam inhalation
	Ginger	Decoction of fresh root
	Peppermint	Inhale a few drops of essential oil
	Yarrow	Make an infusion from leaves/flowers
Coughs	Angelica	Leaf infusion/tincture
	Garlic	Syrup, steam inhalation
	Hyssop	Dilute essential oil to make chest rub
	Licorice	Root decoction/syrup
	Marsh mallow	Use leaves and flowers to make syrup or infusion
	Onion	Syrup from fresh vegetable
	Oregano	Steam inhalation from essential oil
Cuts & grazes	Garlic	Poultice from cloves

Ailment	Herb	Application
Abscesses & boils	Comfrey	Root poultice mixed with comfrey-leaf tea
	Fenugreek	Poultice of mashed seeds
	Marsh mallow	Root poultice – on its own or combined with slippery elm
	Slippery elm	Poultice made from bark
Aches & pains	Birch	Use oil/sap for external massage
	Celery	Infusion from seeds for rheumatism/arthritis
	Lavender	Use flowers or essential oil to make external massage oil
	Rosemary/ Thyme/ Wintergreen	Use leaves or essential oil to make external massage oil
Acne	Chamomile	Use flower infusion/tincture as face wash
	Garlic	Rub with fresh clove
	Marigold	Use petal infusion/tincture as face wash
	Rose	Apply a rosewater lotion
	Sage	Make a lotion using leaves
	Witch hazel	Lotion using distilled extract

Ailment	Herb	Application
Cuts & grazes cont.	Marigold	Petal infusion/dilute tincture on compress
	St. John's wort	Cream or infused oil from flowering tops
Depression	Jasmine/ Neroli/Rose	Essential oil diluted as massage oil or inhalant
	Lemon balm/ St. John's wort	Aerial parts used in infusion/ tincture
Digestive problems	Catnip	Use aerial parts in an infusion—especially for children
	Chamomile	Flower infusion for flatulence
	Dill/Fennel	Seed infusion for flatulence/ indigestion
	Fenugreek	Seed infusion for stomach cramps and upsets
	Lemon balm	Leaf infusion for nervous stomach upsets
	Licorice	Root decoction for ulceration/inflammation
	Parsley/Sage	Leaf infusion as a stimulant
	Peppermint	Leaf infusion for flatulence
	Rosemary	Leaf infusion as a bitter stimulant
	Thyme	Leaf infusion/tincture for diarrhea
Earache	Lavender	Dilute essential oil and massage outer ear
	St. John's wort	Use infused oil on cotton ball as ear plug
Eczema	Chamomile/ Elder	Flowers in infusion as skin wash or in creams
	Evening primrose	Seed oil in capsules or in ointment
	Marigold	Use petal infusion as wash/ tisane; creams and ointments

Ailment	Herb	Application
Eyes, tired/ irritated	Chamomile	Flower poultice/cold teabag on the eye
	Cucumber	Raw slices applied
	Eyebright	Infusion of whole plant in sterilized eyebath
	Fennel	Seed poultice/cold teabag
Headaches & migraine	Feverfew	Fresh leaves in sandwich or as infusion/tincture
	Lavender/ Peppermint/ Rosemary	Dilute essential oil as a massage for temples
Insect bites & stings	Eucalyptus/ Lavender	Essential oil diluted and applied to sting
	Feverfew	Leaf infusion as wash
	Lemon balm/ Sage	Fresh leaves applied to sting
	Onion	Apply slices to sting
	Witch hazel	Apply lotion of distilled extract
Mouth & gum disorders	Sweet Cicely	Use diluted tincture as mouthwash
	Rosemary/ Sage/Thyme	Leaf infusion as mouthwash
Nervous tension	Catnip/ Lemon balm/ Vervain	Use aerial parts in infusion or tincture
	Chamomile/ Lavender	Use flowers in infusion or tincture
Sprains	Rosemary	Leaf infusion in compress
	Thyme	Dilute essential oil as massage or in compress
Throat, sore	Eyebright	Use infusion of whole plant as gargle/mouthwash
	Sage/Thyme	Leaf infusion as gargle
Toothache	Cloves	Apply essential oil to gum area

Use a pot kept specially for the purpose to make your delicate tisanes.

HERBAL TISANES

Herbal tisanes, or teas, are the most widely used of home remedies and among the simplest to prepare. They are made by infusing the aerial parts of a herb, the fresh or dried leaves or petals, in boiling water just long enough to release the active constituents contained in the volatile oils. The infusion may then be enjoyed soothingly hot and, as a matter of choice, sweetened with honey, or refreshingly cold and sharpened with a slice of lemon or lime. If the tisane is administered to someone with a fever, then the tea should be drunk lukewarm.

MAKING A TISANE

Herbal tisanes have a delicate and in some cases almost elusive flavor, and should be made in a glass or china pot, the prettier the better, kept specially for the purpose. The residue of the tannin left in a pot used for infusing ordinary tea could both mask the flavor and detract from the feel-good factor induced by drinking herbal tisanes.

Allow two level teaspoons of dried herbs or two level tablespoonfuls of fresh herbs for each cup. Place the herb in a warmed pot, measure and pour in the required amount of boiling water, and cover. Leave the infusion to steep for 10 to 15 minutes – no longer – before straining. It is not advisable to increase the infusion time in the hope, for example, of intensifying the flavor, since prolonged exposure to heat causes a loss of volatile oils through evaporation.

Herb tisanes, unlike tinctures which are made with alcohol, have a relatively short shelf-life. If you wish to serve a tisane ice-cold, or to make it in larger quantities, cool and strain the liquid, pour it into a jar with a lid, and store for up to 24 hours in a refrigerator. You can then reheat the tisane without boiling in a glass or enamel pan if a warm drink is wanted.

Once you have become accustomed to the benefits of herbal tisanes, you can learn to become your own tea blender. By mixing two or more types of aromatic leaves and flowers it is possible to create innumerable permutations of flavors, and to benefit simultaneously from the perceived healing properties of more than one plant. For example, an infusion of lemon balm and rosemary leaves with hawthorn blossoms, when available, can be helpful in relieving stress and nervous tension; a blend of yarrow, elder flowers, and peppermint makes a tea that has become a classic remedy for fever, and, without peppermint, the combination of yarrow and elder flowers may be taken to alleviate the effects of a hangover.

TAKING HERBAL TISANES

Herbal tisanes made in the proportion suggested are mild medicines which may be taken to relieve symptoms over a period of four to eight weeks. If during this time additional symptoms develop, or the condition worsens, then medical help should be sought. When tisanes are taken for medical rather than social reasons, the normal frequency is two or three times a day, after meals; taking tisanes before meals, as a medicinal aperitif, is not recommended, as they can dilute the gastric juices and upset the digestion.

Whilst some herbal remedies can bring almost instant relief, when they are taken to ease a headache, for example, others take time to strengthen and stimulate the body systems. And so when chronic conditions such as rheumatism are being treated, patience is a virtue.

A guide to herbal tisanes and their attributes

Herb	Use to ease
Basil	flatulence, nausea (avoid in pregnancy)
Chamomile flowers	insomnia
Caraway	flatulence
Catnip	feverishness, insomnia
Hops	insomnia, digestive disorder
Hyssop	mucus on chest
Lady's mantle	menstrual problems
Lavender flowers	headache, nervousness
Lemon balm	headache, insomnia, depression
Marigold petals	indigestion, gall bladder problems
Marjoram	flatulence, nausea, asthmatic complaints
Meadowsweet	acidity in the stomach, feverish chills
Mint	digestive disorders
Parsley	indigestion (avoid in pregnancy)
Peppermint	flatulence, nausea, colic
Rosemary	indigestion, poor circulation, nervousness
Sage	coughs, sore throat, indigestion (avoid in pregnancy)
Thyme	colds, indigestion, asthmatic complaints
Yarrow	flatulence, indigestion

DECOCTIONS, COMPRESSES, AND TINCTURES

Decoctions are made by simmering the roots, rhizomes, or woody parts of plants in liquid to extract the bitter principles and mineral salts. The strained liquid may then be drunk, or added to compresses and applied to the skin, when the beneficial elements will be quickly absorbed. Or, herbs may be steeped in spirits to make a tincture.

COMPRESSES AND POULTICES

Compresses and poultices, which are particularly effective in the treatment of bruises, strains, and inflamed areas, help the body to absorb beneficial herbal compounds through the skin.

A compress is made by soaking a piece of clean cloth such as linen, cotton, or gauze in a decoction or infusion and applying it as hot as can be tolerated. When the compress has cooled, it can be soaked again and again in the reheated liquid and reapplied until the condition has been relieved.

Poultices, which have been widely used in self-help medicine for centuries, consist of parts of the herb itself, rather than a decoction or infusion, and are applied directly to the skin, or made into a paste and wrapped in a sterile gauze pad.

Among the most widely used poultices, which are particularly effective in the localized treatment of abscesses and boils, are those made of powdered marsh mallow root or slippery elm, both of which are available from herbalists. The poultice is made by mixing one tablespoon of the powder to a thick paste with hot cider vinegar, or hot water. The paste is spread between two pieces of gauze and applied hot to the affected area. A hot-water bottle pressed against the poultice will keep the heat in for as long as possible. Once it cools, it should be changed and another, as hot as possible, applied in its place.

Other forms of poultice can be made with fresh herbs. The application of fresh parsley leaves or marigold petals moistened with a little hot water can help to relieve styes, the inflammation of the glands at the base of the eyelashes.

A well-known way of relieving tired and strained eyes is to apply a slice of chilled cucumber to each eye. Puffy eyelids can be relieved and the swelling reduced by the application of grated raw potato. In each case, it is probable that resting in a quiet room with closed eyes adds to the beneficial effects of the poultice.

Comfrey

Culpeper says . . .

Nicholas Culpeper, the seventeenth-century herbalist, attributed the delightfully scented herb southernwood (Artemisia abrotanum) with powerful healing and restorative properties. He claimed that, "boiled with barleymeal, it removes pimples and wheals from the face or other parts of the body . . . The ashes mingled with old salad oil, helps those that are bald, causing the hair to grow again." The herb has been known by the popular names of garde-robe, (because it was hung as a moth repellent), old man, lad's love, and maiden's ruin.

Decoctions

A decoction of valerian is an example of a classic herbal medicine which may be used, for a limited period only, to relieve nervous disorders.

1 oz roots or woody part of plant
4½ cups water

Put the plant material into a glass or enamel pan and add the cold water. Bring to a boil, reduce the heat, and simmer for 15–20 minutes. Strain the decoction through a non-metallic strainer, and press the material against the sides with a spoon. Let cool. The decoction can be stored in a covered jar in the refrigerator for up to 24 hours. If it is to be taken or applied hot, slowly reheat without further boiling.

Tinctures

Tinctures, which are usually bought from herbalists, may be taken undiluted or in hot drinks, or added to skin applications.

4 oz herb
2½ cups alcohol such as vodka

Put the herb in a jar and pour on the alcohol. Seal the jar, shake well, and leave in a warm, dark place for 14 days, shaking once or twice a day. Strain into a dark-glass bottle, and store in a cool, dark place.

To take in a drink, measure out undiluted tinctures in dropfuls. Tinctures may also be mixed with compresses and ointments, or added to a bath.

Curled parsley

Marsh mallow

Pot marigold

SKIN PROBLEMS

It should be possible to treat skin problems, acne, eczema, abscesses and boils included, in two ways: in the short term to alleviate any irritation or inflammation of the skin, and in the longer term to reinforce the body's own immune system and its ability to function healthily.

Poor diet or nutritional deficiency may contribute to such complaints. A gradual movement away from animal and other saturated fats and sugar and other refined carbohydrates will almost certainly bring about a noticeable improvement in general health.

Fresh fruits and vegetables have a positive part to play in a healthy routine, and the increased use of herbs in cooking and salads adds more than nutritional value. These aromatic plants add interest and flavor to dishes of all kinds. Some vegetables and salad leaves are particularly rich sources of the vital chemicals or electrolytes potassium, iron, and sulfur. Among them are carrots, celery, radishes, scallions, spinach, and bell peppers, and herbs including dandelion leaves, parsley, and watercress. Inclusion of these, especially, in your diet should help clear up skin problems.

Eczema

Eczema, which can be caused by fatigue, stress, or an allergy, notably to dairy products, can be relieved by evening primrose oil.

Gamma linolenic acid – GLA – the active constituent of oil of evening primrose, has proved beneficial to many eczema sufferers. Capsules and ointments are available from healthfood stores and herbalists.

FLORAL TISANES
A tisane made from marigold can also help. Make the tisane by infusing one teaspoon of dried flowers or one tablespoon of fresh flowers in a cup of boiling water for 10 minutes. The infusion may be drunk hot three times a day.

GRASPING THE NETTLE
Wearing rubber gloves or thick gardening gloves, gather young leaves of stinging nettles where they will not have been contaminated by pollutants. Make them into a purifying tea, using a handful of leaves to 2 cups of boiling water. For a less painful alternative, use a nettle tea bag.

HERBAL WASH
To tackle the problem of dry, flaky skin from the outside, make a tisane in the usual way from the flowers of chamomile or elder, and use it as a face wash.

Pot marigold

Yarrow

Dandelion

Acne

Acne, caused when the sebaceous glands of the face and neck become blocked, has a demoralizing effect on teenage sufferers.

Scrupulous cleanliness is essential, with natural herb soaps and cleansing creams preferred to synthetically perfumed products. Herbal tonics, face washes, poultices, and tinctures can help, with marigold (calendula), chamomile, sage leaves, and witch hazel among the most beneficial plants.

HERBAL TONIC

Mix equal parts of witch hazel and rosewater (not triple rosewater) and keep it in a stoppered bottle in a cool place. Dab it on your skin after washing or cleansing.

HERBAL FACE WASH

Fresh or dried flowers infused in boiling water can be used as a soothing and cleansing face wash. Elder flowers, chamomile, lavender, and yarrow flowers are all suitable. Infuse a handful of flowers in 1 pint boiling water for 10 minutes, cool, strain, and keep in a stoppered bottle in the refrigerator. Splash on the affected areas, or dab on with cotton.

COMFREY POULTICE

For a "drawing out" poultice, mix one teaspoon powdered comfrey root to a paste with hot comfrey tea or hot water, and spread it over the affected areas. Gently remove it by dabbing with cold comfrey tea, made by infusing the dark green leaves in boiling water. The plant contains allantoin, which stimulates cell growth and can help healing.

MARIGOLD COMPRESS

Benefit from the healing and soothing properties of marigold by mixing one teaspoon calendula tincture (available from herbalists) with ¾ cup distilled water. Apply it to affected areas, or use the mixture as a face wash. Store it in a stoppered bottle.

Boils and abscesses

A tendency to boils or abscesses is an indication that something is wrong internally. It is wise to seek medical advice.

These localized infections often occur in people who suffer from a general malaise or poor nutrition. Stimulating and healing remedies should be accompanied by adequate exercise and a healthy diet.

LEMON LORE

When it comes to bringing boils to a head, the answer is a lemon.

Squeeze out the juice and use it to soak a piece of sterilized gauze, held or bandaged against the eruptions. Alternatively, bind a thin slice of lemon directly on the affected site.

Country folk used to put their faith in baked or boiled onions. Cook an onion until it is soft, skin it, and bind it, as hot as can be tolerated, over the affected area.

TEA TIME

Fenugreek tea has internal and external applications. Crush one teaspoon of dried seeds, and boil them in a cup of water for 10 minutes. Strain, and drink the infusion hot. Reserve the seeds, wrap them in sterilized gauze, and use them as a poultice.

Chamomile

Fenugreek

Common sage

NERVOUS DISORDERS

Nervous tension, anxiety, and depression may be caused by a wide variety of personal and psychological problems and can be the cause or the effect of widely differing physical disorders, too. A lackluster approach to life, a state of permanent tiredness, loss of energy, and severe physical pain may all be experienced.

The case for hops

John Gerard, the sixteenth-century surgeon and apothecary to England's King James I, made a convincing case for hops as a tranquillizer when he wrote in his herbal that beer was more of a medicine than an ordinary drink.

To enjoy the benefits of hops in other ways, infuse three fresh or dried heads in a cupful of hot water for 10 minutes and drink the tisane hot. To reinforce the effect, take a warm bath into which a strong hop infusion has been added, and retire to bed with a sleep pillow filled with dried hops. CAUTION: *Hops should be avoided by people suffering from depressive illness; their bitter resins lower male sex drive.*

As more is understood about the interrelationship of mind and body, it is realized that depression, one of the most widespread of nervous disorders, can have a variety of causes, not all of them psychological. In some people, depression may be symptomatic of an allergy to certain foods, chemical food additives, or gasoline or other fumes. It can be an after-effect of an illness such as influenza or liver complaint and thus prove a severe hindrance to complete recovery, or it can be a sign of vitamin deficiency. And as is well known, many women suffer postnatal depression, a condition that can have far-reaching effects on family life. When an acute or severe form of depression is experienced, from whatever cause, it is imperative to seek medical advice at once.

Some drugs, too, can have depressant side-effects, especially when a high dosage is taken. Among these are some antibiotics and painkillers, and tranquillizers that may themselves be prescribed

Borage

Catmint

True valerian

to treat nervous disorders.

For anyone suffering from a mild nervous complaint, some herbs offer a gentle, nonaddictive means of toning, strengthening, and nourishing the nervous system, and of easing day-to-day stress and tensions. Tisanes made from catnip, chamomile, lemon balm, valerian, and vervain have been taken as mild tranquillizers for centuries. Now recent scientific experiments have proved what exponents of folk medicine and young readers of Beatrix Potter have long known: that chamomile, one of the mildest herbs, has relaxant and sleep-inducing properties. Peter Rabbit's mother, it will be recalled, put him to bed with a cup of chamomile tea after his anxious encounter in Mr MacGregor's garden.

The tisanes can be made from fresh or dried herbs. Dried chamomile flowers can be bought in health-food stores and from herbalists, and are among many herbs available in powdered form and sold as teabags, an up-to-date way of taking age-old remedies.

Vervain

Quick tips

• Enjoy the twin benefits of two relaxing herbs by adding a sprig of fresh catnip foliage to a chamomile infusion.

• Lemon balm tea, another long-standing self-help medicine, is usually drunk cool. As an anti-depressant, it is especially effective taken at bedtime.

• To make chamomile tea from dried flowers, infuse a heaped teaspoon in a cup of boiling water for 10 minutes, and drink it hot.

• Add a pinch or two of lavender flowers to chamomile tea, or to any other relaxing tisane, to increase its effectiveness.

• Valerian is an example of an old belief – if a medicine tastes foul, it must be good for you. You can buy the powdered root from herbalists to make a decoction. Stir in a few lemon balm or peppermint leaves and a spoonful of honey to help make the three-times-daily dosage a more pleasant experience.

• Rosemary may help you to see the brighter side of life following an illness. It is high in calcium and has been found to be effective in relieving post-illness depression. Drink rosemary tea hot and sweetened with honey, if you wish.

• Some essential oils, which you can buy from herbalists, can be diluted with vegetable oil and used for a healing massage to relieve depression. Among the most effective are lemon balm, jasmine, orange, and rose.

RESPIRATORY DISORDERS

From the common cold to laryngitis, respiratory disorders are always irritating and may be temporarily disabling. In mild forms, when the patient is disinclined to consult a doctor, their effects can be minimized by self-help medicine. Other related disorders including tonsillitis, bronchitis, and asthma may call for urgent medical attention.

Common cold

At the first signs of a cold – which may be sore eyes, a runny nose, or a sore throat – resort to the folk-medicine principle of sweating out the cold with the following infusions.

Soothing herbs such as marsh mallow ease respiratory problems. Others can help in specific ways. Those which have antibiotic volatile oils include eucalyptus, hyssop, lavender, rosemary, and thyme. Among the herbs which can, for example, help to dry up mucus, are agrimony, eyebright, and elder flowers.

ELDER-FLOWER AND YARROW TEA
Infuse one teaspoonful each of elder flowers and yarrow flowers in a cup of boiling water for 15 minutes. Strain, sweeten with honey if you wish, and drink hot every two or three hours, especially at bedtime.

AROMATIC INFUSION
Slice 1 oz fresh gingeroot and put it in a small glass or enamel pan with a crumbled stick of cinnamon, six

cloves, one teaspoon coriander seeds and half a lemon, sliced. Add 2½ cups boiling water, cover, and bring to a boil. Simmer for 15 minutes, strain and drink hot, sweetened with honey if you like, every two or three hours, especially at bedtime.

STEAM HEAT
Put eight to ten drops of lavender, thyme, and eucalyptus oils – any one or a mixture of two or three – into a bowl and pour in 2 cups boiling water. Cover your head with a towel and inhale.

CATARRH MIXTURES
The build-up of mucus that results from the irritation of the mucous membranes can be relieved by gently sniffing a warm infusion. Effective mixtures are the juice of half a lemon in a cup of warm

water, and fenugreek tea which is also a soothing drink.

FENUGREEK TEA
Lightly crush one teaspoon fenugreek seeds and simmer them in a cup of water for 15 minutes. Strain, cool, and sniff gently. Sweeten the remainder with honey, and drink hot.

VAPOR RUB
An old remedy valued more for its antiseptic and bactericidal properties than for its aroma, a chest rub of crushed garlic cloves and petroleum jelly can be helpful, especially at bedtime. Crush six large garlic cloves and put them into a small glass or enamel pan with one tablespoon petroleum jelly. Heat just until the jelly melts, then pour it into a sterilized jar and cool. Rub on the chest and back.

Hyssop

Anise

Fenugreek

Sore throats

Sage, thyme, vinegar, lemon, and honey are the ingredients to keep on hand to ease sore throats. Gargles, infusions, and compresses also relieve the discomfort of tonsillitis.

HERBAL GARGLE
Choose between the combinations of sage and vinegar or thyme and lemon juice to make a soothing gargle, which is also helpful in cases of laryngitis. Infuse one teaspoon fresh herb leaves in a cup of boiling water for 10 minutes. Add one teaspoon vinegar or lemon juice depending on the herb. Gargle with a little of the infusion and drink the remainder.

Tonsillitis is a condition that calls for medical attention. Herbal gargles may soothe the burning sensation. Sage or thyme infusions may be used as compresses and held or bandaged with gauze against the throat.

Coughs

Coughing dislodges the excess mucus produced when the membrane lining the throat or airways becomes irritated or infected (as in bronchitis). Blended tisanes help soothe and heal.

COUGH MIXTURE
A combined decoction and infusion makes an effective three-way cough medicine. Simmer one teaspoon lightly crushed aniseed seeds and one tablespoon powdered licorice root (available from herbalists) in 3 cups water for 20 minutes. Pour the decoction over two teaspoons thyme leaves, cover and infuse for 10 minutes. Strain through cheesecloth and drink one cupful, hot, three or four times a day.

KITCHEN REMEDY
Peel a large onion, slice it into rings, and put it into a bowl. Pour in three tablespoons clear organic honey, a powerful antiseptic and expectorant. Cover and leave it overnight. Strain and take one spoonful four times a day.

GARLIC ELIXIR
The antiseptic properties of garlic and honey come together in a country remedy for bronchial coughs. Chop eight garlic cloves, put them in a jar, and cover them with four tablespoons clear organic honey. Enjoy one teaspoon of the elixir at two-hourly intervals.

BREATHE IN!
The essential oils of herbs such as lavender, oregano, and thyme are effective as inhalants. Sprinkle one or two drops on a handkerchief, as Victorian ladies used to do, or add about six to eight drops of one of the oils to a bowl containing 1 pint of boiling water. Cover your head with a towel and breathe in. Alternatively, and less sweetly, crush three large cloves of garlic and add them to the steaming water.

Garlic

Licorice

Common thyme

ACHES & PAINS

The aches and pains that can make daily life an uphill struggle range from the inflammation of muscles and joints that results in rheumatic pain to the nervous conditions or food allergies that can trigger the debilitating headache and sickness of migraine.

Headaches and migraine

The first question to ask when you have a headache is why? There are a number of causes, indigestion, high blood pressure, tension, fatigue, low blood sugar, and menstrual problems among them.

Frequent or recurring headaches should always be reported to a doctor. Those brought on by nervous tension may be relieved by any of the infusions suggested on page 183.

HERBAL RUBS
Massaging the temples with an oil, such as peppermint or rosemary, diluted with a vegetable oil, can be helpful. An alternative is to sprinkle one or two drops of oil on a handkerchief, rest in a darkened room, and inhale the aroma.

FEVERFEW TEA
Infuse one teaspoonful of the dried leaves or one heaped tablespoon of fresh leaves in a cup of boiling water, in the usual way, and drink it hot, not more than two cups each day. It will almost certainly be necessary to sweeten the infusion with honey.

SWEET LAVENDER
Lavender is especially helpful in the relief of nervous headaches. Sprinkle two or three drops of tincture of lavender on a lump of sugar and dissolve it slowly in your mouth, or rub the oil into your temples. Sipping a cup of warm, sweetened lavender tea, made from the flowers, is a third option from this plant.

MIGRAINE
Any of the remedies suggested for tension headaches may help relieve the throbbing and often one-sided migraine. Recent research has given migraine its own herbal remedy, feverfew, a medicinal herb now known to have an action similar to that of aspirin. The bitter leaves are made more palatable by spreading them, two or three at a time, in honey sandwiches.

The case for feverfew

In his Herball *in the sixteenth century, Gerard said that feverfew "is very good for them that are giddie in the head or with the turning called Vertigo".*

Scientific research has taken his assertions further. Extracts of feverfew have been found to inhibit the production in the body of substances called prostaglandins, which play a part in causing inflammation and pain. The herb is now used in the treatment of migraine and for rheumatism and arthritis.

Peppermint

Rosemary

Sprains

Sprains and suspected fractures require professional attention, but minor cases respond to herbal compresses and ointments.

Treat sprains with comfrey root ground to make a poultice.

Mix two tablespoonsful of dried comfrey root powder (available from herbalists) to a thick paste with boiling water. Simmer very gently for 15 minutes, moistening the paste by adding water a little at a time if necessary.

John Wesley in his book of home remedies, *Primitive Physick*, prescribed comfrey for strained tendons: "Boil comfrey roots to a thick mucillage or jelly and apply this as a poultice, changing it twice a day." A modern version of the "jelly" can be made by boiling three tablespoons dried comfrey root powder with 8 oz petroleum jelly. Cool and strain through cheesecloth into a small pot. Rub on the affected areas.

Muscle and joint pain

Minor muscle strain or fatigue caused by overexertion can be eased by gentle massage with a herbal oil. It is more effective if the area to be treated is first bathed in hot water.

It is advisable to consult a doctor or herbal practitioner to find the underlying causes of rheumatism, which may include stress, inadequate diet, and arthritis which may be a result of injury.

To make a soothing oil, put 1 cup olive oil in a small pan and add two tablespoons lavender flowers, dried rosemary, or thyme leaves, or a few sprigs of the fresh herbs. Warm the oil gently, turn off the heat, and leave it to steep for 10 minutes; strain the oil and use it warm, to ease the affected muscles.

A STINGING REPLY
The young tops of stinging nettles can be gathered freely in spring and summer and are rich in vitamins and minerals and highly alkaline, which can counteract excessive acidity and ease rheumatic aches and pains. You can also buy them dried out or, conveniently, as teabags to make nettle tea.

CELERY MILK
An old country medicament for the treatment of rheumatism and arthritis is celery milk, made by chopping three large sticks of celery and simmering them in 1 cup milk for 20 minutes. The resulting mixture, which was also known as "celery mess," is taken warm as a soup.

Celery seeds, too, have a high alkaline content and can be used to make a helpful infusion. Lightly crush one teaspoonful of the seeds and simmer them in a cup of water for five minutes. Cover, leave for 10 minutes, strain and drink warm.

A NATIVE AMERICAN CUSTOM
Native Americans used wintergreen oil as a treatment for rheumatism. A similar oil, now obtained from birch and sometimes called sweet birch oil, can bring relief when rubbed into affected parts.

Some herbalists recommend adding extract of birch leaves to a hot bath to relieve arthritic and rheumatic pains and stiff joints.

Lavender 'Twickle Purple'

Lavender 'Munstead'

Comfrey

CUTS & BRUISES, BITES & STINGS

Minor accidents that might occur in the home, yard, or playground, and result in cuts and abrasions, bruises and burns, bites and stings, can respond to self-help medicine. More severe injuries of any kind call for urgent medical help. Where children are concerned, the combination of a gentle remedy and a sympathetic touch works wonders.

Cuts and grazes

The first requirement when the skin is broken is to clean it thoroughly. One way to do this is to stir ½ teaspoon tincture of calendula in 1 cup boiled water and bathe the wound.

Culpeper says . . .

Nicholas Culpeper, whose seventeenth-century Complete Herbal *set out to identify the medicinal properties of plants and define their uses, had something to say on the treatment of wounds and cuts, and of certain bites. He described feverfew as "one of the most singular wound herbs". And of mint he wrote that, "applied with salt, it helps the bites of mad dogs . . . and is good to wash the heads of young children with, against all manner of breakings out, sores and scabs . . ."*

Sterilized gauze wrung out in a fresh batch of the solution held in place with a bandage has good healing properties. Smaller areas can be treated with one or two drops of tincture of calendula on the sticking plaster gauze.

GARLIC AS A POULTICE

As a healing plant, garlic has a long and far-reaching history. The Chinese applied slices of raw garlic to heal wounds, and garlic dressings were used to treat battle wounds in World War I.

You can put its reputation as a protection against infection to the test, and make a poultice of thinly sliced garlic wrapped in sterilized gauze. As an alternative, you can harness the twin properties of garlic and another known antiseptic substance, organic honey. The garlic elixir recommended on page 185 for bronchial complaints can be spread thickly on cuts and grazes and held in place with sterilized gauze and a bandage. If you find the smell of raw garlic unacceptable, spread honey on the open wound.

Spearmint

Feverfew

Chamomile

Bruises

*Comfrey is an herb with a variety of medicinal properties, and recent
research supports its folkloric use as a treatment for bruises.*

Bathing the affected area in hot comfrey tea, or applying a tisane as a compress should help alleviate pain and reduce discoloration. Comfrey ointment, obtainable from herbalists, harnesses the plant's properties in another form.

Some of the plant's old country names, "knitbone" and "knitback" among them, and its botanical name, *Symphytum*, which comes from the Greek word for union, refer to its ability, when used as a compress or poultice, to help torn flesh heal cleanly.

The early settlers in New England learned some of their herbal medicine from local American Indian tribes, who had long used extract of witch hazel to treat severe bruising. Keep a bottle in the medicine cabinet and use it, soaked on cotton, to reduce the discomfort level.

Burns

*Severe burns and scalds are a matter for urgent medical attention,
but the immediate concern is to cool the affected area.*

Further tissue damage can be halted by immersing the burn in cold water or pouring cold water over the affected part.

Solutions of cold water with a few drops of tincture of calendula or hypericum can be applied to minor burns and scalds. Apply one as a compress with sterilized gauze, or dab it on with cotton. If you do not have any of the tinctures to hand, cold chamomile tea or comfrey tea can both be used in a similar way.

In cases where the skin is broken, a paste made of organic honey and either of the herbal tisanes is both soothing and healing.

Bites and stings

*Bee stings should be pulled out at once. The most effective
on-the-spot treatment is bathing with an alkaline solution of water
and baking soda (bicarbonate of soda).*

Quick tips

- Ant bites also respond quickly to a water and baking soda (sodium bicarbonate) solution.

- Dab bites and stings with witch hazel, the colder the better. It pays to keep a bottle in the refrigerator.

- Perhaps the most widely-known antidote to stinging nettle stings is the immediate application of a dock leaf, a wayside poultice in its simplest form.

- Oil of eucalyptus or essence of lavender dabbed on an insect bite or sting with a clean finger both take away the heat.

- Country folk reached for an onion to soothe painful bites and stings. A thick slice of onion can be used as a poultice, held in place with sticking plaster or a bandage. Alternatively, make a compress with grated or sliced onion in sterilized gauze.

- Feverfew tea, made by infusing 2 tbsp of the flowerheads in a cup of boiling water, is an old country remedy to soothe bites and stings. Dab it generously on the affected areas and allow it to dry.

- The same infusion was used by country folk as an insect repellent. The plant contains camphor which bees and other insects do not like.

DIGESTIVE DISORDERS

Many digestive disorders can be attributed to an injudicious diet or even to the manner of eating. Foods that are high in saturated fats and refined carbohydrates and, most of all, low in dietary fiber; drinks that have a high caffeine, tannin, or alcohol content; and a rapid, hurried, fast-eating routine can all contribute to indigestion, heartburn, flatulence, and colic, acidity of the stomach, and disorders of the bowel and colon.

It cannot be emphasized too strongly that when a severe condition is suspected, medical advice should be sought at once. Home remedies can bring considerable relief in cases of minor disorders, but should never be used to mask symptoms of a more serious condition.

Tisanes and decoctions might have been invented to ease the discomfort of indigestion and related problems.

DANDELIONS

Dandelion is a versatile plant with good medicinal credentials. The root, which can be used to make a decoction, is helpful in cases of dyspepsia, and as a mild but bitter laxative. Due principally to its taraxin content, dandelion stimulates the liver and gall bladder and significantly increases the flow of bile to aid digestion.

The leaves have a reputation as an efficient diuretic, a function attested by the plant's old country French name of *pis en lit* (or piss-the-bed). They may be lightly cooked and served, like spinach, sprinkled with lemon juice and pepper, or included in mixed green salads. The light, bright green young leaves, gathered in the spring, are especially good tossed with watercress. (Watercress is also a diuretic. It helps to relieve fluid retention, ridding the body of toxic wastes from the tissues and blood, and stimulates the digestion.)

LICORICE ROOT

Country children used to be given a stick of licorice root to chew "to keep their stomachs in order," and the plant has long been used as a remedy for indigestion. Its ability to lower the level of acid in the stomach makes it effective against heartburn. It can also ease spasms of the large intestine and contribute to the healing of stomach ulcers. A decoction can be made from powdered licorice root available from herbalists.

NOTE Licorice should not be taken by those who suffer from high blood pressure.

Dandelion

Watercress

Dill

Top tisanes

PEPPERMINT
The terms peppermint and indigestion are inextricably linked. The herb contains flavonoids which stimulate the liver and gall bladder, increasing the flow of bile. It can be an effective remedy for colic and flatulence, and has an antispasmodic effect on the smooth muscles of the digestive tract.

ROSEMARY
A cup or two of rosemary tea can ease flatulence and stimulate the digestion, the liver and the gall bladder by increasing the flow of bile. This is brought about by the action of rosmanicine which, as it breaks down in the body, stimulates the smooth muscle of the gall bladder and digestive tract. Rosemary should not be taken in large doses as it can irritate the digestive tract.

ANGELICA
An infusion of lightly crushed angelica seeds, with their pungent, bitter taste, stimulates the digestion and can ease colic and flatulence. It also has diuretic properties which can be beneficial in the treatment of urinary infections.

THYME
One of the many benefits of an infusion of thyme is its ability to soothe the digestive system and ease flatulence. This is due to the antispasmodic effect on smooth muscle of the plant's volatile oil.

PARSLEY
The herb is a strong diuretic which is useful for treating urinary infections and stones, as well as fluid retention. It is a rich source of vitamin C and iron and aids digestion. It should not be used during pregnancy.

DILL
The name is sometimes said to come from dilla, an Icelandic word meaning "lull," and dill water made from the herb has been used for generations to promote good digestion and improve the appetite. The herb is still a constituent of children's digestive medicines, valued for its ability to ease colic and flatulence. The tisane is made by infusing one teaspoon lightly crushed seeds in a cup of boiling water.

FENNEL
Both the seeds and the root of this umbelliferous plant can aid digestion and soothe discomfort, though fennel tea made by infusing the lightly crushed seeds is more usual. You can buy powdered fennel root from which to make a decoction from herbalists. The tisane is good for easing colic in babies, and heartburn and indigestion in adults.

LEMON BALM
The valuable volatile oils in the leaves may be lost during the drying process, so it is best to use the herb fresh, or frozen. A cup of hot lemon-balm tea sipped slowly after meals is an excellent aid to digestion, and it can relieve colic and flatulence. This is due to the antispasmodic effects of the essential oils, notably eugenol.

SWEET MARJORAM
The wide use of the herb in cooking as a flavoring for egg and meat dishes, probably derives from its properties as an aid to digestion. Marjoram tea is all the more fragrant if you include a spoonful of the tiny purple flowers.

EYE, EAR, & MOUTH PROBLEMS

The unrelated problems of puffy eyes and aching ears can be relieved with the use of a single plant, according to Nicholas Culpeper. In his definitive herbal, he noted of parsley that "the leaves laid to the eyes inflamed with heat or swollen, helps them . . . the juice dropped into the ears with a little wine, eases the pain." He had a remedy for sore mouths, too. In such cases, he recommended mint, with the words, "The decoction gargled in the mouth, cures the mouth and gums that are sore, and amends an ill-favoured breath."

Eye problems

Sore, inflamed, and itching eyes may be caused by lack of sleep, stress and strain or exposure to cigarette smoke. The traditional remedy is a cold compress placed on each eye and rest in a cool, dark room.

Ice-cold water used to soak cotton pads is helpful, but cold herbal teas are better. Fennel tea, made by infusing the seeds, is an old country remedy. More up-to-date is to use cold fennel or chamomile teabags, having first enjoyed the tisane hot or cold.

SOOTHING EYEBATHS
Sore and red eyes may be treated at home with one of a number of soothing eyebaths. Conjunctivitis and other eye infections call for medical attention. Scrupulous attention must be paid to cleanliness and hygiene. First sterilize an eyebath in boiling water or steam. Then use any of these infusions or blends to bathe the eyes. Cool the solution before use,

keep it in a stoppered bottle in the refrigerator for up to 24 hours, and discard the used solution after each application.

Chamomile tea made with the flowers.

Fennel tea made with the seeds.

Calendula eyebath solution Mix two drops of tincture of calendula with 1 tbsp distilled water for each bath, for each eye.

Marigold petal compress This is soothing to tired eyes and can be helpful in dispelling styes, as can torn parsley leaves wrapped in hot, sterilized gauze.

Eye brightness

Culpeper credited Euphrasia officinalis *– eyebright – with remarkable powers: "If the herb were as much used as neglected, it would spoil half the spectacle-makers' trade."*

To make an eyebright solution, mix five drops tincture of eyebright with one tablespoonful rosewater, for each bath. Use a new solution for each eye and each application.

An infusion of the leaves may be taken as a tisane, or cooled and used as an eyebath or compress. As a mouthwash or gargle, the infusion is also helpful for sore mouths and sore throats.

Pot marigold

Fennel

Myrrh/Sweet Cicely

Ear problems

An earache can be the after-effect of a cold, or it can be a symptom of an infection. It is important not to take any chances, and to consult medical opinion at once.

Minor cases of earache can be relieved by the use of a warm herbal oil. You can make one with 20 drops tincture of myrrh and one tablespoon almond oil. Keep the mixture in a stoppered bottle. To use it, pour a little into a teaspoon preheated in boiling water. Apply the oil carefully on a piece of cotton used as an ear plug.

St John's wort oil is another simple remedy. It can be bought in capsule form. Use it as described above, piercing one capsule and emptying the oil into a heated spoon.

Lavender oil diluted with almond oil or olive oil can be massaged around the outer ear to reduce the risk of infection.

Mouth problems

Toothache and sore or infected gums are symptoms that should be checked by your dentist.

Herbal mouthwashes can help to relieve soreness and act as bactericides. Vitamin supplements, especially vitamin C, and the B vitamins are also helpful.

HERBAL MOUTHWASHES
Tisanes made in the usual way can be used as soothing mouthwashes in cases of sore gums or toothache. Swish the infusion around in your mouth and retain it there for as long as possible. The following solutions should be helpful.
Rosemary tea Use fresh or dried leaves.
Sage tea Use fresh or dried leaves.
Thyme tea Use fresh or dried leaves and, if possible, a few flowers.
Lavender tea Use flowers.

Tincture of myrrh Dilute the tincture in warm, boiled water. Use in the proportion of eight drops to ½ cup water.
Oil of cloves This is used as a local anesthetic to ease nagging toothache. Pour a few drops onto a cotton swab and massage it on the gums around the affected tooth. Repeat every two to three hours as require.

BREATH SWEETENER
Any of the tisanes or solutions mentioned above will also help when bad breath is a problem; although the underlying cause will need to be determined. Other ways to freshen the breath are to chew a few caraway, cumin or fennel seeds, or parsley or mint leaves.

Chamomile

AROMATHERAPY

The use of essential plant oils as a means of promoting emotional and physical well-being, the practice of aromatherapy, was widely appreciated by ancient cultures around the world. It formed a significant part of medical practice in both China and Egypt, where the therapeutic powers of the oils were well recognized.

Aromatherapy harnesses the therapeutic properties of essential oils to heal and cure both physical and psychological ailments and to enhance well-being. Oils can be administered by way of the skin, with massage; the airways, in inhalations; and the digestive tract, in tisanes.

Combined with all these are the olfactory pathways along which aromas reach the brain. Neurons – nerve cells – in the lining membranes of the nasal passages enable information to be relayed rapidly to different parts of the brain. *Kyphi*, the blend of oils developed by the ancient Greeks, had well-documented mood-altering properties.

The use of oils in body massage is one of the most widely known aspects of aromatherapy. The skin, our largest organ, absorbs the volatile oils, which are taken up selectively by different tissues in the body. They also reinforce the body's own natural healing processes. There is an added benefit, since massage is soothing and relaxing.

Just as the oils themselves are complex, so their action is complex and cannot be fully understood without extensive study. It is, for example, possible to take essential oils internally, but because they are so highly concentrated and have such diverse properties, this is not recommended unless under the supervision of a qualified practitioner.

One of the most intriguing aspects of aromatherapy is the blending of more than one essential oil to make what are known as

Purple sage

Apothecary's rose

Coriander

synergistic compounds, each one formulated to have unique properties and actions. This, too, is an area on which it is advisable to take expert guidance.

USING ESSENTIAL OILS

Essential oils should never be used undiluted – they are far too highly concentrated – but diluted in the proportion of a maximum of five drops of essential oil to 1 tsp of a base or carrier oil. This may be a single oil or a mixture of two or more, chosen from, among others, grapeseed, peanut, hazelnut, walnut, soybeans and almond oils. Usually one teaspoonful of oil is enough for a whole body massage.

Inhalation is another way of harnessing the benefits of essential oils. One drop of, for example, lavender oil on a handkerchief can produce enough aroma to be both calming and relaxing, while two or three drops of an essential oil in a large bowl of hot water produces a strong vapor. To maximize the effects of this aromatic steam, hold your face about 10 inches from the bowl, cover your head with a towel, close your eyes, and breathe deeply through your nose for one minute. The act of deep breathing also contributes to the benefit of this age-old remedial procedure. WARNING   Essential oils must not be used during pregnancy. Many are slightly toxic, or could induce a miscarriage.

Lavender
'Twickle Purple'

Choosing an essential oil

These are some of the oils which can be used for massage, as inhalants or added, three or four drops at a time, to a bath.

SANDALWOOD
The sandalwood tree, native to the province of Mysore in India, has to be 30 years old before its essential oil is fully developed. The luxurious oil is used to combat anxiety and reduce nervous tension.

JASMINE
It takes eight million hand-picked jasmine blooms to make about 2 pounds of the "absolute" from which the oil is made. It is used to aid relaxation and sleep, and to soothe anxiety.

YLANG YLANG
This intensely sweet oil, extracted from the blossoms of "perfume trees" grown in the Philippines, is both a sedative and an anti-depressant. Its aroma can be somewhat cloying, and it should be used sparingly.

FRANKINCENSE
Extracted from the gum resin from the tree Boswellia sacra, this oil has a calming effect. It is particularly effective when used in a vaporizer as a relaxing environmental perfume.

NEROLI
This relaxing yet stimulating oil, which comes from the bitter orange tree, can ease nervous tension and anxiety and encourage sleep.

GERANIUM
Sometimes sold as geranium Bourbon-la-Reunion oil, for the island where the plant originated, the essential oil is soothing and relaxing.

LAVENDER
This oil is used for its steadying influence on the nerves and as a relaxant. It is effective both as a massage oil and, used two or three drops at a time, as an inhalant.

BERGAMOT
The oil is used to lift depression and encourage a more positive outlook.

CHAMOMILE
This golden oil is used to calm anxiety and dispel anger. It is also effective, used two or three drops at a time, as an inhalant.

MELISSA
Distilled from lemon balm leaves, the oil is used to lift depression and induce a sense of well-being.

ROSEMARY
The essential oil can lift exhaustion and stimulate the senses and can be used to aid concentration.

GRAPEFRUIT
This is the oil to use when a confidence booster is needed. It is warming and soothing.

CORIANDER
To produce this oil, coriander is harvested when the fruit is fully ripe. Its stimulating effect can help to combat tiredness and lethargy.

ROSE
Distilled from centifolia, damascena and gallica roses, rose oil, or attar of roses, is used to ease tension and soothe anxiety, and is especially helpful in post-natal depression. It takes about 5 tons of roses to produce 2 pounds of the oil.

CRAFTS

Herbs were once the mainstay of many home crafts, used in dyeing and for decoration. Many decorative uses have their origins in symbolic or religious beliefs – St. John's wort tied in bunches at the window to ward off evil spirits, for example, or mistletoe hung to bring good fortune and fertility. Today, many of these symbolic meanings are preserved in Victorian "language of flowers" listings, even though our seasonal decorations are more usually regarded as pure ornament. The traditional herb dyes have not been forgotten, however. Many craft weavers and spinners still prefer the subtle and variable shades they give compared with standardized chemical products.

Tansy flowers dry well and are attractive in arrangements.

Wreaths look good all year, not only at festive times.

Herbs for dried flower arrangements and wreaths

The colors in dried flower arrangements can be richer and more varied than the familiar shades of muted brown and green. The list below shows herbs that work particularly well in arrangements, retaining color when dried. It also includes some that make interesting shapes. When choosing herbs to dry, pick them just after they open – their colors when dried will be richer if they have not begun to fade at the time you harvest them.

HERB	PARTS USED	COLORS WHEN DRIED
Bay	leaves and stems	deep green
Bee balm	flowering stems	scarlet
Caraway	seedheads	tan and brown
Chamomile	flowers	yellow-gray
Chervil	seedheads	green and brown
Dill	seedheads	green and brown
Eucalyptus	leaves	silvery gray
Fennel	seedheads	light gray-brown, umbrella-shaped seedheads
Lady's mantle	flowering stems	yellow-green
Lavender	flowering stems	shades of purple and dark blue
Pennyroyal	flowering stems and leaves	purple
Rosemary	stems and leaves	deep green
Sorrel	seedheads	shades of green
Southernwood	stems and leaves	green
Tansy	flowering stems	bright yellow
Yarrow	flowering stems	pink, white, deep yellow

The language of herbs

The chart shows the symbolic meanings of a number of herbs. These could be taken into account if you are making an arrangement for a special occasion.

Herb	Symbolic meaning
Bay	honor, loyalty and unchanging affections, faithfulness
Basil	best wishes, warm friendship
Borage	courage
Chamomile	patience, meekness, resignation
Chervil	sincerity, warm feelings
Coriander	hidden worth, concealed feelings
Elderflower	compassion, sympathy
Evening primrose	inconstancy, uncertainty
Fennel	strength, flattery
Geranium	comfort, consolation
Lavender	silence, the acceptance and recognition of love
Marjoram	happiness, joy
Mint	wisdom
Myrtle	love, a first declaration of love
Nasturium	conquest
Parsley	celebrations, festivity
Red rose	true love
Rose	silence
Rosemary	remembrance
Rue	repentance
Saffron	marriage
Sage	esteem, friendship
Southernwood	constancy
Thyme	activity

Herbs for dyeing

Herbs can be used to produce a wide range of natural dyes with colors that are softer and more subtle than the synthetic dyes used commercially. Mordants both fix the dye in the fabric and affect the final color: those suggested below are for dyeing wool. If you want to try dyeing at home, start with a small amount of fabric in a natural cotton or wool – a wool scarf would be suitable. Mordants can be purchased at a craft store; consult directions on the packaging and use exactly as directed. You should only think about dyeing with herbs that you have in plentiful supply – because the color is gentler than that in commercial dyes, you will need quite a large quantity of the herb to achieve a deep enough color. The following herbs give a good result; the mordants suggested are for wool.

Herb	Part used	Color	Mordant
Elder	leaves	green	alum
	berries	blue/lilac	alum/salt
	berries	violet	alum
	bark	black	iron
Marigold	petals	pale yellow	alum
Parsley	leaves and stems	cream	alum
St. John's wort	flowers	red	tin/acetic acid
Tansy	flowering tops	dark yellow	alum
Woad	leaves	blue/lilac	ammonia

Garlands of fresh herbs can be used to soften hard lines, creating a more natural effect.

WREATHS & GARLANDS

It was the practice in years gone by to create wreaths and garlands on a core of grass, bittersweet, and other supple stems and bind them, like with like, with more of their own kind. To this day, the *stefani* rings hung on doorways in Greece in celebration of May Day are made, often by children, by binding posies of fragrant flowers on a circular hoop of grasses.

More substantial wreath forms can be made – or purchased in florists' shops – of supple clematis, grapevine, willow, or other twigs twisted and interwoven to form the base for further decoration. These circular forms, as well as long, thick raffia or vine plaits, provide sprays and posies of herbs with support but not a moisture source. They are suitable for short-term decorations, and for use with evergreen herbs such as bay, rosemary, and sage and all those flowers which will dry naturally in warm air. Bergamot, caraway, chamomile, chive, feverfew, lady's mantle, lavender, tansy, and wild marjoram are floral examples; the seedheads of herbs such as chervil, dill, fennel, and sorrel have similar properties. A ring or garland of any one of these herbs, or a fragrant medley of many, will dry attractively day by day until it forms a long-lasting decoration that will have lost little of its original glory, or its fragrance.

Wreath bases and garland cores made of natural materials may form not just the structure of the design, but a visual element of the decoration. A ring of dried grass stems underpinning overlapping bunches of marjoram flowers can provide an acceptable and attractive texture contrast.

Wire, rope, string, cord, plastic, and other core materials can be masked by covering them with dry sphagnum moss or hay. This should be bound on with green twine concealed beneath the mass of natural stems. The design for a long-lasting herbal wreath uses this technique.

Sweet bay

Pot marigold

Chervil

Fresh herbal wreath

Delight the senses with a wreath of fresh herbs that gives off a sweet fragrance as it dries.

selection of herb leaves such as bay, lavender cotton, lavender, rosemary, and sage
selection of herb flowers such as chamomile, chive, feverfew, lady's mantle, lavender, and oregano
green twine
dry hay
double copper-wire ring frame, 10 inch in diameter
silver wire
medium-gauge stub wires, cut in halves

Tie one end of the twine to the ring frame. Press handfuls of hay against the frame and bind it on with twine. Gather the herb leaves and flowers into small posies, either of separate or mixed plant materials. Cut the stems to equal length and bind them with silver wire. Keep the posies in water until you are ready to complete the decoration. Bend the stub wires to make U-shaped staples. Hold one

of the posies flat against the covered frame and secure the stems in place with the staple. Position successive posies so that the heads of each one cover the stems of the one before. Continue around the ring in this way. You may, if you wish, leave a section of the hay uncovered.

Hang the herbal wreath in a dry room away from direct sunlight. The herbs will dry *in situ*.

Table garland

Decorate a summer party or bride's table with a short-lived garland of fresh herb leaves and flowers.

long sprays of, for example, variegated mint and golden marjoram leaves
flowers such as damask roses or marigolds
thick cord or coiled paper ribbon in colors to complement the flowers
silver wire
hot-glue gun or clear, quick-setting glue

Plan to make the decoration as close as possible to the opening of the festivities, and keep the plant materials in water until you are ready to start.

Measure around the edge of the

table, or across the front, allowing for loops in the garland if you wish. Cut the cord or other core material to length. Bind the herb stems to the core with silver wire, taking two, three or more together, depending on the thickness you want the garland to be and the density of the foliage. Cut off the flower stems and glue the flowerheads over the foliage stems. Spray the design with cool water to keep it fresh.

Variegated apple mint

POSIES & NOSEGAYS

Nosegays, posies, herbal bouquets, tussie-mussies, call them what you will, have their roots in both country lore and the learned professions. In Elizabethan England, people carried these sweet-smelling or pungent posies to sweeten the air around them, and as a protection against the plague and other diseases; the disinfectant herbs such as lavender, rosemary, and rue were favored for this purpose.

In Victorian times, would-be lovers exchanged small floral posies made of plants chosen to convey a secret message. In accordance with the traditional language of flowers, there might be sprays of rosemary which, Ophelia tells us in Shakespeare's *Hamlet*, is "for remembrance;" sweet basil to signify best wishes; coriander for hidden worth (on whose part, it might not be clear); elder flower as a sign of compassion; fennel as a symbol of strength; and parsley for festivity. A red rose would be almost mandatory in a love posy,

as an expression of true love.

Herbal posies can be composed with informality, or created more precisely in the Victorian manner, with concentric rings of aromatic leaves and flowers arranged around a central bloom, traditionally a small rosebud. A simple posy could be given as a token at each place around a dinner table.

FESTIVE BOUQUETS

A herbal posy arranged in the hand makes a delightful bouquet to be carried by a bride or her attendants at a wedding. Boutonnières and

corsages can follow a similar theme, the stems of short-lived plants given a moisture source by being inserted in an orchid holder.

Matching posies can become part of the setting for a festive occasion. Attach small herbal posies, made up and then kept in water until the last minute, to a leafy garland edging a table, wind them around tent poles or drape across the front of a tablecloth. For an equally charming effect, you can pin small posies to the tablecloth front, arranging them in rows or at random.

A nosegay

Make a herbal nosegay as prettily informal as you please, as artless as a bunch of flowers gathered by a young child.

selection of herbs and flowers such as feverfew, clove pinks, pink bachelors' buttons, purple sage, and variegated mint

Compose the nosegay in your hand or on a flat surface, with the longest stems—they may be the mint or the sage—at the back and the flowering herbs in graduated heights below them. In that way, when the nosegay is put into a

small vase, each herb will be seen to its full advantage. Loosely tie the stems with raffia or twine so that the planned shape—which should look entirely artless—is not disarranged.

Lady's mantle

True valerian

Lamb's ears

Decorating candles

Candles made in plain cylindrical, square, or cone-shaped molds can be decorated with pressed leaves or petals. Pressed rose petals arranged to form flower shapes would be appropriate around rose-scented candles. Establish a color link by decorating a yellow candle with orange pressed marigold petals or nasturtium flowers. Citrus-scented candles could be accented with small sprays of a lemon-scented herb, and candles perfumed with lavender could be decorated with pressed purple sage leaves and flowers. Use a thin, clear papercraft glue to glue the herbs in place, or lightly brush over them and the surrounding surface of the candle with clear melted wax.

You can also buy flexible candle molds in shapes that suggest the aroma. Orange- and lemon-shaped candles could be scented with the appropriate essential oils. Perfume cone-shaped candles with sandalwood oil to evoke the aroma of incense.

A Victorian posy

It takes a measure of patience to compose a Victorian-style posy of flowers and foliage arranged in concentric rings. For the neatest effect, grade the flowers and leaves according to size.

selection of flowering herbs such as rosebuds, feverfew, chamomile, lavender cotton, marjoram
fine twine or silver wire
coordinating ribbon

Cut away any thorns from the rose stems. Hold a rosebud in one hand. Surround it with a ring of well-matched flowers, feverfew for example, with the heads at a slightly lower level than the rosebud, and then with sprays of foliage, their tips slightly below those of the previous ring.

Adjust and readjust each stem until the rings are even and

concentric, then bind the stems with twine or silver wire. Continue making rings around this central core, binding the stems at intervals.

Finish the posy in the traditional way, with a ring of large protective leaves such as those of lady's mantle. Tie the ribbon around the stems and finish the ends neatly. Spray the posy with cool water and stand it in water.

Lavender cotton

Feverfew

Sweet marjoram

HOUSEHOLD PREPARATIONS

In the days before conveniently packaged polishes and detergents, herbs were an important tool for the housewife, used for all sorts of homemade cleaners and disinfectants. One important use was the daily spreading of scented plants on floors to absorb dirt and smells in a far less hygienic world than our own. Plants like lady's bedstraw, meadowsweet, and sweet clover were often used to give houses a rather more attractive fragrance. Potpourris have their origins in the Middle Ages, too, while the rich would carry pomanders – not only to have something pleasant to smell, but in the belief that they would ward off pestilence and plague.

Water basil regularly if your windowsill is very sunny.

Lavender has many household uses, from candles to insect repellent.

Applications	Herb	Part used	How to use
Candles	Bergamot	flowers	Add crushed to melted wax
	Costmary	leaves	Add crushed to melted wax
	Lavender	oil	Add to melted wax as scent
		flowers	Add crushed to melted wax
	Mint	leaves	Add crushed to melted wax
	Neroli/ Orange	oil	Add to melted wax as scent
	Rose	oil	Add to melted wax as scent
	Rosemary	oil	Add to melted wax as scent
		leaves	Add crushed to melted wax
	Sandalwood	oil	Add to melted wax as scent
Fabric rinses	Costmary	leaves	Use strained infusion as final rinse for bedlinen, etc.
	Bergamot mint	leaves	Use strained infusion as final rinse for bedlinen, etc.
		flowers	Use strained infusion as final rinse for bedlinen, etc.
	Lemon verbena	leaves	Use strained infusion as final rinse for bedlinen, etc.
	Rosemary	leaves	Use strained infusion as final rinse for bedlinen, etc.
Household cleaners	Cedar	oil	Add to beeswax and turpentine polishes and creams
	Lavender	flowers	Add to beeswax and turpentine in furniture creams
	Lemon balm	leaves	Traditionally added to furniture polish; infuse in linseed oil and turpentine
	Soapwort	leaves	Use infusion for washing fabrics and upholstery
		root	Use decoction for washing fabrics and upholstery
Insect repellents	Basil	whole plant	Grow on a windowsill
	Lavender cotton	leaves	Deters moths if hung in closets or combine with southernwood and other moth deterrents in muslin bags
	Lavender	flowers & stems	Deters moths if hung in closets

Applications	Herb	Part used	How to use
Insect repellents cont.	Pennyroyal	whole plant	Grow around flowerbeds, to deter ants
	Rosemary	leaves	Combine with southernwood and other moth deterrents in muslin bags
	Rue	leaves/stems	Deters flies and wasps from a room or picnic table
	Southernwood	leaves	Deters moths if hung in closets
	Tansy	leaves/stems	Deters flies and wasps from a room or picnic table
Mice repellents	Mint	leaves	Strew in affected area
	Pepper	ground seed	Sprinkle in affected areas
Pillow stuffers	Chamomile	flowers	Use to help sleep
	Hops	strobiles	Use to help sleep
	Lavender	flowers	Use or for scenting linen and lingerie drawers
	Rose	petals	Use for scenting linen and lingerie drawers
Pomanders	Cloves	flower bud	Stick into dried orange
	Rose	buds	Use to decorate dried oranges
		powdered	Use to scent beeswax pomander beads
		petals	
		oil	Use to scent beeswax pomander beads
Room fragrances	Bay	leaves	Use in incense cones
	Bergamot	flowers	Use in potpourri and sachets
	Borage	flowers	Use in potpourri
	Cardamom	seeds	Use in incense powder
	Coriander	ground seeds	Potpourri; use in incense cones and powder
	Fennel	seeds	Use in potpourri
	Lavender	prunings	Burn on an open fire
		flowers	Potpourri or store in a stationery box to scent stationery; use in incense cones
		stems	Use for lavender "bottles" to scent drawers, etc.
		oil	Use in incense cones
	Lemongrass	leaves	Use in potpourri and sachets
	Lovage	seeds	Use in potpourri
	Marigold	petals	Use in potpourri and sachets
	Marjoram	flowers	Use in potpourri and sachets
	Myrrh	resin	Use in incense powder
	Orris	root	Fixative for potpourri
	Rose	petals	Use in potpourri and sachets
	Rosemary	leaves	Potpourri
		flowers	Use in potpourri and sachets
		pruned clippings	Burn on open fires
	Sandalwood	powder	Use in incense cones & powder
		oil	Use in incense cones

Victorian ladies used to carry pomanders. Now, they are used to delicately scent rooms and cupboards.

Herbs can be used not only to scent candles but also to decorate them.

HOUSEKEEPING PREPARATIONS

Herbs and other aromatic plants can be utilized to keep homes fresh and clean, sweet-smelling and welcoming. Making and using herbal polishes and household soaps offers both a sense of satisfaction and continuity with the past that manufactured products cannot match.

Lavender furniture cream polish

Apply this sweet-smelling cream sparingly, and polish with a soft, dry cloth.

2 oz beeswax
1 cup pure turpentine
2 oz pure soap flakes
¾ cup lavender infusion

Put the beeswax and turpentine into the top of a double boiler and stir until the ingredients are well blended. Remove from the heat and cool slightly.

Put the soap flakes and lavender infusion into a small pan and heat gently. Beat the mixture until it is frothy, then remove from the heat and cool slightly.

Stir the lavender mixture into the beeswax to make a thick, creamy consistency. Pour into an airtight tin or covered jar, cover, and label.

To make about 2½ cups

Household shampoo

This mild soapwort shampoo has been entrusted with the delicate task of cleaning old tapestries and antique carpets.

1 oz dried soapwort root, soaked overnight, or 3 handfuls of fresh soapwort stems
2 pints water

Drain the soaked root, cut it into small pieces, and crush it with a rolling pin or a hammer. Cut fresh stems into short lengths. Put the soapwort in a pan, pour in the water, and bring to a boil. Cover and simmer for 30 minutes, stirring occasionally. Set aside until it is cool. Strain off the liquid, discarding the herb. Pour it into bottles, cover and label.

To make 2 pints

Soapwort

Insect repellents

Herbals and country lore abound with ways of ridding yourself of unwelcome pests. Lavender clippings were burned on open fires to deter insects and to scent the room, and in the Middle Ages sprays of mint were strewn on the floor to keep rooms fresh and deter not insects but mice, which were said not to like the smell. Other effective strewing herbs were rue, southernwood, and tansy. Tansy leaves were also rubbed over meat and fish to impregnate the food, before covering them with fresh sprays of the herb.

Basil, which has been grown in the Mediterranean region since ancient times, is cultivated in windowsill pots more to repel flies than to flavor tomatoes. By growing pots of herbs such as bergamot mint, peppermint, basil, and thyme on the windowsills, hanging bunches of herbs to dry in a warm airy room, and arranging pots of chamomile and pennyroyal, lavender cotton and southernwood around the home, you can discourage an insect invasion.

KEEPING MOTHS AT BAY
Southernwood, lavender cotton, lavender, and rosemary protect woolens from moths. If you wish to try herbal moth repellents, wrap the herb sprays in cheesecloth, or place them between layers of tissue paper to avoid having to remove silky leaves and tiny seeds later.

MOTH-REPELLENT BAGS
To make sweet-smelling moth-repellent bags, mix together 6 tablespoonsful of dried southernwood leaves with 2 tablespoonsful each of dried chamomile flowers and dried, crumbled rosemary leaves, 1 tablespoonful of crumbled dried bay leaves, 2 crushed cinnamon sticks, 1 teaspoonful each of ground cloves and orris root powder, and 1 tablespoonful of salt. Store in an airtight container for two weeks, shaking every day or two. Use the matured mixture to fill satchets for closets and drawers.

Household soap

Create a pleasant ambience around the home as you use this soap for household cleaning. It is especially useful for brightening paintwork.

8 oz pure soap flakes
2 tbsp corn oil, plus extra for brushing
5 tbsp clear honey
1 tsp oil of cloves

Put the soap flakes, corn oil, and honey into the top of a double boiler and stir occasionally until the ingredients have blended. Stir in the oil of cloves, and continue stirring until the mixture thickens and resists the movement of the spoon.

Turn the mixture into greased molds or individual dessert dishes and put them in a warm, dry place to set. This may take two weeks or more, depending on the volume of each bar. Unmould the soap, and polish with a soft cloth.

To make ¾ lb

Pennyroyal

Rosemary

SWEET-SCENTED LAVENDER

Probably more than any other garden herb, lavender has long been associated with serenity and calm, with fresh, clean smells and an aura of luxury. Whoever said that cleanliness is next to godliness must have had a favorite aunt who made use of the herb to perfume every room in her home

For many people lavender evokes bygone days, of Victorian drawing rooms scented with lavender bags tucked between cushions or hung from chairbacks beneath antimacassars. Sachets were even popped inside writing boxes to scent stationery. These and other fragrant notions have as much relevance today and can greatly enhance our personal environment. If the sweet scent of lavender alone does not create the ambience you seek, spice it up with, say, crushed coriander seeds, a crumbled cinnamon stick, a few allspice berries, and dried tansy flowers.

Fragrant fillers

You can use herbs and other aromatic plants to transform everyday household objects into fragrant decorations.

TEAPOT MATS
Cut heavy cotton fabric into circles, squares or rectangles, or fancy shapes like strawberries or pumpkins. Sew two matching shapes together and fill the "bag" with a sweet or spicy mixture. Every time you put a hot dish on the mat, you will release the scent.

SWEET BAGS
You can use the sleep-pillow mixture given right, or a similar one of your choice, to fill sachets. These can be used to scent drawers and closets, hung on a door handle, or used as a
pull for a light or window-shade.
Small spherical bags, tightly packed with the flower mixture, can be used as "comforters" to handle in times of stress. Tossing them from hand to hand or squeezing them releases the soothing aroma.

PINCUSHIONS
Make a pincushion in any shape you choose, an apple or pear, heart or hat, and trim it with ribbon or braid, beads or sequins. Pack it with the sweet-bag mixture or with a single herbal fragrance such as dried coriander leaves and lightly-crushed
coriander seeds. Each time you insert or withdraw a pin or needle, the pincushion will release the aroma.

SCENTED PAPER
Tuck a sweet bag into a box of stationery or face tissues or, for a more long-lasting effect, sew some flower mixture between pieces of cheesecloth. Place these cloth bags between sheets of paper, wrap the paper in foil or put it in an airtight box. Leave it for two or three weeks, by which time the paper should be well impregnated with your favorite herbal fragrance.

Lavender "bottles"

Sometimes known as lavender rattles for their resemblance to babies' rattles, lavender "bottles" have a practical design concept.

22 long supple stalks of lavender
in full flower
2 feet approximately of satin ribbon,
¼ inch wide

The lavender flowers are held in a "cage" of interwoven stalks and ribbons, so they will not spill out. These decorations were originally used to separate linen stacked in chests into dozens and half-dozens, scenting it at the same time.

Gather the lavender stems together, with the flowerheads level. Tie them together with one end of the ribbon just below the flowers. Turn the bunch upside-down and bend the stalks downward, from just below the ribbon, so that they cover the flowerheads. Space out the stems

in pairs and weave the free end of the ribbon over and under alternate pairs of stems so that it encloses the flowers. Pull the ribbon more tightly at the top and bottom of the design, so that the "bottle" has more fullness in the center. Tie the ribbon in a bow, finish the ends, and trim the stalks.

Tuck a lavender "bottle" into a drawer with underwear or woolens, hang one on a coat-hanger, or arrange three or more in a dish in a bedroom or bathroom.

To make one "bottle"

Sleep pillow

Make a small pillow from the prettiest fabric you can find, fill it with this relaxing herbal mixture, and rest assured, at home or on an airplane, that it will soothe you to sleep.

2 oz dried lavender flowers
1 oz dried chamomile flowers
1 oz dried fragrant rose petals
2 tbsp coriander seeds, lightly crushed
1 small cinnamon stick, crumbled
2 tbsp dried orris root powder

Mix all the ingredients together and store them in a covered jar for two weeks, stirring or shaking the contents every day. Pack the dried-flower mixture into a small pillow made of closely woven fabric.

If you decide to vary the mixture, be sure to include the orris root powder, which acts as a fixative.

Lavender
stoechas

Chamomile

ROOM FRAGRANCES

Use herbs from your backyard or windowbox to contribute to the mood of the moment. Potpourri, a fragrant blend of dried flowers and petals, leaves and seeds, is a delightful way of enjoying the scents of summer long after the flowers have faded. You can turn back the clock and create both light and fragrance by burning aromatic oils in a traditional burner, or you can perfume candles with fragrant oils to create a romantic mood or an air of luxury.

The most creative element of the craft is in the blending. You can blend the dried plant materials by fragrance – rose petals with rose-scented geranium leaves is a perfect example; by color, creating a sunshine mixture of golden thyme and golden marjoram leaves with pot marigold petals and those from lemon-yellow roses; or simply by season. Few potpourri mixtures could be more evocative or romantic than one composed of myriad flowers and leaves gathered all on a summer's day.

The origins of potpourri as an air freshener go back to the Middle Ages when even the heaviest fragrances could scarcely mask the unwelcome odors of daily life! The craft is enjoying a revival of popularity today, when the blend of sweet or pungent aromas, the variety of textures, and the limitless color permutations make potpourri one of the most delightful accessories for the home.

Although the concept began as a blend of the most fragrant flowers in the herb garden, damask rose petals and lavender flowers, it is possible to include some plant materials which have little or no fragrance, and compensate by adding another pinch or two of a ground spice and a couple of drops of an essential oil.

There are two types of potpourri. The first, made by what is known as the "moist" method, has the longer pedigree and was made in the still-rooms of the great European estates. The second type, made by the dry method, is simpler and more versatile.

THE DRY METHOD

To make potpourri by the dry method, it is necessary to have all the materials completely dry; so dry that they rustle like tissue paper. Mix them together with the spices and other fragrances, and store them in a covered jar for three or four days, stirring daily. Add the fixative and essential oil, cover and leave for six weeks, stirring daily if possible. The potpourri will then be ready for use.

Rosemary

Rose garden potpourri

Make the potpourri as described for the dry method.

2 cups dried damask rose petals
1 cup dried rosemary flowers
and leaves
1 cup dried chamomile flowers
1 cup dried lemon verbena leaves

1 tbsp ground allspice
1 tbsp ground cinnamon
1 tbsp ground orris root powder
4–5 drops rose oil

Rainbow potpourri

Make the potpourri using the moist method.

1 cup partly dried marigold petals
1 cup partly dried bergamot flowers
1 cup partly dried marjoram
flowers, stripped from the stalk
1 cup partly dried lemongrass
leaves, finely chopped
1 cup partly dried lemon verbena
leaves

1 cup partly dried borage flowers
3 cups fine-textured salt
1tbsp aniseed seeds
1 tbsp fennel seeds
1 tbsp ground coriander
1 tbsp dried orris root powder
5–6 drops essential oil, such as
bergamot

more sophisticated alternative to simply filling a glass container with potpourri, you can embed a nosegay of dried herbs in a block of florists' foam and conceal the block with potpourri. To conserve the color and fragrance, store it in a covered jar and lift the lid on the aroma only when the room – a guest bedroom, perhaps – is in use.

The mixture can also be stuffed into sachets and drawstring bags, sleep pillows, and other decorative items; there are more details of these notions on pages 206 and 207. A potpourri blend can be used to create three-dimensional decorations by glueing it evenly over the surface of styrofoam balls, piled high in a shallow dish to make a pretty display. A dry foam ring or a heart shape can also be covered in this way. A final flourish of a dried-flower posy tied with ribbon completes a romantic design.

THE MOIST METHOD

To make potpourri by the moist method, partially dry the leaves and petals and layer them with salt in a covered container. Leave them without stirring for two weeks. During this time, the salt will have acted as a desiccant and drawn out the remaining moisture from the plant materials. Break up the block which will have formed, add the spices, the fixative (ground orris root powder) and a few drops of essential oil. Stir well, cover, and leave for six weeks, stirring every day if possible. Choose a wide-necked container and mix the developing potpourri with your fingers; it is remarkably relaxing.

USING POTPOURRI

Potpourri can be displayed in an open bowl, placed where people can stir it with their fingers as they pass, or in traditional "pomander" bowls with perforated lids. As a

REVIVING POTPOURRI

When your potpourri loses a little of its original color and fragrance, it is time for revival tactics. Discard any especially faded petals and leaves, replacing them with more colorful (and fully dried) materials. Put the mixture into a covered container, shake on a little more spice and essential oil, stir well and cover the jar. Set it aside for about two weeks, stirring it each day.

Borage

Pot marigold

Wild marjoram

Rosebud pomander

*Hang this pretty decoration over a dressing table, on a bedpost, a
door handle, wherever it will give you most pleasure.*

styrofoam ball, about 3 inches diameter
2 tbsp cloves
36 small dried rosebuds, approximately
a handful of potpourri
half a medium-gauge stub wire
narrow ribbon to hang

Stud the foam ball all over with
cloves. This will give the
decoration the pungency of the
traditional "clove oranges," or
dried-fruit pomanders. Cut the
stems of the rosebuds to a length of
about 3/8 inch and press them into
the foam, making neat rows or
rings. Continue all around the ball

until it is covered. Wrap the
pomander in potpourri in several
layers of tissue, or a paper (not
plastic) bag. Leave it in a dry, warm
place for several weeks. Remove
from its wrappings, pierce the top
with a U-shaped staple, and attach
a ribbon by which to hang it.

To make one pomander

Scented candles

*A few drops of the essential oil you use in home remedies and
cosmetic preparations or homemade fragrant oils are all you need to
scent candles of all shapes and sizes.*

9 tbsp paraffin wax
1 tbsp stearin (stearic acid)
candle dye (from craft stores)
3–4 drops essential oil such as rose,
orange, or lavender, or 1 tsp fragrant oil
1 wick
1 wick rod, or pencil or toothpick
1/4 pt candle mold, or yogurt container

Melt the wax in the top of a double
boiler. Stir in the stearin, which
strengthens the wax and slows
down the rate of burning, and the
dye. Stir in the fragrant oil and stir
until well blended. Remove from
the heat and cool slightly.

Cut a piece of wick 3 inches
longer than the depth of the mold.
Dip the wick in the melted wax and
tie it, close to one end, around the
center of the wick rod. Lay the rod
across the top of the mold and
thread the other end of the wick
through a hole in the center of the
mold base. Stand the mold base
upright. If it is an uneven shape, it
may be necessary to support it in a

jar or box.

Pour in as much wax as the mold
will take, taking care to keep the
wick vertical. Tap the mold to
release any trapped air and leave
the wax to set slightly. As it does
so, a depression will form in the
top. Gently reheat the remaining
wax and pour it into the mold to
level the surface. Leave the candle
to cool completely, overnight if
possible.

Remove the wick rod. Peel off
flexible molds, or tap rigid ones to
release the candle. Trim the wick
and polish the candle with a soft,
dry cloth.

To make one candle

Lavender
'Hidcote'

Coriander

Myrrh/
Sweet Cicel

Incense powder

If you have an open fire or are lighting a barbecue, sprinkle a little of this aromatic powder on the glowing charcoal, but make sure that the room is well ventilated if you are using it indoors.

1 oz sandalwood powder
½ oz coriander seeds, lightly crushed
½ oz cardamom seeds, lightly crushed
1 tsp myrrh crystals
1 oz dried lavender flowers, ground to a
powder
1 oz gum benzoin powder
2–3 drops essential oil

Mix together the sandalwood, coriander and cardamom seeds, myrrh crystals and lavender flowers. Stir in the gum benzoin, which acts as a fixative and "holds" the fragrances, and then the essential oil. Store the mixture in an airtight container. Sprinkle a few large pinches over a fire.

To make about 4 oz

Incense cones

Incense cones bring a hint of the East to a living room or hall, and may be used to freshen the air after a party.

5 tbsp gum arabic crystals
6 oz charcoal, crushed
1 oz gum benzoin powder
1 tsp sandalwood powder
1 tsp ground coriander
1 oz dried bay leaves, finely crumbled
1 oz dried lavender flowers, ground to a
powder
4–5 drops essential oil such as
sandalwood or lavender

Put the gum arabic into a small bowl and mix it to a stiff paste with water. Mix together the charcoal, gum benzoin powder, sandalwood, and ground coriander and stir in the gum arabic paste. Stir in the crumbled bay leaves and lavender flowers and add the essential oil. Stir until the ingredients are thoroughly blended. Form cones about 2 inches high and leave them in a warm place for about two days. When dry, wrap the cones in foil to keep in their aroma. Unwrap and light the tip to burn.

To make about 20 cones

Fragrant smoke

This simple form of incense captures the fragrance of home-grown herbs in a wisp of smoke. Select the herbs to suit the mood of the occasion. Rub or grind them to a powder, put them in a small flameproof dish, and set them alight.

FOR A ROMANTIC MOOD
Lavender flowers or rose petals.

FOR A REFRESHING AROMA
Lemon balm, lemongrass, lemon mint, peppermint, rosemary, sage or thyme leaves, dill or fennel seeds.

FOR AN EXOTIC AROMA
Bay leaves, coriander seeds or cumin seeds.

Sweet bay

Apothecary's rose

HERB USES

Herb	Aromatic	Cosmetic	Craft	Culinary	Household	Medicinal
Agrimony (*Agrimonia eupatoria*)		skin care			roots: yellow dye	diuretic
Angelica (*Angelica archangelica*)	mildly aromatic			fruit, cheese dishes, candied stems		appetite stimulant, digestive
Anise (*Pimpinella anisum*)	licorice-like, pungent			seeds: curries	infusion of seeds: insecticide	seeds: breath freshener; tisane: digestive, for cough
Basil, sweet (*Ocimum basilicum*)	clove-like		herb wreaths	tomatoes, cheese, salads	insect repellent	tisane: flatulence, nausea
Bay, sweet (*Laurus nobilis*)	sweet, woody		wreaths	meat dishes, sauces, soups	potpourri	mild sedative, stomach upset, antiseptic
Bee balm (*Monarda didyma*)			wreaths, posies, potpourri	flower: flavoring teas		
Bergamot (*Monarda didyma*)	sweet, light fragrance	oil: perfumery	flowers: floral decoration	salads; flowers: garnish	oil: scented candles	tisane: relaxant; inhalant: chest troubles
Borage (*Borago officinalis*)		skin lotion		leaves and flowers: soup; garnish; fruit punches		leaves: infusion for feverish colds
Caraway (*Carum carvi*)	pungent aroma of seeds		seedheads: wreaths	seeds: cakes, bread, cheese		tisane: flatulence
Catnip (*Nepeta cataria*)	pungent	skin care, hair care				tisane: insomnia, colds
Chamomile (*Anthemis nobilis / Chamaemelum nobile*)	apple-scented	skin care, hair care	dried flowers: floral wreaths		orange or green dye; flowers: potpourri	tisane: insomnia, digestive; mouthwash; poultice
Chervil (*Anthriscus cerefolium*)	licorice-like	skin care	seedheads: wreaths	*fines herbes*, salads, meat, fish		poultice
Chicory/ Belgian endive (*Cichorium intybus*)				salad, braised vegetable; dried root: drink		
Chive (*Allium schoenoprasum*)	onion-scented			*fines herbes*, salads, egg dishes		mild antiseptic

Herb	Aromatic	Cosmetic	Craft	Culinary	Household	Medicinal
Chive, garlic (*Allium tuberosum*)		hair care		savory dishes, soups, oils, garnish		
Clary (*Salvia sclarea*)	balsam scent			soups, sauces, wine-making		eye lotion, gargle, antiseptic
Comfrey (*Symphytum officinale*)		skin care, hair care			yellow dye	poultice: abscesses, burns, bruises
Coriander (*Coriandrum sativum*)				seeds, leaves: Mexican, Oriental dishes, salads	ground seeds: incense	tisane: digestive; oil: aromatherapy
Costmary (*Chrysanthemum balsamita/ balsamita major*)	strongly aromatic	skin care, hair care		salads, soups, sauces	insect repellent, potpourri	tisane: digestive
Cumin (*Cuminum cyminum*)	strong, pungent			seeds: curry, stews, bread, cakes		seeds: breath freshener
Dandelion (*Taraxacum officinale*)		skin care		salads, soups; flowers: wine; dried root: beverage	roots: magenta, brown or orange dye	appetite stimulant, laxative, diuretic
Dill (*Anethum graveolens*)	caraway		seedheads: wreaths	fish, sauces, garnish; seeds: pickles, vinegars, oils		decoction of seeds: sedative, digestive
Evening primrose (*Oenothera biennis*)						oil: skin ailments, menstrual problems
Fennel, Florence (*Foeniculum vulgare dulce*)				bulb: salads, vegetable		
Fennel, sweet (*Foeniculum vulgare*)	licorice-like	skin care, hair care	seedheads: wreaths	stews, fish dishes, salad dressings; seeds: bread		infusion: digestive, diuretic; eyebath
Fenugreek (*Tribonella foenum-graecum*)	bitter aroma			roasted seeds: curries; sprouted seeds: salads	seeds: yellow dye	seeds: digestive, breath freshener
Feverfew (*Chrysanthemum parthenium*)	bitter	skin care			moth repellent	tisane: headache; tonic
Garlic (*Allium sativum*)	strong flavor	hair care		savory dishes, oils, vinegars		antiseptic, diuretic
Germander (*Teucrinum chamaedrys*)						diuretic

Herb	Aromatic	Cosmetic	Craft	Culinary	Household	Medicinal
Ginseng (*Panax quinquefolius*)						mild stimulant and relaxant
Good King Henry (*Chenopodium bonus-henricus*)				salads, vegetable		
Horehound, white (*Marrubium vulgare*)	bitter					tisane: chest troubles, digestive
Horseradish (*Cochlearia armoracia/ Armoracia rusticana*)	pungent when bruised	skin care		root: sauces, fish, meat, fish dishes		fresh root: chest troubles
Hyssop (*Hysoppus officinalis*)	musky			salads, meat dishes	insect, moth repellent	tisane: chest trouble, gargle, bruises
Lady's mantle (*Alchemilla vulgaris*)		skin care	posies, wreaths			tisane: menstrual troubles
Lavender (*Lavendula*)	strongly and sweetly scented	skin care, hair care	wreaths	scented oils, sugars	potpourri; laundry rinse; furniture polish; insect repellent; oil: scented candles	tisane: headache, nervousness; oil: aromatherapy
Lavender cotton (*Santolina chamaecyparissus*)	strongly aromatic	oil: perfumery		flowers: garnish	insect repellent	
Lemon balm (*Melissa officinalis*)	lemon-scented	eau de Cologne		vegetable dishes, milk custards	laundry rinse; potpourri; furniture polish	tisane: headache, insomnia; insect bites; oil: aromatherapy
Lemongrass (*Cymbopogon citratus*)				Oriental cuisine	potpourri	
Lemon verbena (*Aloysia triphylla*)	lemon-scented	skin care, hair care		meat and poultry stuffing; flavoring syrups	potpourri; sachets for linens	infusion: digestive, mild sedative
Licorice (*Glycyrrhiza glabra*)	sweet			candy		digestive, laxative
Lovage (*Levisticum officinale*)	celery aroma	skin care, deodorant		soups, salads, casseroles, Indian cuisine		diuretic; infusion: digestive
Lungwort (*Pulmonaria officinalis*)						leaves: infusion for coughs, diarrhea

Herb	Aromatic	Cosmetic	Craft	Culinary	Household	Medicinal
Marigold, pot (*Calendula officinalis*)	petals spicy	skin care, hair care	garlands	petals: rice, cheese, meat dishes, salads	petals: pale yellow dye	tisane: digestive; poultice: styes
Marjoram, sweet (*Origanum majorana*)	honey-scented	hair care, soap	wreaths, garlands	bouquet garni, meats, stuffings, salads, oils, vinegars	insect repellent; potpourri	tisane: digestive, asthma
Marsh mallow (*Althaea officinalis*)		skin care, hair care		salads		decoction of dried root: sore throat; bruises, strains
Meadow-sweet (*Filipendula ulmaria*)	honey-scented flowers		wreaths, posies			tisane: digestive; antiseptic, diuretic
Mint (*Mentha*)		skin care, soap	garlands	meat sauces, cheese, jellies, syrups, oils, vinegars	insect repellent, scented candles, laundry rinse	tisane: digestive, sedative, appetite stimulant; infusion: antiseptic
Mugwort (*Artemisia vulgaris*)						digestive; regulates menstruation
Myrtle (*Myrtus communis*)				flowers: garnish, flavoring for sweet custards		
Nasturtium (*Tropaeolum majus*)	spicy	hair care		seeds: as capers; flowers: salads, garnish		tisane: chest troubles; urinary tract infections
Onion, Egyptian (*Allium cepa proliferum*)	onion-like			as onions		
Onion, Welsh (*Allium fistulosum*)	onion-like			bulbs as onions; tops: garnish		
Oregano/Wild marjoram (*Origanum vulgare*)				meat, vegetable dishes, salads, oils, vinegars		
Orris root (*Iris germanica* var. *florentina*)	violet-scented	dried root: hair care			fixative for pot-pourri; herb pillows	
Parsley (*Petroseleum crispum*)		skin care, hair care		*fines herbes*, sauces, salads, egg dishes, soups, garnish	green or cream dye	dispels halitosis
Pennyroyal (*Mentha pulegium*)		skin care			insect repellent	plants in flower: colds, nausea; insect stings and bites
Peppermint (*Mentha × piperata*)	menthol-scented	skin care, hair care		beverages	insect repellent	tisane: digestive, antiseptic

HERB	AROMATIC	COSMETIC	CRAFT	CULINARY	HOUSEHOLD	MEDICINAL
Rose (*Rosa*)	sweet, intensely floral	skin care, soaps, powder	garlands	jam, jellies, decoration, rosehip syrup	potpourri, scented candles, scenting linen	rose vinegar: headache; rose honey: sore throat
Rosemary (*Rosemarinus officinalis*)	pungent	skin care, hair care, soap	posies, wreaths	bouquet garni, roast meats, potatoes, vinegars	potpourri	tisane: digestive, nervousness; diuretic
Rue (*Ruta graveolens*)	bitter				insect repellent	eye disorders; gargle
Salad burnet (*Poterium sanguisorba*)				salads, sauces, beverages		
Sage, garden (*Salvia officinalis*)	pungent	hair care, tooth cleanser		bouquet garni, meats, poultry stuffings	insect repellent	tisane: coughs, digestive; mouthwash; oil: aromatherapy
Sage, pineapple (*Salvia elegans*)	pineapple-scented			stuffings		
Sandalwood (*Santalum album*)	musty				incense	oil: aromatherapy
Scented geraniums, (*Pelargonium*)	lemon-, nutmeg-, orange-, clove-scented	skin care		flavored sugar, sorbet, cakes, desserts, decoration	potpourri, insect repellent	
Selfheal (*Prunella vulgaris*)						infusion: mouthwash
Soapwort (*Saponaria officinalis*)		skin care; dried root: hair care, soap			soaps, furniture polish	skin conditions
Sorrel (*Rumex acetosa*)	lemon-scented		seedheads: wreaths	soup, vegetable, salads	yellow and green dye	diuretic
Sorrel, French (*Rumex scutatus*)			seedheads: decorations	vegetable, sauces for fish, egg dishes, salads		
Southern-wood (*Artemisia abrotanum*)	sweet, refreshing	hair care		stuffing for meat, poultry	potpourri, insect and moth repellent; stems: yellow dye	stimulant, antiseptic
Summer savory (*Satureia hortensis*)	spicy			stuffing for meats; bean dishes		tisane: digestive, antiseptic, diuretic; insect stings
Sweet Cicely/ Garden myrrh (*Myrrhis odorata*)	sweet, licorice		posies, wreaths	fruit salads, tarts; seeds: beverages	seeds: furniture polish	

Herb	Aromatic	Cosmetic	Craft	Culinary	Household	Medicinal
Sweet violet (*Viola odoratum*)	highly floral scent	skin care		honey flavoring; crystallized flowers		chest troubles
Sweet woodruff (*Galium odoratum*)	like freshly mown hay			beverage	scenting linen	
Tansy (*Tanacetum vulgare*)	pungent		wreaths	meat, cheese, custards	orange dye; insect repellent	tisane: digestive
Tarragon, French (*Artemisia dracunculus*)	sweet scent			*fines herbes*, salads, tomatoes, poultry, oils, vinegars		
Thyme (*Thymus*)	strongly fragrant	skin care, hair care		bouquet garni, stuffings, marinades, roast meats, oils, vinegars	potpourri, insect repellent, scented candles, scenting linens	tisane: colds; digestive, antiseptic
Valerian, true (*Valeriana officinalis*)	repelling aroma					decoction: mild sedative, headaches
Vervain (*Verbena officinalis*)						tisane: mild sedative, headaches, gallstones
Watercress (*Nasturtium officinale*)				soups, salads, butters, cheeses, omelets		chest troubles, digestive
Winter savory (*Satureja montana*)	peppery			game, meats, soups, bean dishes	scenting linens	infusion of flowers: digestive, antiseptic, diuretic; insect bites, stings
Woad (*Isatis tinctoria*)					blue dye	
Wooly betony (*Stachys byzantina*)			wreaths			
Wormwood (*Artemisia absinthium*)						tisane: digestive
Yarrow (*Achillea millefolium*)	strongly aromatic	skin care	wreaths	salads	insect repellent	tisane: digestive, colds, poultice: minor wounds

PLANT ZONES

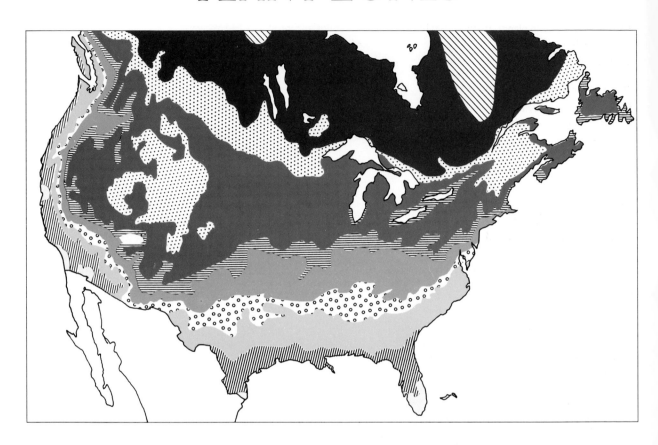

ZONE 1		below −45°C	below −50°C
ZONE 2		−45°C to −40°C	−50°F to −40°F
ZONE 3		−40°C to −34°C	−40°F to −30°F
ZONE 4		−34°C to −29°C	−30°F to −20°F
ZONE 5		−29°C to −23°C	−20°F to −10°F
ZONE 6		−23°C to −18°C	−10°F to −0°F
ZONE 7		−18°C to −12°C	0°F to 10°F
ZONE 8		−12°C to −6°C	10°F to 20°F
ZONE 9		−6°C to −1°C	20°F to 30°F
ZONE 10		−1°C to 5°C	30°F to 40°F

This map provides a guide to plant hardiness – the range of temperatures for growing plants. It indicates the lowest temperatures at which a plant will usually survive. The zone number at the end of each Directory entry corresponds to a zone or region on the map.

While the zone system of defining plant hardiness is broadly accurate, temperatures still differ widely over quite small areas of land. The resulting "micro-climates" mean that it is often possible, in a warm or sheltered location, to grow a plant in a zone that is theoretically too cold for it.

PLANT CLASSIFICATION

Family A category in plant classification which gathers together a group of related genera.

Genus (pl. genera) The category in ranking between a family and a species. Species with closely similar characteristics are grouped within a genus.

Species The category ranking below genus, linking very similar plants with specific characteristics.

Subspecies A division within a species.

Cultivar/Variety The term "cultivar" is abbreviated from "cultivated variety". It denotes a plant cultivated for specific distinguishing characteristics. In plant identification, cultivars are labelled "cv" and their names are contained within single quotation marks. The term "variety" denotes a variant within a species, which occurs naturally, rather than being deliberately cultivated. It is labeled "var."

Hybrid The offspring of two different species with the same genus, or, more rarely, of species in different genera. A hybrid is signified by a multiplication sign.

SPECIALTY HERB SUPPLIERS

Bountiful Gardens
18001 Shafer Ranch
Willits, CA 95490
(707) 459-6410

Caprilands Herb Farm
534 Silver St.
Coventry, CT 06238
(203) 742-7244

Cedarbrook Herb Farm
986 Sequim Ave. S.
Sequim, WA 98382
(206) 683-7733

Companion Plants
7247 N. Coolville Ridge Rd.
Athens, OH 45701

Farmer Seed & Nursery
818 N.W. Fourth Street
Faribault, MN 55021
(507) 334-1623

George Park Seed Co.
P.O. Box 31
Greenwood, S.C. 29648
(803) 233-8555

Gurney Seed & Nursery
Company
110 Capitol St.
Yankton, SD 57078
(605) 665-4451

Harris Seeds
60 Saginaw Dr.
P.O. Box 22960
Rochester, NY 14692
(716) 442-0410

Henry Field Seed & Nursery
415 N. Burnett
Shenandoah, IA 51602
(712) 246-2110

Herb Gathering
5742 Kenwood Ave.
Kansas City, MO 64110
(816) 523-2653

Hidden Springs Nursery
170 Hidden Springs Ln.
Cookeville, TN 38501
(615) 268-9889

Hilltop Herb Farm
P.O. Box 325
Romayor, TX 77368
(713) 592-5859

Johnny's Selected Seeds
Foss Hill Rd.
Albion, ME 04910
(207) 437-9294

Le Jardin Du Gourmet
Box 75
St. Johnsbury Center,
VT 05863
(802) 748-1446

Logees Greenhouses
141 North Street
Danielson, CT 06239
(203) 774-8038

Meadowbrook Herb Gardens
Rt. 138
Wyoming, RI 022898
(401) 539-7603

Nichols Garden Nursery
1190 N. Pacific Highway
Albany, OR 97321
(503) 928-9280

Penn Herb Co.
503 North Second St.
Philadelphia, PA 191123
(215) 925-3336

Redwood City Seed Co.
P.O. Box 361
Redwood City, CA 94064
(415) 325-7333

The Rosemary House
120 S. Market St.
Mechanicsburg, PA 17055
(717) 697-5111

Sandy Mush Herb Nursery
316 Surrett Cove Rd.
Leicester, NC 28748
(704) 683-2014

Seeds Blum
Idaho City Stage
Boise, ID 83706
(208) 342 0858
Fax: (208) 338-5658

Shepard's Garden Seeds
6116 Highway 9
Felton, CA 95018
(408) 335-6910

Southern Exposure
P.O. Box 170
Earlysville, VA 22936
(804) 973-4703

Stokes Seed Company
P.O. Box 548
Buffalo, NY 14240
(716) 695-6980

Sunnybrook Farms Nursery
9448 Mayfield Rd.
P.O. Box 6
Chesterland, OH 44026
(216) 729-7232

Taylor's Herb Garden
1535 Lone Oak Rd.
Vist, CA 92084
(619) 727-3485

Territorial Seed Co.
P.O. Box 157
Cottage Grove, OR 97424
(503) 942-9547

Thompson & Morgan
P.O. Box 1308
Jackson, NJ 08527
(908) 363-2225

Well Sweep Herb Farm
317 Mount Bethel Rd.
Port Murray, NJ 07865
(908) 852-5390

INDEX

PHOTOGRAPHIC CREDITS

Key: *a* above, *b* below, *l* left, *r* right

Ace 130*a* (Brian Green), 131 (Anand Razdan), 141 (Mauritius), 173 (Bo Cederwall);
A-Z Botanical Collection 7*r*, 17 (Francois Merl), 33, 44, 57, 70, 73, 95, 109, 110, 179;
J. Allan Cash 6*b*, 114, 182; et archive 8*a* & *b*, 9*l* & *r*, 10*b*, 11*a*; Greg Evans 180; Derek
Fell 1, 65, 80, 121*b*, 122, 123*r*, 124/5, 127; Peter McHoy 16, 19, 20, 22, 28, 31, 32,
34, 35, 36, 37, 39, 41, 42, 45, 46, 47, 48, 49, 50, 52, 53, 55, 56, 58, 59*l* & *r*, 61, 62, 63,
67, 71, 76, 78, 79, 81, 82, 85, 86, 87, 89, 90, 91, 92, 93, 96, 97, 98, 99, 102, 103,
105*a* & *b*, 106*a* & *b*, 111, 117, 123*l*, 128, 135, 137, 186; Maggie Oster 115;
Photo/Nats 43; Pictor 133, 188, 206; John Searle 11*r*; Holly H. Shimizu 118; Harry
Smith Collection 23, 25, 26, 29, 30, 68, 74, 101, 104, 107, 119, 120, 121*b*, 129, 160*b*,
202*a*.

All additional photography by Paul Forrester,
Nelson Hargreaves and Chas Wilder.